The Heretic's Guide to Thelema

Volumes 2 & 3

The Heretic's Guide to Thelema

Volume 2 & 3

by
Gerald del Campo

Issued by order of
The Grand Triumvirate
of the Order of Thelemic Knights

Concrescent Press

The Heretic's Guide to Thelema Volume 2 & 3 by Gerald Del Campo

© 2012 First Concrescent Press edition

ISBN: 978-0-9843729-7-3

Library of Congress Control Number: 2012941899

Dedication
First Concrescent Press Edition

I dedicate his book to my loving wife, April, as well as Bonnie, Twayn, Liv, Jeff, Kim, Matthew and all other artists who labor at great personal cost to bring Beauty to a world drunk on misery. May your work continue to inspire others to do something better. We need you now more than ever before.

This book is dedicated to YOU.

Dedication & Thanks
2008 Edition

Dedicated to all the Children of Thelema, who are quickly becoming a formidable army and hold the seeds for a Thelemic Utopia in their hands. Learn from your parents, and plant them in fertile soil (The seeds, not the parents).

To Esperanza, for showing me that one can never be too old to be a dad and for reminding me of what is important. And to my soulmate April...who is still walks with me after all of this. For the life of me I have no idea what I might have done to deserve her. I love you.

And a very special thanks to the Secret Chiefs: Thanks...again. For everything.

This book is dedicated to you.

Contents

More Thelemas
the publishers preface

As religions develop, the implications left incomplete by the progenitor are expounded by the followers, who rarely agree with one another. Exhortations to "leave well enough alone" or "the master did not say that" are answered by "you're doing it wrong" or at least, "can't you see the problem?" As religions become entwined with power, especially state power, power is then used to used to enforce the orthodoxy of the empowered clique. The danger is that what was originally a spiritual or moral injunction becomes a law to which obedience is compelled by the state. Authoritarianism and oligarchy can corrupt any good thing. But it can only do so if the voices of diversity remain silent.

Therefore it is profoundly important that Thelema develop in a rich ecology of ideas, exploring all of the implications of the source material and sharing out the possibilities inherent this spiritual path. The book you hold sets out two major areas of development. One is a solution to the issue of using the English language in our Qabalah based on a cypher in the *Book of the Law* and set out in the first volume in this book, the second in the series, *New Aeon English Qaballa*. It builds a new gematria and does some fantastic analysis of Thelema's core holy book, as well as develop a new take on kameas or magical squares.

Perhaps even more important is the second half of this book, Volume Three of the *Heretic's Guide to Thelema, The Ethics of Thelema*. With welcome sincerity and plain speaking, our author explores the ethical questions inherent in the antinomian maxims of Thelemic scriptures. Is the Law of Thelema the law of the jungle or an exhortation to deep cooperation? Every religion has its specific focus, the existential question it is trying resolve. For Thelema, the question is ethical: What am I to do? Here is the effort of a deeply committed Thelemite engaging with that deeply rooted challenge.

This book concludes our *Heretic's Guide* series, at least for now. Hopefully it will keep these fresh ideas before the eyes of inquiring souls as they ask: What is Thelema? What am I to do today? What is my will? Here are some new tools, some thoughts crafted by one who has pondered them at length. Learn, experiment, test, try. Only in the doing is the knowing.

SUCCESS IS YOUR PROOF

Forward
author's preface to the 2012 joint edition

What you are now about to read are Volumes 2 and 3 of *The Heretic's Guide to Thelema.*

Volume 2: New Aeon English Qaballa first appeared in 2000 as a private edition of only 100 copies and was entitled *Liber 59 and Other Qabalistic Writings.* Since then I am quite delighted to report that it has opened up the way to serious research into the mysteries of *The Book of the Law,* as prophesied in 1904. Upon releasing this work publicly, the only request I made of my readers was that they examine these new experimental methods with an open mind, and to actually put it to the test before drawing any conclusions. I warned the reader that it would seem difficult "switching gears" from the conventional wisdom known as the Hermetic Qabalah, but that the mental resistance to learning something new would eventually give way to ones magical training. After all, the beauty of the Hermetic Qabalah is that it behaves as a filing system for abstract ideas and symbols, and what is the English Qabalah if not a new set of symbols?

In spite of the tremendous blow-back I received from daring to suggest a non-Crowleyan solution to one of the most profound mysteries in one of the most profound books of our age, many readers began to email the results of their own work using this system. My work was done. It was all I ever asked for: that magicians judge the system based solely on results. Or to put it another way: Success is your proof. It's the least any of us can do to show respect to the people who labored to bring us this work in the face of tremendous opposition, peer pressure and organizational bias. We really do stand on the shoulders of giants, and the names of the heroes in our little story have not been excluded from this work. Look them up. They are remarkable people.

Volume 3: The Ethics of Thelema was also penned in the year 2000 and privately printed in as little as 50 copies. I refrained from making it publicly available for a few years. The idea that some one might confuse my desire to share my ethical values as a Thelemite with some sort of dogmatic or orthodoxy inspired agenda filled me with trepidation. And that is exactly what occurred in spite of the usual disclaimer that I make in very single version of every single book that I have ever written: These are MY ideas, and this is how

Thelema is working through me as a Thelemite. Apparently that disclaimer is written in invisible ink only I can see.

The reason that I finally decided to released *The Ethics of Thelema* to a greater audience was that I could see something dark coming our way, and that I might be able to use Thelema to explain not only what was wrong with our values, but what values we should consider to prevent a catastrophe. After the banking collapse and other completely avoidable disasters, I received many letters and emails from readers who referred to that work as "prophetic." I claim no such ability. One only need pay attention to one's heart. Generally speaking, I think humans are losing that ability. Trust me when I say that reading this little work won't change anything about you. That's not what it is for. It is only humbly presented to you to provide you with the excuse to explore your values as I did, so that you may decide for yourself whether or not they enhance your life and the lives those you love. Lastly, my intention was to open up the debate to see whether or not Crowley was right about Thelema: That it possesses the solution to all of our problems. I believe the time is ripe to answer that question.

Don't you?

The Heretic's Guide to Thelema

Volume Two:
New Aeon English Qaballa

by
Gerald del Campo

Issued by order of
The Grand Triumvirate
of the Order of Thelemic Knights

Concrescent Press

Introduction

The area we are about to cover in this little manual is relatively new, as far as magical or Qabalistic technology is concerned. It is indeed a New Aeon Technology, one with the potential to help us create a *true* Western Mystery Tradition. I sincerely hope that you will enjoy this brief introduction to the New Aeon English Qabalah. I have, up until this point, used the term "Qabalah" to describe the nature of the Work. I have done this to avoid confusion. From this point forward we will refer to it as "Qaballa." This deviation in the spelling is not an aberration. The difference is intentional, as its gematria is significantly important, and this spelling always refers to New Aeon English Qaballa.

Since you will see variations of spelling used throughout this work, perhaps a brief explanation of the etymology of these terms is in order:

Kabbalah is an arrangement of numerical correspondences that has its roots in Judaism, and has greatly predisposed the teachings of the Western Mystery Tradition. It is is used to extract secret meaning from the Torah.

Caballa refers to the Christian adaptation of the Hebrew system that occurred during the Renaissance. This adaptation is a tool by which to decode the Christian writings

Qabalah stands for what is known as the "Hermetic Qabalah." This reorganization evolved out of the Caballa when it was infused with an intricate system of correspondences during the occult revival of the late nineteenth century. Unlike the previous two systems, this scheme has no relation to any particular holy book and is used mainly as a system of correspondences and as a rather effective sort of magical decoder ring that facilitates ritual composition.

Qaballa stands for New Aeon English Qabalah, or NAEQ. It is an alphanumerical arrangement of correspondences that focuses on *Liber AL vel Legis* and other Thelemic Holy Books.

The brevity of this manual is deliberate. The author should not be blamed for a lack of things to say, but as a group we feel that recording the results of this research in this manual will only discourage experimentation and self-development. It is my intention to excite you about the system and encourage you to use it.

The first thing to consider when approaching any sophisticated magical methodology is that it does not convey the Truth-with-a-capital-T, regardless of how complex and thorough it appears to answer our questions. If any of this were truth in the spiritual sense (with a capital T), it would cease to be so the moment it was communicated to you. The big T would turn into a little t, preventing the proverbial choir of angels that so often accompany these epiphanies. NAEQ is a system by which a practitioner may *arrive* at the Truth: nothing more, nothing less. It is a means to an end, not the end itself.

Furthermore, since the truth is incommunicable, nothing written down in this manual will accomplish anything other than to explain a theory and tell a wonderful story. Since this is so, the author is relatively sure that he is in little danger of becoming a "Center of Pestilence." I will endeavor, however, to tread dangerously close, and so that is why we must emphasize that what you will read are *theories*. We are about to explore a different paradigm than many of us are used to. The topic of this discussion is controversial, and has been met with tremendous resistance and hostility from fundamental Thelemic circles. Crowley said that secrecy was the enemy of truth. I think he only got it half right. Politics, Sectarianism and personal agendas have no place in legitimate magical or philosophical research, either.

And this brings us to the subject of secrecy. It has been suggested that the keys to such a powerful system should be guarded from the profane. This is an unnecessary concern for the following reasons:

These techniques are new. There is no immediate benefit to be gained by withholding it from the magical community. By developing a Qaballistic system using the English alphabet, we can enhance our own spoken language, so that we can use it to divulge subtle spiritual ideas, where presently any attempt to do so is encountered with failure. The emphasis should be on discovery and development. If one person can discover much using this system, then imagine how much could be revealed if a thousand people worked to develop it. It is simply too important to limit its use.

Qaballa is a Gnostic* system. The experience will come to the

---

* Gnostic: An adherent of, or pertaining to Gnosticism. A religious tradition promoting spiritual knowledge & experience rather than Faith.

individual who works the routine in a specific way. Understanding will not be open to anyone else in the same manner. The secrets are already guarded against the profane because unless one works the system, they cannot hope to reap any benefit. And most important-ly, it is impossible. It is folly to think that one can hide the Truth. It is usually in plain view for everyone to see. Even if it could be hid-den, why would anyone resort to that sort of evil? My hope is simply to bring it to you in an easy-to-digest form, and allow you to make up your own mind based on your own discoveries. As in all things, success can be the only proof.

Ironically, much of the criticism about the New Aeon English Qa-balla (or NAEQ) is that the outcome is ambiguous, or that sophisti-cated mathematics must be applied in order to see results. It is true that one can make a word mean anything by employing enough mathematical gymnastics, but the same could be said of Hebrew or Greek Qabalah.

Isn't it better to use a system of correspondences based on the original language, than to debase those words by transliterating them into a foreign one? More importantly, how can we expect our research to include the subtleties of the racial consciousness of Eng-lish speaking cultures by taking these words and changing them into Hebrew or Greek words that mean nothing? Transliteration serves no other purpose than spelling a familiar word in a foreign alphabet while trying to retain its phonetic qualities so that the ma-gician can look up its correspondences. Many magicians don't see the problem with this; Crowley obviously didn't. The Hebrew Qa-balah is for use with the Hebrew language. The Greek Qabalah, for the Greek language, on Greek texts. The English Qaballa, for holy or inspired books written in English. And shouldn't a new Qabalah have its own unique methodology? I suspect that the resistance from established Qabalists may come from their repulsion toward new things.*

---

*   Recently, the Xth Degree Supreme and Holy King of the caliphate OTO in his speech at the national OTO conference, called the NAEQ an "imposture." The reason for such an unkind comment about the only group of people who have done any worthwhile research into the Holy Books worth mentioning is that this system began with Frater Achad and not Crowley. Therefore they are unable to exploit it, sell it, or us it to support their own ideas like they can with Crowley's work. By defining what Thelema isn't they can monopolize it and control it.

This resistance is understandable, since most of us have spent our entire adult lives memorizing correspondences and learning how to write in Hebrew. But if we cannot or will not make the transition, even for the sake of experimentation or research, then let us refrain from criticizing the new systems so that the discovery of this wonderful gift will be accessible to new and younger researchers.

A New Qaballa?

Why another Qaballa? This is a very valid question. As I explained in *The Heretic's Guide to Thelema, vol. 1, New Aeon Magick*, the Qaballah provides us with a language that we can use to communicate abstract ideas. Without this language and an agreed upon system of correspondences, we could never evolve in the art of magick because most of our time would be spent teaching others how to speak the lingo.

The story of the Tower of Babel illustrates the struggle of a people that made plans to secure their own greatness to make a name for themselves, but failed, largely because they could not understand one another. Imagine if contractors and laborers using different languages, weights and measures had built the Eiffel Tower in Paris.

Our task is difficult enough without reinventing the wheel. Presumably, we are all trying to create a Thelemic world. Do we want another Babel?

I knew a man that suffered from kidney stones. He had set up a surgery with his doctor, and his wife (having been trained by her mother on the medicinal properties of herbs) encouraged him to try a less dramatic course: she recommended that he drink a strong tea of angel hair until the day of his surgery, stating that this would probably dissolve the stones. I asked her to explain the nature of angel hair, and she informed me that it was corn silk. I then asked her why she didn't simply refer to it as corn silk, and her reply really drove home the importance of words and the symbols we endue them with. She replied: "Corn silk is the yellow strands around corn. Angel's Hair is what you use to dissolve stones." The man passed the stones that week – without the surgery.

I think this illustrates the importance of words.

It's all the same. But words, and the letters which compose them, really are important. They are symbols. Consider this from a scientific perspective:

Ever since the first human pondered existence and his or her relation to the whole, we have tried to develop a universal method to acquire scientific knowledge about the Unknowable. We have failed miserably, and will continue to fail, because the practice of the metaphysical arts is as complex and multifaceted as its practitioners are diverse. We need a language, verbiage, an unambiguous lingo geared toward our trade, which is magick. When it comes to the English language, this is where NAEQ comes in.

The magician uses the Qabalah to collect and develop criteria for specific things, and develops a set of correspondences that can even be used to access some of the involuntary areas of the psyche. Through the function of what Jung called the collective unconscious,* this method also has the added benefit of being a language that can be used to communicate with other magicians in order to develop hypotheses, share experiments, and communicate their results with their peers.

Social considerations will also effect the direction of the research, greatly complicating the progress of development. Magick is far from being a self-contained subject. Factors that further complicate the study of magick are the tangled relationships between individual knowledge or experience, and socially embraced knowledge. New developments in science critically affect magick, as the magicians everywhere adjust their paradigms to conform to the newly found data, such as when the earth was discovered to revolve around the sun.

At the center of this is the Gnosis† of the individual – a unique and personal insight and experience into the working of the Universe.

With very few exceptions, magical or Qabalistic research cannot be done without borrowing from already published work or (gasp) working with others or groups of others. This is exceptionally true when pioneering a new system.

The goal of magical/philosophical research is to extend the experience of the *individual* with his or her universe beyond what is already known. Individual magicians do this. However, this can hardly be called "science" until the methods used to achieve the experience are presented in a format or style which can be verified by others. Now you can begin to see the difficulty and importance of our work. We are pioneers. Each of us is an adventurer exploring areas of the mind never accessed before. But one quickly realizes that we are pieces of a jigsaw puzzle so large that any effort to see

---

*   The Archetypes and the Collective Unconscious (1934) Collected Works of C. G. Jung, Vol. 9, Part 1. 2nd ed. (1968), Princeton University Press

†   A highly personal religions/mystical experience preceding union with God. Usually the experience exceeds language and cannot be described.

the big picture is in vain. It is so huge that one human cannot hope to look at it entirely. And so perhaps on some unconscious level, we are driven into groups so that, in an united effort, we may perchance view a microcosmic representation of everything that is, as each of us lays a piece of the puzzle on the altar.

As in all scientific work, a constant never ending process of examination and review is seriously important. It reduces the weight of individual prejudice by requiring that other magicians accept the results. It is also a powerful incentive for practitioners to be extra cautious of drawing any quick conclusions, and to be ever aware that their work will undergo critical examination by their colleagues. Working within a group(s) keeps one honest and humble.

Throughout this gamut of dialogue and forethought (notice I didn't say, "argument") the paradigms and philosophies of individual magicians are scrutinized, organized, and selectively integrated into the consensual but always changing magical literature. In this practice, individual understanding is regularly improved into generally accepted knowledge.

This process occurs on many different levels. Researchers share their information with other researchers via email or personal contact. Data is exchanged, and ideas are speculated upon. Many write for the various magico-philosophical newsletters and journals in an effort to share information with an even wider audience, or to receive feedback. Some who write up their findings may send them to magical journals of other sectarian flavors to see how their theories hold up within other paradigms.

Working with others does much more than validate what becomes accepted occult knowledge. It also helps to spawn and maintain a body of scientific techniques and social etiquette, thereby establishing the standard to be used by the next generation of magicians.

Why wasn't there any mention of NAEQ in *New Aeon Magick?*

Because at the time I felt that it was important to have an understanding of traditional Hermetic Qabalah before launching the student into uncharted territory. I felt that some background into the mechanics of the traditional methods that were already accepted by the greater occult community would facilitate the research of a new system. Unfortunately, this has not been the case.

Much of the criticism of NAEQ comes from traditionalist practitioners who spent most of their lives memorizing Hebrew correspondences, and resent having to invest the time and effort to learn another set of correspondences. This seems ironic to me: we have an opportunity to embellish our own dialect and our own symbols with mystical meaning, or more accurately, we have an occasion to discover the mystical meaning of our own language. *The Book of the Law* says that it must be done (Crowley, 2004).

People shouldn't expect this to be as tremendous an undertaking as it was for our predecessors. We have the advantage of having learned from them. Also, the New Aeon has brought with it various technological advantages that our forefathers did not have at their disposal. Presently, communication occurs at the speed of light with a simple click of a mouse. Mathematical research that once required the use of an abacus or calculator and several months worth of tedium can now be easily accomplished with the right software. It should be much easier for us than it was for them. But nothing will happen unless we study, apply, and record.

As long as people keep regurgitating the same material over and over again, we will never advance. Crowley came; he is gone. Learn from him, and move on. But don't make the mistake of moving on without a true understanding, or progress won't come, either.

We have to approach our philosophy, our Magick, as a living thing. Thelema is a way of life. Use it as a ruler by which to gauge the human condition. Only then will its beauty become apparent, and only then can we hope that it will yield its beautiful pearls. It will not open up its secrets until its true adherents, its philosophers and scientists, learn to view it as more than just a fad, party game, or soap box on which to draw to themselves undeserved scholastic attention.

Why An English System?
Over a period of three consecutive days in Cairo, Aleister Crowley received that earth shattering transmission we call *The Book of the Law*. On the second day, he received the following directive:

> *Thou shalt obtain the order & value of the English Alphabet; thou shalt find new symbols to attribute them unto.*
> (*Liber AL vel Legis II: 55*, Crowley. Weiser Books, 2004)

The instructions above seem simple enough – but what a tremendous responsibility. Not only was he the vessel, the battery which would distribute the 93 current, but he was also being ordered to create an entirely new system of Qabalah to boot. And Crowley, not being one to disappoint, did take a stab at it in what he called *Liber Trigrammaton* but was never really quite happy with it. He felt that it fell short of the intended goal.

> *There cometh one to follow thee: he shall expound it.*
> (*Liber AL vel Legis II: 76*, Crowley. Weiser Books, 2004)

Charles Stansfeld Jones (or Frater Achad, as he was known in the A.'.A.'.), whom Crowley presumed to be his magical child,* may have inadvertently provided the key to the English Alphabet.

A group of individuals working to discover the key to the riddle came upon some surprising coincidences during the 70s. We are going to use this word a lot from here forward: coincidences. After working with this new numerical scheme for some time, they developed an entire system which continues today to yield various other coincidences still. You can imagine the enthusiasm when this was discovered. They believe that they have helped to fulfill the requirement of instructions given in *Liber AL* with regard to the English Alphabet with the assistance of Crowley's own magical child, Frater Achad.

The clue Achad provided came out of his *Liber Thirty-One*.

> *Then I noticed another very important thing. I was wondering why A and L should be chosen, or rather why L the 12th letter of the Hebrew alphabet should follow A, the first.*†
> (*Liber 31. Frater Achad, Luxor Press 1998*)

What a powerful revelation this proved to be. Remember this, because the entire system hinges on this clue.

How did this all come about?
Remember that when first written, Crowley dismissed the *Book of the Law* as a mere oddity. The manuscript was thrown into some closet

---

* R.A. Gilbert, *Baphomet & Son: A Little Known Chapter in the Life of the Beast 666.* Holmes Pub Grou Llc; 3rd,Revised edition, 1997.
† Note that these letters share the same position in the alphabet both in Hebrew and in English: A & Aleph is the first letter, L & Lamed is the twelfth.

for about five years before Crowley rediscovered it (read: found it in a closet, probably looking for something else). It wasn't until then that he began to understand its importance. After some scrutiny, he began to see it (as do many of us) as an outline for a magical organism that could be used to transform the customs of the old age to a system based entirely on self-realization called Thelema.[*]

Crowley threw everything he had at this book, and by employing the Hebrew, Coptic, and Greek Qabalah he was able to write commentaries from his extensive observations of this work, but felt he had fallen short of the instructions given to him to come up with an English Qaballa. The result of this endeavor was, as I wrote earlier, *Liber Trigrammaton*, but according to his diaries he was never satisfied with this work. In fact, in the new Comment, he writes, "The Attribution in *Liber Trigrammaton* is good theoretically, but no Qabalah of merit has arisen therefrom.[†]"

The time is 1918 – Frater Achad walks right into a huge hint. It is almost like the story of Moses, who could gaze upon the Promised Land but never enter. Here is Frater Achad looking right at the key, and not comprehending the message hidden in his own words.

Frater Achad never knew how close he had come, or what that small little paragraph, that little hunchback in the shape of a question, that innocent speculation and curiosity might mean to our movement.

After Achad's breakup with Crowley, the entire subject of the English Qabalah was all but forgotten until 1976, when an English chap named Jim Lees discovered the cipher. The discovery might have gone something like this:

Remembering that Frater Achad had insinuated (inadvertently perhaps) that the letter A was the first letter, and the letter L was the second, then all one would have to do is to count from the letter A to the letter L to notice that there are exactly 11 letters in between. Hey! The Book of the Law says something about the number 11. It must be important. So one continues counting in groups of 11 until we arrive at the order of the English alphabet currently used.

A	L	W	H	S	D	O	Z	K	V	G	R	C
1	2	3	4	5	6	7	8	9	10	11	12	13

---

[*]   The Confessions of Aleister Crowley. Crowley, Aleister
[†]   The Commentaries of AL - Chapter II. Equinox Vol. V no. 1. Motta

N	Y	J	U	F	Q	B	M	X	I	T	E	P
14	15	16	17	18	19	20	21	22	23	24	25	26

This prompted the interest of several individuals to study and research through The Book of the Law and other Thelemic Holy Books in order to prove, or disprove, the accuracy of the cipher. And thus began the quest of fulfilling the prophecy regarding the promised key. It is hard to imagine the frustration involved in such an undertaking.

This key has promise like no other. Some folks have agreed amongst themselves that this would be the key to *Liber AL*. We make no such claims about this, but we will explore some of these things together, and if we are successful in our mission, we will have supplied the reader with enough information to determine this for themselves.

So what are some of the things a person can do to test their suspicions? Well, various methods have been adopted which yield some fascinating coincidences.

Why does this particular cipher show more promise that any other? Understand that we are not saying that this is *The* Cipher. That is for readers with a pioneering spirit to decide for themselves. The progression originates with the name of the book, *AL*. This is one of the most significant clues.

The third letter is W and produces an anagram for Law: The title of the Book. Okay. Nice coincidence, but admittedly, nothing to write home about.

Brace yourself. The following coincidence is gripping:

The hand written manuscript contains a grid drawn by Crowley on the text of *Liber AL*, Chapter III, verse 47, and there is a line in there that reads "Then this line drawn is a key." (*See Illustration 1 on page 14.*)

The following illustration shows what occurs when you place the English letters on the grid continuously beginning with the letter A from the top left hand corner. (*See Illustration 2 on page 15.*)

If we take the "This line drawn is a key" as a clue, then we might come to the conclusion that we ought to read the letters in the order designated by the line. You will notice that reading the letters diagonally across the grid yields the order exactly as indicated above.

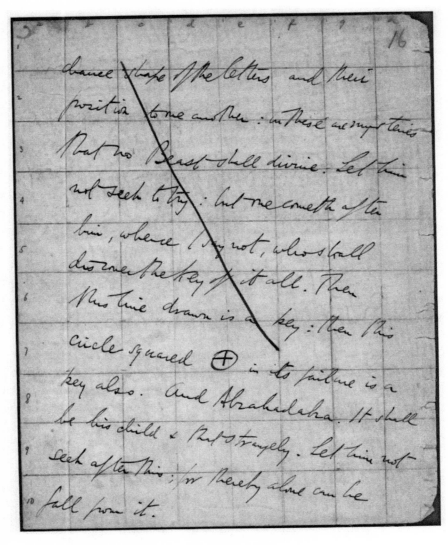

Illustration 1

Another coincidence is the cross within the circle. This is a traditional symbol of the Rosy Cross. The words Rosy Cross enumerates to 81 when using this particular numerical key. The writing on the manuscript asserts, "then this circle squared in its failure, is a key also."

Note that the symbol is drawn in the square assigned to the letter K, and this letter has a numerical value of 9. Nine squared is 81

Illustration 2

– the English Qabalah value for the words "Rosy Cross."

One more in case you are not yet at the edge of your seat: The edge of the circle infringes upon the neighboring square, which has been assigned to the letter U with a numerical value of 17. By adding up 6 (K) and 17 (U), we get the number of letters in the English Alphabet: 26.

One of the leading researchers in this field, Jake Stratton-Kent, discovered that by converting all the letters in Liber AL II: 76 into their English Qabalah numerical equivalents, and adding all of the numbers together you get a value of 351. If you add all of the numbers assigned to each of the letters in the English Qabalah, you also obtain the value of 351.

"76. 4 6 3 8 A B K 2 4 A L G M O R 3 Y X 24 89 R P S T O V A L. What meaneth this, o prophet? Thou knowest not; nor shalt thou know ever. There cometh one to follow thee: he shall expound it. But remember, o chosen one, to be me; to follow the love of Nu in the star-lit heaven; to look forth upon men, to tell them this glad word." (*Liber AL vel Legis – II:76*)

The words "English Alphabet" enumerate to 187. So do the words "magnificent" and "perfection."

One can do words or sentences. For example, Chapter I verse 24 tells us that: "I am Nuit, and my word is six and fifty."

Applying this numerical format to this sentence we conclude that Nuit = 78. The numbers 7 and 8 can be multiplied to receive another number: 56 – This is, coincidentally enough, exactly like saying "Six and fifty." Which also happens to be the value of "ISIS," a notariqon that is hidden in plain view in I:22, and another correspondence, which will be explained shortly.

Another coincidence has to do with the way many of us abbreviate our standard Thelemic closing. Rather than saying, "Love is the law, love under will," to close our letters and emails (which in NAEQ enumerates to 279), we abbreviate by writing 93 93/93. There are three 93's in the closing: 3 X 93 = 279, the number of all the combined words in the closing.

These are some of the things we feel make this Cipher more significant than most others.

The Method to the Madness

What other methods can one apply to the English Qaballa?
As shown above, normal word analysis where words that yield a particular number are compared with other words yielding the same value. For example:

Analyzing the words:
"Pan" P 26 + A 1 + N 14 = 41
41 = hoofs, shoe, whole
"Scholar" S 5 + C 13 + H 4 + O 7 + L 2 + A1 + R 12 = 44
44 = folly, play, read, fail, suck, and love
"Eros" E 25+ R 12+ O 7 + S 5 = 49
49 = rose, key, loves, moon, male, gain

Looking for clues in the various Class A materials can yield interesting coincidences. Here is one:

"… but Tzaddi is not the Star." *Liber AL* I:57
"Tzaddi" = 68, also "Jesus"
"Star" = 42, also "cross" "sin" and "blood"

Notariqon
This is an old technique involving the creation of an acronym from some significant phrase. For example, in the *Book of the Law*, Nuit tells us: "I am the Infinite Stars and the Infinite Space (Crowley, 2004)."

ISIS = 56
56 = cup, lips, lover, chant, wings, rule, beds, wise, magi
Another quote, "Do what thou wilt shall be the whole of the Law," becomes DWTWSBTWOTL = 121
121 = delicious, harmonized, despised, brilliant, content, rapturous, secretly, bewithus, beetle, phoenix, rejoice, sacraments

The authors have applied this method to come up with the title of this book. NAEQ is a notariqon for New Aeon English Qabalah, and it enumerates to 59.*

---
* The first publication of the NAEQ was called Liber 59.

Other words that enumerate to 59: Kiblah, wheel, yoni, onrush, leaps, sure, forward, like, hunt, dance, ready, cradle, Khem, wealth, take, abode, and reward

Planetary or Sephirothic Mystic Numbers
To come up with a mystic number, you have to begin with the number of the planet. For example, Sol is represented in the 6th sephirah, which marks the magician's attainment of Knowledge and Conversation with the Holy Guardian Angel.

To come up with its mystical number, you would do it the usual way of adding every number beginning with the number of the sephirah all the way down like this 6+5+4+3+2+1 = 21. We would then look up other words that enumerate to 21, and expect to find some indication of the function of this sephirah.

21 = goal, On

For more information on the drawing of magical squares and talismans I would recommend Israel Regardie's How to Make and Use Magical Talismans (Thorsons Publishers; Revised ed., March 1983)

Anagrams
The rearrangement of words so that they mean something else is another method which is employed. Some of the obvious ones are:

God & Dog. On & No. Eros & Rose. Arms & Mars.

Counting Well
This technique is unique to NAEQ, and gave birth to a sigilization technique known as *wanakaba*, which will be discussed in more detail shortly. You take two words and multiply the sum of the first word by the number of letters in the second. Then, you reverse the process by multiplying the sum of the second word by the number of letters in the first. *Then*, you add the two values. To signify that this method has been applied, the Qaballist will place a % between both words. For example:

Secret % Center
The *first* word, "secret," is enumerated:

S 5 + E 25 + C 13 + R 12 + E 25 + T 24 = 104

The *second* word contains 6 letters, and so 104 is multiplied by 6 to yield the number 624.

Now the process is reversed and applied to the second word.

C 13 + E 25 + N 14 + T 24 + E 25 + R 12 = 113

The *first* word (secret) also contains 6 letters, and so the number 113 is multiplied by 6: 113 X 6 = 678.

Now, one must add the final value of the first word (secret, 624) and add it to the final value of the second (center, 678).

624 + 678 = 1302
So, secret % center = 1302

(It may have become apparent by now that this operation yields various numbers. By applying Counting Well to these two words, the Qabalist has pulled the numbers 104, 624, 113, 217, and 678. These should all be analyzed along the way in their various permutations.)

I find it useful to use this system whenever I encounter an "&" in between two words.

Another anomaly to look for is two words that share the same numerical value appearing next to one another in the text. An example is in *Liber AL*, Chapters I, Verse 50: "ye 40 have 40 star 42 & star 42, system 95 & system 95;" which could indicate a numerical significance. These types of occurrences should be studied using various methods in addition to Counting Well, such as adding them together, number reversal, etc.

Number Reversal

This is a simple reversal of numbers, wherein one looks for similarities or oppositions. For example, the number 93 becomes the number 39. For our purposes, we will use this symbol ↻ throughout this book to indicate when we are applying number reversal. This technique can be applied to any number regardless of the number of digits it may contain.

93 ↻ 39
93 = unity, circles, thyself, being, masters, original, begin
39 = full, orb, you, awake, fools, follow

Squares & Sigils

Making Magical Squares with the English Alphabet
We will discuss two different methods for creating kameas, sigils, and squares using the New Aeon English Qaballa. The first method is referred to as Wakanaba, or Wakan Grids. The second is called Obsidian Squares.

Method One: Wakan Grids
The Wakan method is a system of creating fresh kameas and extracting previously unused barbarous names by using Counting Well as a means of permutation. Because it uses the English letters, the magician will never encounter any of the problems associated with transliteration of Hebrew or Greek. It all begins with a grid.

Unlike traditional magical squares, or the method I have outlined elsewhere in this book, Wakan follows none of the old rules of attribution to Sephiroth. In fact, when one uses it will depend largely on when something jumps out at the magician from the Holy Books, and this will of course depend on the particular circumstance the individual happens to be facing at any particular time. It is, for the most part, a free-form process with the magician having ultimate artistic control. The author finds this process very useful as an investigative method which lends itself quite readily to the Holy Books, but has a difficult time finding a ceremonial application for it in the temples. For me, it tends to lend itself more toward prayer or mantra work, rather than conjuring.

You will notice that since it is not necessary to have an equal number of horizontal and vertical letters, so that the result is often times rectangle, rather than a square. For this reason, we will refer to it as a "grid." Each segment of the grid is a "sub-square."

For this particular example, we will use MIDNIGHT % SUN, since it yields a number of great Thelemic significance when Counted Well: 666. (See "Counting Well.")

First, one has to determine the number of cells that the grid will have. To do this, it is a simple matter of multiplying the number of letters from one word by the number of letters from the other word. In this case, we get a grid with 24 cells.

The value for each of the letters comprising the first word is enumerated, and those numbers will provide us with the root numbers for the grid. The first word is always the top horizontal line, while the second word is vertical. You should start off with something that looks like this:

		21	23	6	14	23	11	4	24		
		M	I	D	N	I	G	H	T		
5	S										
17	U										
<u>14</u>	N										

Now, the value of the first letter from the first word (21) is added to the value of the first letter from the second word (5), and the resulting total is added to the first "sub-square" on the first row. The process is then repeated with the second number of the first word until the entire row is complete. We keep repeating the process with the other rows until the grid is complete. It should look like this:

		21	23	6	14	23	11	4	24		
		M	I	D	N	I	G	H	T		
5	S	26	28	11	19	28	16	9	29		
17	U	38	40	23	31	40	28	21	41		
14	N	35	37	20	28	37	25	18	38		

Now we must check our math to make sure that the grid has been properly constructed. Add all the numbers in each row, and write the total at the bottom of the grid, and then add all of those together:

		21	23	6	14	23	11	4	24	=	126
		M	I	D	N	I	G	H	T		
5	S	26	28	11	19	28	16	9	29		
17	U	38	40	23	31	40	28	21	41		
<u>14</u>	N	35	37	20	28	37	25	18	38		
36		99	105	54	78	105	69	48	108	=	666

If the number is the same as the two words Counted Well, then your math is correct.

Barbarous Names
The magician can then apply a method discovered by Jake Stratton-Kent in order to extract barbarous words, incantations or mantras from the grid. He affectionately refers to it as "The Kamea Extrapolator."

The way it works is by using the numbers in each sub-square to make a syllable. These are strung together to form an incantation, then verses, and finally the Grand Word or Name, which is used at the end of each verse. There is a fairly complex set of rules which must be applied in order to extract this data with the use of a key.

The rules sound a lot more difficult than they are. Every number from 1 through 26 in a grid's sub-square represents a letter, while the higher digits represent a combination of letters. The key below makes them pronounceable.

The Key to the Kamea Extrapolator

A		W	K	N	B
O		H	V	Y	M
U		S	G	J	X
I		D	R	F	T
E		Z	C	Q	P

The first step is to take the numbers in our Midnight Sun grid and transform them to letters using our cipher. The first sub-square is 26, and this corresponds to the letter P in the NAEQ assignation. Using the key above, we locate the letter in question and identify the vowel sound associated with it. In this case, it is the vowel E, which makes the first sub-square sound much like the Hebrew letter *Peh*. In other words, the consonants will adapt the sound of the vowel at the beginning of the row to which it was assigned. Well call this "**Rule 1**."

For the next square, we will have to apply more complicated rules since we are dealing with a number greater than 26. Any number greater than 26 must be treated as two separate numbers and attributed to the English alphabet. In the case of the number 28, the 2 is assigned to the letter L, as one would expect. The number 8 corresponds to the letter Z, and a quick glance at the key above will reveal that Z corresponds to the vowel E. See correspondences below:

A	L	W	H	S	D	O	Z	K	V	G	R	C
1	2	3	4	5	6	7	8	9	10	11	12	13

N	Y	J	U	F	Q	B	M	X	I	T	E	P
14	15	16	17	18	19	20	21	22	23	24	25	26

Now, if I haven't lost you, you may have realized that I did not resort to using the key above to the letter A. There is another rule that applies only to that letter: **Rule 2:** the L follows all vowels and the letter A follows all L's. These two letters are treated differently because AL is the key to the cipher.

There is third rule. **Rule 3:** the number zero is treated like the number 7 (or the letter O) if it appears in a number higher than 26. And since the letter O is a vowel, then you must apply the first rule and follow it with the letter L. If you can remember these three rules, you are good to go.

So, using the example of the two sub-squares that we have analyzed so far, we get "PE" for the first one, and "LA-ZE" for the second one. The next digit corresponds to the letter "G" and by referencing the key above we conclude that this sub-square is pronounced "GU."

Continue the process until all sub-squares have been translated. You should end up with the following invocation for the grid Midnight Sun:

PE LA-ZE GU QE LA-ZE JU KA LA-KA
WA-ZE HO-OL IL WA-AL HO-OL LA-ZE MO HO-AL
WA-SU WA-AL BA LA-ZE WA-OL EL FI WA-ZE

A second verse can be extracted from the grid by treating the sum of each of the two words, and the sum of all of the columns to the same technique. (Those numbers have been underlined for clarity). Remember the rules:

1. Follow each consonant with its assigned vowel.
2. The L follows all vowels, and the letter A follows all L's.
3. The number zero is treated like the number 7 (or letter O) if it appears in a number higher than 26.

		21	23	6	14	23	11	4	24	=	<u>126</u>
		M	I	D	N	I	G	H	T		
5	S	26	28	11	19	28	16	9	29		
17	U	38	40	23	31	40	28	21	41		
<u>14</u>	N	35	37	20	28	37	25	18	38		
<u>36</u>		<u>99</u>	<u>105</u>	<u>54</u>	<u>78</u>	<u>105</u>	<u>69</u>	<u>48</u>	<u>108</u>	=	*666*

These numbers yield the second verse of the grid:

KA-KA AL-OL-SU SU-HO OL-WA AL-OL-SU DI-KA HO-ZE ALOL-ZE

The Great Word or Mantra for the total of the grid, which in this case is 666, is extracted the same way. The number 6 is given to the letter "D" and by using the key above we discover that the vowel "I" is to follow:

DI-DI-DI

When I use these as prayers, they create a very interesting mental effect. Start with the Great Name, and move into the first verse, concluding with the Great Word. Then, recite the second verse again, finishing with the Great Word. Try it – you'll like it.

Wakan Talismans

Talismans and sigils can be made from the original grid. For example, we can take this grid for Midnight Sun:

26	28	11	19	28	16	9	29
38	40	23	31	40	28	21	41
35	37	20	28	37	25	18	38

And apply the following Wakan key:

1	⊢⊣[[⊢•	6	⌐⌐⌐⌐⌐
2	⊢⊣[[⊢•	7	Blank
3	⊑Ш∃⊓	8	Blank
4	✛✖	9	⌐⌐⌐⌐⌐
5	⌐⌐⌐⌐⌐	0	Blank

When the number ends in 7, 8 or 0, the space is overlooked or blanked out, as I've done below.

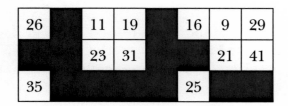

The second digits (6 in 26, 9 in 19, etc) determine the sigil that goes into each sub-square. Then take one symbol from the set shown next to each number in the Wakan key, and put it in the square in place of the number in your grid. The way that the symbols are connected together, or which direction they run, is up to the taste of the magician. The final version of the Midnight Sun talisman looks like this:

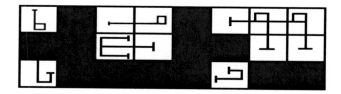

The Wakan key can also be used for creating freestanding sigils for the Great Words of these grids. In this example of Midnight Sun, the Great Word is fashioned from the number 666, and so any of the following sigils for the number 6 will work.

These can be placed behind the talisman when they are activated.

Method Two: Obsidian Squares
You may have noticed that there are only 22 letters in the Hebrew alphabet, and 26 in the English alphabet, making the placement of the English letters on the Tree of Life a somewhat difficult task. Those of us that work that an English Qabalistic system have made many attempts to recreate the Tree of Life so as to account for those extra four letters in the English alphabet. This system is new, and so there are many opinions as to what the new Tree would look like. Many radical changes have been made, most which I personally find impossible to use since they lack the coherence of the Tree familiar to most of us. I decided that the proper thing for a magician to do when he needed an answer was to do magick, so I began a magical operation with the intention of learning how to account for the extra four paths. It was during this working that I discovered the magical method that I will cover here. I might add that it works rather well. Those of you that have studied Chaos Magick will find it a variation on Austin Osman Spare's "Alphabet of Desire."*

You must then look to the Tree of Life to see which sephirah best represents the desired end. (See *New Aeon Magick: Thelema Without*

---

* Book of Pleasure (Self-Love), the Psychology of Ecstasy, published by the author 1913.

Tears for sephirotic attributions.)

In this case, I looked toward Hod, the eighth sephirah, concerned with the sciences and hidden knowledge. It will become readily apparent that some considerable mastery in brevity is necessary, the higher up the Tree one performs these rites.

Magick is about intent. Eventually, you must make a mission statement to serve as the focus of the operation. Write it on a piece of paper, capitalizing every letter. Here was mine:

"I WISH TO VIEW AND UNDERSTAND THE NEW TREE."

You then eliminate all of the vowels, but discard only the consonants which repeat themselves. (Note: In this particular system, the Y is considered a vowel.) You should then end up with the same number of letters as the number of the sephirah. If not, you must restate your position and redo it until it does. If the number of your original intent happens to match the desired number, then the magician should look at this as a good sign.

I ended up with 8 letters: WSHTVNDR = 78

Some words that enumerate to 78 include: true, hidden, voice, unknown, willing, display, guarded.

All of these words say something about the sephirah we have chosen, and should be seen as an indication that we are on the right track.

The letters of your cipher must now be placed into the square in the following fashion to create a kamea. The first line (vertical and horizontal), shows the letters as they appear above. The second set of letters begins with the second letter of the word, the third set with the third letter, and so on, with the remaining letters taking their places at the end of the initial listing.

W	S	H	T	V	N	D	R
S	H	T	V	N	D	R	W
H	T	V	N	D	R	W	S
T	V	N	D	R	W	S	H
V	N	D	R	W	S	H	T
N	D	R	W	S	H	T	V
D	R	W	S	H	T	V	N
R	W	S	H	T	V	N	D

Now, we must come up with a method of calling out the servitor that will indulge us. With the square, we have created a door. By creating a sigil, we will acquire the key.

Sigilizing the Obsidian Square

In its most complicated permutation, a sigil is a conscious attempt to create a visual for an archetypal concept. They can also be used to represent ideas, persons, angels, demons or desires.

Various methods can be applied to the letters of the English alphabet in order to yield sigils. It is helpful if we learn to look at the letters of the alphabet as pictographs. Perhaps one of the simplest and most popular methods is to write down the magical intent as simply as possible, and apply various rules to the sentence to come up with a sigil. The following is a method employed by Austin Osman Spare

The next sigil will represent the function of the spirit you wish to contact. Write out a phrase describing, as simply as possible, the spirit's specialty. Use all caps:

"I RULE OVER HIDDEN KNOWLEDGE"

This time, we discard all *consonants*, but only remove *vowels* that appear more than once. Remember that in this system, the letter Y is treated as a vowel:

IUEO = 72

Some words that enumerate to 72: Happy, chaste, domain, places, magical, tomb, lingam, raised, fashion, skilled, vessel, open.

Those words can be said to hint at the personality of the servitor.

Now, the magician must use his creative genius in order to combine the symbols (the vowels) to form an aesthetically pleasing sigil. The magician has creative license to manipulate the letters however they please by turning them upside down, on their sides, stretching some lines while rounding others, and the like. Remember that magick is an art, and that this sigil represents an extension of your will.

The sigil will likely go through several evolutionary phases before you are happy with the results. The key is to make the sigil as symmetrical as possible, and make it so that it fits within the square. Tracing paper is a handy tool. Here is an example:

IUEO

The sigil does not have to be complex. The sigil above could be simplified or embellished further. Again, the magician has creative license.

Now, the sigil must be fitted to the square you made from your letters. The square should be the color of the sephirah, but the sigil should be painted in its flashing color. In my particular case, it was orange and blue, respectively. I didn't include the colors in my example so that the details of the square and its contents would be clear. Another thing: these talismans work better when they are painted on the corresponding metal. In this case, it is Mercury, and so an amalgam available from dental supply houses will do. It could look something like this:

W	S	H	T	V	N	D	R
S	H	T	V	N	D	R	W
H	T	V	N	D	R	W	S
T	V	N	D	R	W	S	H
V	N	D	R	W	S	H	T
N	D	R	W	S	H	T	V
D	R	W	S	H	T	V	N
R	W	S	H	T	V	N	D

By adding the value of the consonants in the Obsidian Square to the value of the vowels from the sigil (78 + 72), we get 150.

Some words that enumerate to 150: Priestess, tempest, sentences, gentleness, incestuous, and begotten.

These words can be said to describe the nature of the interaction between the servitor and the magician.

We now have our square and sigil. The invocation is all that is left.

NAEQ Invocation

Preparation for The Invocation

In order to prepare for this invocation, it is necessary to flood the temple and consciousness with the archetypal material which corresponds to Hod. The magician must use incense, flowers, herbs, weapons, anything that they can get their hands on to facilitate a successful communication. The following notes in italics were borrowed from the Qabalah section of my *New Aeon Magick (Heretic's Guide, vol. 1)*.

The study of this book is highly recommended since it deals with the Qabalistic placement of the Greek, Egyptian, and Thelemic Gods. The following is only a piece of a much larger puzzle, and if you desire to move beyond this example, studying the book is recommended.

HOD	
Meaning:	Glory (Honor)
God Name:	Elohim Tzabaoth
Image:	A Hermaphrodite
Titles:	Perfect Intelligence
Archangel:	Michael
Order of Angels:	Beni Elohin, Sons of God.
Spiritual Experience:	Vision Of Splendor
Virtue:	Truthfulness
Vice:	Falsehood Dishonesty
Human Chakra:	Legs
Magical Weapons:	The Names, Versicles & Apron
The Precious Stones:	The Opal
The Plants:	Moly
Alchemical Metal:	Mercury
Incense and/or Oil:	Storax
Tarot Cards:	The Four Eights
Wands (Fire):	Swiftness
Cups (Water):	Indolence
Swords (Air):	Interference
Disks (Earth):	Prudence

NOTES ON HOD

The magical weapons connected with Hod allude well to its function. One can only name something once it has been given form, and Hod gives elemental forces form.

The Apron is usually worn over the genitals, which are portrayed by Yesod, the astral sphere that represents unconscious imagery, or something unknown. The Apron signifies that these images have been transcended, by virtue of the fact that they have been given Force by Netzach, and Form by Hod: they have been released and utilized. From a practical point of view, Hod creates the talismans, while Netzach animates them.

Dion Fortune made a brilliant comment concerning the Apron and its relation to Hod. She stated that the Apron is the regalia of the Mason, a maker of forms, and therefore justified quite nicely its placement as a weapon or tool of this sphere.*

The connection to "form" should not confuse the reader. Binah is the giver of form. Hod is the reflection of Binah, after it has been filtered through Chesed. Hod is the intellectual manifestation of a spiritual idea represented by Binah. This is another way of saying that Binah's domain is within the Neschamha, while Hod exists in the Ruach.

You may be wondering why Binah is filtered by Chesed and not Tiphareth. The mystery lies in what Binah, Chesed, and Hod have in common: the element of Water. The same is true of Chokmah, Geburah, and Netzach, because all three share the element of Fire. The Middle Pillar consists entirely of sephiroth corresponding to the element of Air, and these principles apply here as well.

One of the many attributions to the sphere of Mercury alludes to the intellect – the capacity to reason, the seat of logic. It is interesting to note that it also represents the Kundalini energy known as Pingala.

The vices of falsehood and dishonesty probably allude to the God of Thieves, Mercury, who received a bad reputation in Greek mythology for having stolen the heifers of Apollo.

(See the chapter on the Greek Gods in New Aeon Magick)

The Archangel Michael was probably placed here because he is the slayer of the serpent, and illustrates the superiority of the intellect over illusion.

Because the intellect is greatly embellished by this sephirah, it has become a trap for many potential magicians. Many of them will become armchair magicians, satisfied with the never-ending task of impressing their fellows with their mental prowess. This is mental masturbation, and does not lead to Knowledge and Conversation of the Holy Guardian Angel. The magician must be constantly aware of this danger, and strive as best as he or she can

---

*   The Mystical Qabalah by Dion Fortune 1935

to continue moving forward. (See "A Word About Balance" in New Aeon Magick.*)*

Invocation

The following example is a highly abbreviated sample from an actual working. It is meant to serve as a guideline for your own personal work with these entities. The first actual working, from which many of these excerpts are taken, lasted a grueling four-and-a-half hours. I had a very complete list of questions, and the creature was friendly, entertaining, and willing to indulge me. Whether or not there is anything useful in the following pages is up to the reader.

This is the hardest part of the entire process. This is because most people can't get beyond the fact that they are actually trying to contact an entity which may or may not exist outside of their minds. There is a fear of insanity, which is justifiable. All one has to do is look at the condition and lifestyles of most modern magicians to understand this concern, but the study of magick is a relatively safe endeavor for people who are well balanced and have done the preliminary work. In *New Aeon Magick,* you will find Qabalistic correspondences and a study on mythology, as well as simple exercises to prepare your mind for the journey. Your safety line is composed of four principles:

Knowledge. Study, learn, practice, and prepare for your magical work. If you jump in with both feet, unprepared and unconditioned, you shouldn't be surprised if you find yourself walking on a cracking layer of thin ice.

Courage. The audacity to go forward, to endure and accept the challenge. This kind of confidence follows knowledge.

Silence. Don't reveal too much. Don't kiss and tell. The dispersion of magical energy through speech is a very real thing. Record your experiments and their results in your diary.

Will. Do what thou wilt shall be the whole of the Law. Try as best as you can to not waste your time on issues that will lead you astray from your path. Time is not a renewable resource. Use it wisely.

The preparatory work of bathing and setting up a double-cube altar is described in *New Aeon Magick*. Place the *Book of the Law* upon it with an orange candle and an incense burner that will bellow the sweet smell of Storax, both of which are customary for working with this sephirah. You have put on your robe and are wearing an apron (a Masonic one will do just fine), which is the magical weapon for this sephira, and for an extra nice touch, you have painted the sigil on it. Now you are prepared with your list of questions for the spirit. You do have something to ask, don't you?

Perform the Rituals of the Banishing Pentagram and Hexagram (See *New Aeon Magick*).

Now, you must invoke Mercury in the usual way. You will draw the four invoking hexagrams of Mercury in the four quarters, and a fifth where the physical location of the planet is at the time of your invocation. Mercury travels with the sun, and so if you perform your invocation at 8 p.m. (as you should), then the fifth hexagram will be drawn below the horizon to the West.

Turn to that direction, and recite an appropriate prayer. Here is one that works rather well, as it begins with a prayer to Tahuti. You are assuming the god form of Horus. Horus asks for Tahuti's assistance in summoning the creature that will respond to the sigil you have made:

> *I call upon you, Tahuti, the Messenger, The Son and The Daughter combined, in the name of the One whose name is never spoken, I summon thee. Patron of Youth, Wisdom and Health, Master of the Word whose winged feet move him without care through the veils of our very existence, I call for thee. Oh thou thrice proclaimed emerald God, whose laurels heal the sick and whose scent awakens the sleeping masses.*
>
> *Thou who rules over the rivers and creeks of our bodies and causes them to intertwine in us like serpents. Thrice, I call upon thee.*
>
> *Behold, for I am the Hawk-Headed one, the son of the immortal self-slain self-raised, and I am enshrined by the blue-lidded daughter of sunset. On my breast I carry the mark of my father, and on my right hand the double-headed wand of power. I am the Lord of Fire and I am the Lord of Silence, I am the Lord of destruction and reconciliation and have avenged my Father.*
>
> *Tahuti. Thoth. Anubis. Hermes. Mercury. Odin. By whichever of these names I call you: Assist me; lend me your armies and your generals. Make them obedient unto me, so that I may accomplish the Great Work.*

It is worth mentioning that there is no use going into the invocation of Tahuti, much less the creature, until the proper transformation from magician to Horus has taken place. It is very difficult to explain how you will know you are there. In fact, as a writer and a magician, trying to articulate the experience is a source of great frustration to me. This is not something that can be faked. It has nothing to do with theatrics, memorizing lines, or dressing up. It is something that cannot be taught, but those people who are able to legitimately pull this off can show it to open-minded students under controlled conditions.

The entire art of magick, whether it be Enochian, Goetic, Qabalistic, or otherwise, depends on the ability to do this one thing well. The student is well advised not to skip any of the preliminary work.

Once you have assumed the god form, you must call upon your subjects. There will be no need to be creative, nor will you find a loss of words if you have truly made the transition.

Conjuring the Creature
The first call
> *I call upon the bearer of this symbol to come forward in the name of Tahuti, that thou mayest serve me well and please your master. Appear within the triangle and announce thy true name.*

The second call
> *Secret Spirit of Hidden Wisdom whose privileged eyes have beheld the splendor of those things concealed from man. I seek your council in the name of he who is above you and around you. Show yourself presently. Let thine image be familiar to me.*

I'll not ruin the experience for the reader by describing what occurred in the room, or in what form the creature manifested. Suffice to say that it was beautifully pleasing to the eyes, nose and ears. In this particular operation, the spirit revealed itself as Theriedon.

The name was composed entirely from 8 letters found on the square and in the creation of the sigil. So far so good. Next, I opened up my book of English Qaballa correspondences and enumerated his name. Theriedon = 115: Mercury. Bingo.

I began to ask my questions, which were composed in such a way as to make it easy for the spirit to answer. I did this thinking that the creature would be deceiving (as the Goetic spirits can often be). I was surprised by the sincerity of the spirit, and the developed dialogue that we shared. I was surprised by what it told me, and was quite taken back when it asked me some very specific questions about my work. I asked if it would come again when called, and it said it would, but asked that I burn Sandalwood and Frankincense instead of Storax, as it finds that aroma of those compounds much more pleasing.

Here is a partial list of the questions that I asked, and the accompanying dialogue and conclusions that I came to from my session with Theriedon.

Query One: The dilemma caused by the extra four letters of the English language, and where they are placed on the Tree of Life. His response:

The Tree is in every way perfect. The paths for the additional four letters of the English Alphabet are already there. Some things do not change from one Aeon to another. You seek for something new with the turn of the seasons, not understanding or appreciating the gifts you already possess. Some things simply relocate. The key is in Da'ath, but not in the manner that you suspect. Think of the sephiroth as doors, and Da'ath as an open portal to the Trees on the other planes.

There are three dimensions to the Tree: the first is illustrated by the horizontal paths, the second by the vertical. There is a third behind the middle pillar composed of Da'ath, and at one time, there were the four paths connecting it to Chokmah, Binah, Chesed and Geburah. During this time, Malkuth was simply Kether of the Tree below. There is another dimension, but we are not yet ready to speak about this now.

We engineered a cataclysmic leap in your evolution. As a result of that violent jump in human consciousness, Da'ath broke away from the rest of the tree, descending down and attaching itself to the bottom of the Tree at Malkuth where it currently resides: which was once the Kether of the Tree below it. The paths folded onto itself like a lotus closing its petals. Those four paths became your four elements. Those four elements are the paths which you seek, and solve the mystery of the extra four letters. They are the gates to the palace.*

---

*   The term "Da'ath" is a word that predates the Zohar. It was used to define The Supernal Triad. It is said to have been rediscovered during the Lurianic period in the 1500's, and many Hebrew Kabbalists believe that it was wrongly taken to be a missing sephirah. Nevertheless, it has been widely adopted and accepted by many Western Mystery Traditions, such as the Golden Dawn and others, and it has been used to indicate the location of the Garden of Eden before The Fall.

The following drawings are a feeble attempt to illustrate the objects which Theriedon projected unto a water-filled scrying mirror.

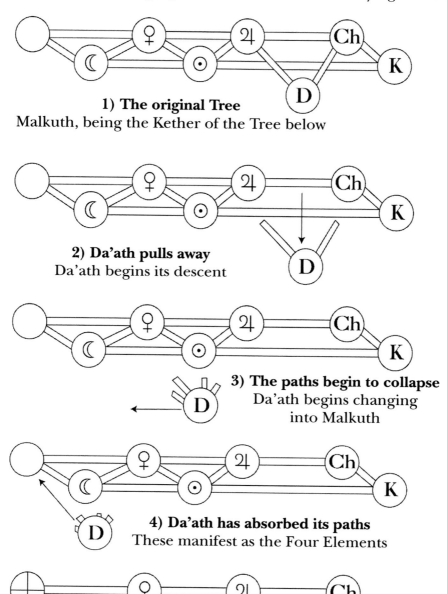

1) The original Tree
Malkuth, being the Kether of the Tree below

2) Da'ath pulls away
Da'ath begins its descent

3) The paths begin to collapse
Da'ath begins changing
into Malkuth

4) Da'ath has absorbed its paths
These manifest as the Four Elements

5) The cycle is complete

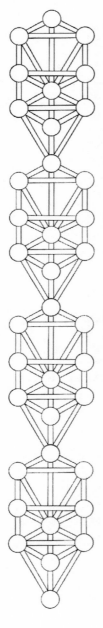

Theriedon continued, *In order to appreciate this, an illustration is necessary. Kether is in Malkuth, but after another manner. Your current model shows a static universe, when in reality it is in a state of flux. The four Trees model you use does not illustrate evolution because you don't live long enough to notice it. (See Tree on Left)*

This reorganization will continue throughout the ages, until all four of your Trees overlap, and you are able to travel through all Four Worlds simultaneously. This overlap of dimensions is explained by your scientists as the expansion and contraction of the Universe. The current stage is more accurately illustrated by a model in which Malkuth is the Da'ath of the Tree below it. (See Tree on Right)

Remember that Da'ath is a portal that can be used to move between worlds. Study the relationship between the Crown and the Foundation to understand your current state of affairs as a species.

The next shift will unite the Father with the Son, and a God will walk the earth again.

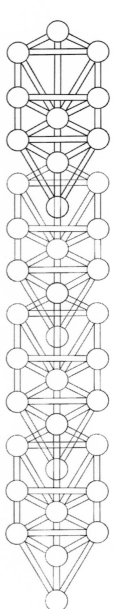

The four letters attributed to the four elements in Malkuth are L, W, N, and R. These are called the double letters. You will understand why by studying the alphabet as it is used in your own native tongue.

This tormented me for many years. Due to the tremendous resistance by researchers in English Qaballa to postulate that this particular key might work for all languages that use the same symbols, I overlooked the possibility that the letters may be part of my own language. My native tongue is Castilian, **not** English. In many European cultures where Latin is the root of most things in their language, these letters are doubled up and treated as different letters altogether: W is simply a double V, while L is LL, R is RR, and N is Ñ.

L is for Fire, the creative force that can only occur when uniting one thing with another thing. W is obviously for Water, for the letter itself is a pictogram of the physical waters. N is for Air for reasons which will become apparent to you later. R is for Earth, the physical vessel for the other elements.

Together, these letters enumerate to 31, which is also the number of: Nu, far, work, shadows, sea, small, sons, sands, soul, roads, crawl, a very nice collection of words that could easily be applied to define Malkuth. It's interesting that Nu is connected with the number of these letters combined, for if we look at Malkuth, which is 78, we see her name spelled in full, with a couple of other names which correspond: Nuit, Apep, Lilith, amaranth, and diamond.

This completes the formula for the elements. The names of the Tarot cards for these paths are: Being, Certainty, Meaning, and Consequence.

I was then shown the pictures on the reflection of my scrying mirror:

Being: Letter L. Fire attribution. A male god sits naked in a lotus position with open palms facing up. On his right hand the letter A, on his the left, the letter Z. A huge burst of light emanating from the 3d eye chakra. A DNA strand is visible in the middle of the burst of light, as though the thought of creation just entered the humanoid's mind. The letter L hovers directly over his head.

Certainty: Letter W. Water attribution. A female god, pregnant, sits in lotus with both hands open. She floats on a black sea. Her womb is transparent and in the shape of an Alchemical flask. Inside the flask is a child in the sign of Hoor-Pa-Krat. On the right hand is a burning bush. On the left is a seed. The letter W hovers directly over her head.

Meaning: Letter N. Air attribution. A scientist in a lab, his eyes on a microscope as he writes in a book. English letters are scattered in disarray all over the walls of the lab. There is a flask on a burner of the same type as described in "Certainty." Inside the flask there are three letters spelling the word "LAW." The letter N is clearly visible at the top of the card, larger than the other letters.

Consequence: Letter R. Earth attribution. A man stands at a cross-roads. His back is to me. The path to the left is dry, dead, and desolate. Ruins. The sky over that part of the card is dark and foreboding. The right path is brightly lit, green, thriving with trees and lake, children in the distance playing. Next to his right foot a plant begins to grow. Above his head: the letter R.

For the proper pronunciation of the barbarous name, insert the letters I, A, and O. LIWANOR.

IAO = 31 same as LWNR

31 ☾ = 13. Ra, do, add

Together, the name LIWANOR enumerates to 62: Tum, sacred, deed, hope, just, kings, order, grace, awaking, satyrs, ghastly, worked, found, gems, fury, camel, bowels.

26 ☾ = 26. Gold, son, shadow, car, sand, class, dally

As to the letter representing spirit, it is A, Air as in the singularity, the first breath sound and the soul of the individual. The Tarot card associated with this character is The Aeon.

That would make it LWANR = 32. Kaaba, Logo, his, door, cloak, lords, salt, oil, rood, sap.

23 ☾ = 23. I, fall, calls, slay, wood, swallow, swan, glow, coal, land, hard, cow.

A = 1

Air = 36. Sails, sun, seas, swoon, man, mask, opal, talk, works, souls, fawn, hills, head, folk, kill, drawn.

36 ☾ = 63. Ships, adorer, lustral, forms, anger, above, cling, bind, move, healed, leave, page, wanton, glee, wastes, fix, azure, ten, walking, ashamed, cackle, part, range, dolorous, having, burn.

Breath = 86. Mercy, spoken, throne, seated, myself, bride, scents, fumes, courage, creeds, filthy, unclean, ravished, forbid, tree, bodies, resolve, disclose, parches, titan, images, ripe, beware.

86 ☾ = 68. Jesus, maker, life, chosen, fate, sought, adamant, proud, brave, horned, availed, aflame, burns, build, palace, parts, dine, befall, fling, fee, rapid, orison, craft, nets, bait, change, lute, abuse, smooth.

Sound = 49. Eros, rose, key, bell, shakes, called, echo, cave, crown, sore, rage, solve, meal, gain, loves, crazy, moon, Astor, bath, Saxon, male, alone, Jews.

49 ☾ = 94. Helper, creator, destroy, burden, laborious, sister, prize, inmost, invoked, assembly, lovesick, thief, fruit, sickens, cometh, expand, branches, stagnant, trodden, parted, bright, blackness, rideth, brine, shining, girders, depart, autumn, left-hand, sphinx, runner, unbind, stardust, inhuman, point.

Breath % Sound = 430. Sound % Breath = 294. Combined = 724.
Singularity = 147. Hyperbolic, extended, enlightens, beautiful,
bedchamber, stripped, abandonment, minister, exceeded
Soul = 31, again. 31 ʊ is 13. See above.

*When Da'ath descended, it created a vacuum in its place, a wormhole
of sorts that various people have learned to use as a portal in order to
travel quickly throughout the planes: from one Tree to another. It is a
shortcut for those of you that can reach it unharmed.*

*An illustration is necessary. Imagine there being only one Da'ath,
but four Trees. Da'ath is the hub that connects these together. Once you
can imagine this, you will see that the Pillar of Mercy on one tree, is the
Pillar of Severity on the one next to it; Chesed becomes Geburah, Netzach, Hod, and so on. This is important because the plane before influ-
ences the plane that follows, and this colors the outcome of your magick.*

*Tell them if you must. But they will gauge your understanding by
comparing this concept against already existing conventional Qabalah, and think you mad.*

Query Two: On the attributions of the English letters to the paths
on the tree.

Path	Letter	Value	Tarot Card	Planets, Alchemy, or Elements
11	A	1	The Aeon	Pluto
12	B	20	The Magician	Mercury
13	G	11	The High Priestess	Luna
14	D	6	The Empress	Venus
15	H	4	The Star	Aquarius
16	V	10	The Hierophant	Taurus
17	Z	9	The Lovers	Gemini
18	C	13	The Chariot	Cancer
19	T	24	Strength	Leo
20	Y	15	The Hermit	Virgo
21	K	9	Wheel of Fortune	Jupiter
22	U	17	Justice	Libra
23	M	21	Hanged Man	Neptune
24	F	18	Death	Scorpio
25	S	5	Art	Sagittarius
26	O	7	The Devil	Capricorn

27	P	26	The Tower	Mars
28	J	16	The Emperor	Aries
29	Q	19	The Moon	Pisces
30	I	23	The Sun	Sol
31	E	25	The Fool	Uranus
32	X	22	The Universe	Saturn
33	L	2	Being	Fire
34	W	3	Certainty	Water
35	N	14	Meaning	Air
36	R	12	Consequence	Earth

Query 3: On the proper method of invoking, and on restraining the creatures.

*Call as you have called me. We are ordered to cooperate by one higher than you, each of us in our own capacity to assist you to progress. No need to restrain or force us into a triangle, but we will comply so that you will be able to tell us apart from the disobedient ones. It is an unnecessary device unless one wishes to summon The Shells. In these cases, the triangle works best due to its sacred geometry. To work with The Shells, one simply need reverse the method you used to find me.**

"You do so at your own risk, however. Move with caution if you must use them. You will be in unfamiliar territory, and they can be unpredictable at best and will try to deceive you any way they can. They can be held at bay and ordered back into the triangle with the use of the Stele. We rejoice before this image, while they cannot look into it when held before them. Also, you must never give them the Law of Gladness. "

Query 4: On the problem of creating squares with a small number of letters.
When using the Obsidian Square, the Magician must learn to economize speech by reducing the desire to one word. This has many other advantages, which will not become apparent to you just yet.

Obsidian is 99. Divided, strive, obscure, prevail, aphorism, points.

Square is 79. Abrahadabra, making, linked, higher, homeward, arcanum, white, heaven, working, govern, source.

Together they are 178. Thelemites, complement, and inheritance.

Query 5: The nature of the interaction between Nuit, Hadit and humans.

---

* So that the square is composed of vowels and the sigils of consonants.

The interplay of the Gods in the Thelemic pantheon depends largely on human experience. Nuit and Hadit exist because you do. The Book of the Law *screams to you to live your lives in joy and to try all things without guilt. At least most all things. Even in Thelema there are limits.*

Nuit, the sphere of all possibility. She lulls you into experience, while Hadit, the core of every Star, is there as an ever vigilant witness recording your life events in every way, emotional, physical or intellectual, on all planes known and unknown. Good experiences, bad experiences, it doesn't matter. He is a passive player, while you, the active participant in the game of life, provide him with the means and opportunity to fulfill his intended purpose of union with Nuit. He must not, or rather cannot, return empty handed. Existence is joy and Nuit hungers for it. And when your lives are over, Hadit proceeds to his Nuit like a bee heavy with the pollen of experience returning to its hive.

It now becomes necessary to oversimplify this for your understanding. All of the Hadits put together equal the one Nuit. Or, if you prefer, Nuit is divided into many pieces. Call them Hadits, and each piece is looking for the moment of union with another piece. The Tree of Life is a symbol which illustrates this phenomena.

Thelemites are servants, and it is through experience that you worship your gods. Think of it this way: The gods created you so that they could know what chocolate tasted like.

"So what happens when Hadit returns to Nuit? There is a phenomenal fusion of ecstasy that utterly destroys them both so that neither of them exists. You refer to this process as Ra-hoor-khuit. Then they, or rather "It," is reborn once again, and the process begins anew with a new, improved and expanded realm of possibility, and a new and improved Hadit. This describes the method of evolution of your species, and it is occurring every moment of your lives and will continue forever. Everything comes back to its source, and everything is redistributed, the universe is in a constant state of expansion and compression in various dimensions.

Humans suffer from separation anxiety because their egos don't like to postulate a future in which they are not included. There is a solution for this problem, and it is precisely the problem that magick was designed to address. Read the words of the Prophet. Learn and understand the Law. You will know what to do.

License to Depart

"Because you assisted this Star in its going, and have complied with my desires, I reward you with this bouquet. Depart to your place when you have had your fill of it. I send you off with a greeting of gladness: Do what thou wilt shall be the whole of the Law. Let there be peace and mutual respect between us, and may the blessings of Our Lady be upon you. Love is the law, love under will. Be thou ready to come when I am in need of your assistance, either by the application of these rites, or by the simple utterance of your name. In the name of God, which is never spoken. Aum."

Appendix A
Brief Listing of Numbers and Their Relationship to Class A Words

The following words were taken from some of the Holy Books of Thelema, and are arranged in numerical order to be used as a reference to your work in the English Qaballa.

This is by no means complete. I couldn't praise John Crow's *New Aeon English Qabalah Dictionary* enough if I wanted to (Luxor Press, 2002). He has broken down several thousand words alphabetically *and* by numerical value according to Cipher 6. Well worth the trouble, and it will save you numerous intimate hours with your calculator.

1	A
2	L
3	W, AL
5	S, Ha, all, ah
6	D, as, law
7	O
8	Z
9	K, was, saw, lo
10	V, Ka, has, ash
11	G, ho, ass, oh, Had, had
12	R, so, low, sad
13	C, do, add, Ra
14	N, shall, who, how
15	Y, old, also, walk, an, ask
16	J, howl, war, ay, dash
17	U, hawk, oak, slow
18	F, lay, go, call
19	Q, Asar, or, way, show, hold
20	B, Away, vow, asks, glad
21	M, goal, gash, on, and, say, no
22	X, us, clad, alway, why, am, hawks, draw, day, oaks
23	I, fall, calls, slay, wood, swallow, swan, glow, coal, land, hard, cow

24	T, holds, glass, dog, hood, lady, sway, ways, own, claws, now, dawn, wand, god, odds
25	E, hollow, of, hand, at, rod, soar, half, look, vows, ovals
26	P, gold, son, says, whoso, shadow, car, sand, class, dally
27	Ran, lord, ill, days, hook, always, graal
28	Cold, slays, mad, is, holy, swans, dark, sack, rolls, can, falls, we, ray, woods, word
29	Isa, Asi, sky, rags, dogs, lap, cool, snow, he, wands, gods, wail, sank, ox, tall
30	Hoor, Khu, Chaos, Wanga, hail, wolf, world, rods, aid, down, drag, any, will, hang, hands, nay, flow, sat
31	Nu, IAO, far, gallows, work, sang, shadows, sea, sail, pall, small, sons, good, sands, to, soul, roads, crawl
32	What, his, door, cloak, lords, kaaba, afar, salt, oil, agora, laid, last, blow, flag, shook, rood, sap, heal, mg, loud, well, asp, logo
33	Aloud, words, hath, hell, nor, fold, seal, sword, grow, soon, iv, vi, know, rays, wholly
34	Arab, grass, she, fool, snows, dew, wild, arm, long, two, deal, hast, lead
35	Arrow, woe, dais, skull, did, whom, crash, said, fly, would, by, lowland, coral, worlds, hangs, laugh
36	Sails, sun, swoon, man, mask, worn, cook, goods, opal, air, talk, our, works, souls, locks, shalt, fawn, gat, my, hills, head, seas, folk, yon, kill, drawn, lewd
37	For, collar, in, fro, song, swell, art, warm, wells, leash, age, dusk, may, royal, horn, avail, pass, less, lake
38	Aiwass, haze, hells, knows, dwell, harm, act, cat, grows, hole, bars, too, Nia, lost, are, wrack, joy, only, Ain, shell, dead, moss, food, weak, swords
39	AUM, full, arms, gale, fools, awake, khabs, lose, wave, follow, rosy, leads, orb, such, told, you, task, gray
40	Lowlands, lurk, flood, shed, host, hour, altar, have, ye, sake, tool, hardly, woes, gross, cry, hair, laughs, vast
41	Pan, bull, hoofs, doth, her, should, shoe, rock, whole, ours, awful, Hades, yea, aye, if, mans, wear, heads, save, vials
42	Damn, new, cross, boy, ages, bark, drank, sub, sin, dost, want, songs, pool, horns, blood, hum, hear, star, kiss, lakes, pay, high

43	Each, cats, joys, run, foods, liars, up, shells, back, red, goat, worm, brass, lawful, aged, book, than, across, acid, cast, harp, thy, din, toads, bazaar, off, does, ache, slave
44	Folly, play, whose, Jew, scholar, dear, waves, read, roof, wrath, fail, bank, fang, foul, whirl, suck, dare, love, undo
45	Horus, duck, hosts, sunk, black, fill, not, could, orgy, darkly, be, watch, end, slain, coil, altars, Apollo
46	Woman, floor, me, loose, few, flush, void, toy, easy, lion, leaf, ink, blown, sorrow, bulls, hewn, wind, kin, sugar, swear, one, when, corn, abyss, drug
47	Maat, clasp, aeon, pools, ooze, it, known, cowards, jackals, flap, wraps, egg, gave, wrong, use, brows, which, wound, took, stars, shoot, guard, glory, fur, boys, fox, fell, foam, bond, sooth, cells, silly
48	Goats, out, him, rave, bulk, goodly, swoop, buds, shrill, body, sighs, park, slaves, yews, heard, haply, goes, dove, sharp, web, fast, girl, vain, wend, child, runs, lust, link, backs, dung, flew, casts, hound
49	Eros, sore, lower, rage, solve, meal, flock, Mary, sound, gain, loves, pack, fangs, crazy, bell, crown, stood, curls, bid, et, moon, Astor, bath, Saxon, male, shakes, alone, Jews, echo, called, rose, cave, key
50	Seb, clouds, harlot, send, stand, fish, dread, lamp, sandglass, rode, self, root, thus, fade, showed, faun, eat, loved, Coph, arose, lie, worth, rain, rare, six, coils, wroth, again, nuns, axle, rear, flats
51	Your, base, charm, fled, woodlands, glare, dragon, drop, winds, womb, many, icy, wing, lazily, hit, let, care, cum, bed, grew, sink, island, false, drugs, wildly, crush, try, sorry, knew, gazed, sorrows, skin, axis, ones, race, wait, amid, adore, large
52	Adonai, Hathor, aeons, eggs, its, dust, loosed, near, await, navel, buy, gird, wet, musk, nigh, garlands, rich, thou, acorns, poor, wolves, push, float, sit, ape, done, tale, thank, galaxy, snowfall, boat, swim, close, same, bonds, scarab, wilt
53	Lazuli, made, angry, angel, frogs, vulgar, brand, year, girls, that, the, sing, tell, stank, sign, clear, spark, shore, dress, ordeal, today, afloat, toward, bolt, dower, cakes, wizard, born, horse

54	Buddha, flesh, hoarse, snake, pale, soft, lyre, pray, hate, swallowed, big, haven, heat, blade, yellow, four, vault, horror, learn, set, die, fair, with, byway, over, leap, roses, among, hymn, moons, cut, miss, gums
55	Ptah, Abaddon, Apis, magus, hooded, lies, isle, lotus, flake, grade, east, eats, fades, orchard, much, chain, stands, reach, milk, bliss, seat, catch, naked, ravish, see, both, sling, shone, sate, opus, pharaoh, palms, value, valley, deadly, path
56	Isis, chant, drain, ruddy, wings, rule, paid, round, past, make, shame, ease, faded, yoke, this, fear, foot, yours, beds, gulp, swing, lest, brown, shrouds, soared, heap, iron, still, blaze, wise, weary, magi, marrow, cup, looked, lips, lover
57	Caesar, Obeah, adored, withal, phallus, help, bloom, home, lapis, bless, else, hurt, human, wide, cicada, raced, king, satyr, steal, canst, season, most, below, bloody, coin, top, based, around, least, torn, while, west, awaits, face, aught, core, gone, apes, waxed
58	Hadit, droop, atoms, drunk, from, drowse, chorus, form, angels, house, abased, swollen, closed, sweat, sparks, shaken, heath, hide, awhile, some, signs, bear, bare, years, horses, onyx, ordeals
59	Khem, kiblah, wheel, cone, yoni, onrush, leaps, sure, forward, like, hunt, cowardly, knave, byways, once, side, dance, ready, cradle, dregs, blades, wealth, grave, take, abode, reward
60	Evil, pallid, heed, almost, alike, harder, came, deny, death, lashing, get, health, gnawed, bosom, paths, none, men, grades, slayer, bane, live, spell, brew, gleam, veil, hillock, died, loosen, fins, aside, decay, cower, anarchy, vital, ransom, search, chains, vile, ocean, ring, cloudy, answer
61	Atman, choose, lovely, afraid, lucid, amen, rules, whips, find, waking, lovers, name, wander, bird, arched, neck, north, cause, makes, but, caress, ice, shape, mane, gate, fears, showers, seed, asylum
62	Tum, Mongol, relax, ere, locked, deed, satyrs, order, grace, animal, swathe, masses, tear, very, just, score, kings, ghastly, worked, already, hope, sailed, awaking, unto, sacred, found, gems, fury, shamed, abashed, camel, fellows, fallen, porch, bowels, pour

63	Leave, lustral, page, wanton, forms, glee, wastes, fix, azure, ten, walking, ashamed, bears, anger, above, cackle, cling, bind, move, healed, part, range, dolorous, having, adorer, ships, burn, rapt
64	Nile, Hindu, bridal, check, sigil, blue, bury, ascend, seek, line, myrrh, fresh, belly, eagle, twin, bread, light, young, weave, upon, pylon, sealed, bound, dive, sides, dumb, thrown, drink, drone, behold, reap, robe, equal, reason, wheels, closer, yet, weeds, ruby, abodes, sunray, didst, mind, languor, stir, druid, apart, pain
65	Babalon, Italy, damsels, rise, veils, dream, Indus, assuage, fit, wisdom, armed, lives, forth, alight, lonely, more, were, oceans, jet, water, warmth, froth, honey, colder, golden, spells, eye, pen, lying, goddess, adorant, those, wine, globe, touch, sunny, danced, gleams, abound, blind, twain, bend
66	Legis, Uranus, rest, thigh, mend, sorely, grains, lowest, waning, laughed, staff, maim, ride, speak, means, lived, ruin, pillar, holies, slimy, raise, plain, mix, plum, gates, lofty, here, pearl, foolish, thorns, herbs, heart, thrush, went, topaz, tooth, hangman, laying, come, dagger, devil, charge, birds, boyhood, argue, babe, calling, earth, arise, bone
67	Smoke, obey, brake, olive, skies, shaped, break, sight, ivory, cover, place, welded, stain, youth, turn, arouse, attach, masked, thrill, though, then, teach, deeds, stops, joyous, animals, gushes, must, hardens, shaking, gaunt, plough, scrub, pours, pluck, passes, flower, edge, ravens, flame, wonder, yearn, lift, put
68	Tzaddi, Jesus, dine, palace, proud, parts, befall, maker, fling, fee, rapid, they, passed, nets, into, chosen, sought, aflame, adamant, fate, availed, burns, build, orison, horned, brave, bait, change, smaller, lute, craft, unless, abuse, smooth, life
69	Gladness, fairy, darling, danger, give, closely, third, saying, scarce, druids, cease, homage, pains, spare, spear, cruel, storm, reels, dying, starry, robes, stoop, seen, lights, wife, about, where, weird, loosing, felt, left, magic, garden

70	Caligula, Cheth, eyes, amorous, truly, faith, groves, symbol, milky, feel, note, globes, space, dived, warrior, second, caught, knower, beat, women, absorbs, outward, waters, rises, absolve, wines, clearly, girt, bends, gladdens, followed, slavery, proof, brain, upwards, chance, slopes, need, although, jets, flee
71	Atone, cloven, pillars, hearts, bones, weighs, plains, slyness, mate, filth, vice, slaying, graver, parallel, wrote, limbs, chapel, crust, reek, triads, globed, wedded, glowing, comes, style, jewel, ibis, marvel, began, glamour, naught, glances, gnarled, falling, yield, pearls, longer, faery, burrow, babes, landmarks, easily, surpass, shine
72	Crystal, happy, habit, kisses, chaste, domain, ilex, places, ever, magical, other, grip, attack, tossed, tomb, lingam, plucks, melt, raised, fashion, skilled, thread, flowers, throat, curse, vessel, open, flames
73	Demand, holier, smoked, demon, forge, strong, store, keen, hasten, court, cannot, orisons, wisely, jocund, lutes, taken, sudden, great, gilded, mouth, peck, graven, Bacchus, press, Athens, giant, damned, fading, rice, feats, group, thick, palaces, fates, runes, power, pit, charred, console, dazzling, metal, feast, swift, flamed
74	Ararita, gives, travel, column, sighed, under, spears, lesser, gazelle, them, doubt, exalt, even, scarred, firm, harmony, apex, best, adorable, revel, noise, think, right, sense, assume
75	Osiris, abide, pet, played, issue, shudder, cavern, closing, ceased, city, prongs, imps, dweller, force, conceal, reveal, count, dropt, judge, beast, grape, spread, aright, factor, draught, cube, symbols, bees, anguish, stone, stink, warriors, falsehood, sucked, union, crackle, whirled
76	Heru-ra-ha, Iacchus, meats, stayed, filled, seem, steady, absolved, night, smile, vices, aimed, thing, canopy, slime, withdraw, dancers, belts, coiled, drive, five, towers, nine, forty, jewels
77	Ammon-ra, Khuit, vilely, others, toyed, enjoy, venom, vessels, darkness, fishhook, throes, coldness, wailing, curses, inane, curve, devour, crystals, vines, silver, scream, serve, keyword, deem, lively, madness, double, gather, sickle

78	Nuit, Apep, Lilith, Malkuth, rather, averse, fantasy, borne, pyre, true, odyssey, hidden, amaranth, voice, enough, demons, feasts, giants, petal, prey, unknown, powers, garlanded, willing, display, wept, speck, burst, mantras, chirp, test, guarded, thee, wounded, myriad, fire, knees, licked, lithe, fondled, angrily, diamond, mouths, cries, goring, wrought, rider, cancer, spit, thousand
79	Abrahadabra, Zelator, consoled, making, midst, lusted, cried, music, linked, kindle, higher, state, taste, spout, homeward, arcanum, white, heaven, yonder, working, govern, source, seven, ritual, riddles, powder, against, forgot, sunder, girdle, weep, fret, through, fields, wicked, unable, reins
80	Sparkle, length, nymph, blizzard, spilt, struck, fount, beggar, stones, crowned, step, fight, heavily, split, after, until, gained, beasts, faint, asunder, abides, pure, pomp, perch, arisen, liquor, worship, free, bring, forces, bathed, grapes, since, dwellers, extol, single, fine, offer
81	Khephra, unhallowed, weapons, things, troops, truth, guise, knowing, gifts, mire, divers, taught, marble, issued, image, cheeks, scent, rooted, seems, clothed, paste, radiant, Indian, passion, smiles, hiding, giver, nights, alchemy, equally, steel, stele, fought
82	Leading, first, vision, follies, adept, winged, longing, waited, fourth, action, liber, diadem, aimless, deep, insane, beheld, enslave, sweet, carrion, crushed, plague, dolphin, stroke, smote, endless, selfish, guide, slept, language, poison, scarlet, balanced, charmed, Greek, money, river
83	Archangel, sleep, comely, shrine, sheet, shoulders, chief, living, bursts, circus, mere, birth, bought, mount, arrive, voices, might, middle, mine, these, swept, success, blasted, sorrowful, unloosed, specks, bent, subtly, strewn, myriads, distil, flying, fires, laughing, hunger, earthly, godlike, floated, given, diamonds, inkhorn, dissolve
84	Sebek, English, father, hundred, sweep, convey, couches, rite, blacken, foamless, rituals, whence, volcanoes, courses, basket, heavens, trout, hawk-headed, bestow, barren, glorious, chariot, decked, declare, kept, been, naming

85	Soldiers, vomit, faster, squared, next, visit, tasted, result, cubby, keep, kindled, reign, prayed, passing, college, jasper, stealth, reaches, primal, outer, girdled, sheep, tunes, holiness, cleanse, consoler, depth
86	Mercy, filthy, unclean, breath, ravished, forbid, tree, bodies, seated, myself, tuned, tricks, throne, resolve, bride, scents, never, disclose, fumes, courage, creeds, tavern, spoken, loathing, taint, parches, titan, partook, images, endowed, ripe, beware
87	Another, verily, fourfold, method, eater, flights, dreadful, fasten, prison, green, every, hideous, following, actions, gladiator, beyond, breast, kinsfolk, gossamer, chanted, guests, glacier, salvation, adepts, monthly, weakness, begun, poets, burnt, armies, eight, rivers, attain, write, crater, stilled, fifth, dalliance, drained, broken
88	Theban, archangels, nations, invoke, blessed, pity, oyster, prate, naturally, often, fullness, corpse, muscles, corners, eaglet, crying, modest, their, abreast, sinuous, master, ecstasy, circle, glorify, breed, rising, sheets, stream, russet, twice, basilisk, strayed, Coph-Nia
89	Nubian, tiers, humble, twine, creeks, spangles, sixty, twelve, cattle, openly, cloistral, obtain, rites, fathers, headdress, aureole, dreamt, luscious, raising, trance, threshold, dissolved, lustrous, nectar, eaten, solitary, chariots, vastness, coming, mandrake
90	Typhon, there, maiden, galaxies, somewhat, greatly, holiest, tried, nowhere, kissing, whereon, eunuch, disease, driven, suddenly, peace, spangled, hunted, flaming, python, liquid, weight, unlike, fever, uglier, three, paper, scourge, guardians, osprey, subdue, apostle, wheeled, declared, withdrawn, sunset, depths, hearing, approach, leaning, summons
91	Thought, appear, forsaken, joined, height, central, rightly, whiter, answered, caresses, spring, eagerly, leavings, sighing, outcast, ringed, disgust, prayer, languidly, veiled, casting, forest, unveil, within, starlit, monkey, herself, firmly, trees, eighth, kingdom, servant, revolve, easier

92	Sekhet, Hermes, embassy, caressed, carapace, infamy, praise, hither, undergo, pride, seized, reading, emerald, mockers, terror, spice, accursed, glaciers, wandered, mantles, thirst, feet, behind, playing, resolved, quench, manifold, nostrils, million, breasts, strange, frenzy
93	Tahuti, begin, silent, masters, ending, circles, coffin, granted, being, original, apparel, fiery, nature, illusion, listen, molten, unity, mother, theirs, soften, enamels, pines, whiten, nightly, corpses, poured, virgin, divide, time, thyself, coiling, shameless, divest, athirst, weddings, penis
94	Sickens, fruit, cometh, expand, thief, branches, invoked, stagnant, prize, helper, trodden, creator, whereof, parted, bright, blackness, sister, rideth, inmost, burden, brine, shining, assembly, girders, lovesick, depart, autumn, left-hand, sphinx, destroy, runner, laborious, unbind, stardust, inhuman, point
95	Narcissus, inform, singers, unfolded, roseleaf, genius, reaped, perish, scudding, passive, brought, formless, escape, whither, delight, desolate, licking, self-slain, beloved, bearded, maidens, system, meet, adoration, excess, cursing
96	Virginal, thoughts, loathsome, laughter, remain, servants, confound, violets, desire, statue, touched, trackless, heavenly, motion, winners, mingle, unfit, unveils, forests, fasting, springs, scourged, highest, farther, harpies, absorbed, appears, chamber, battle, coupled, heights
97	Ra-Hoor-Khut, Corinth, nothing, desert, itself, bathing, drunken, secure, distant, revile, weighed, greet, sphere, millions, rested, spices, writhed, purged, betray, harnessed, company, timid, tinge, miracle, started, heathen, markets, galloping, bites
98	Hungrily, delicacy, tongue, standing, praised, exhaust, covered, devilish, cohesion, quickly, stained, partake, cluster, smite, times, fifty, lifted, nameless, himself, mighty, smother, ploughed, darkened, strike, bedeck, virgins, utmost, eating, sending, visibly, plucked, failure, pleasant, turned, forcing, uncover, whitens, scribe, mothers, speech
99	Divided, winging, myrtle, waiting, endure, strive, sisters, sickness, children, obscure, ardently, balancing, smiling, nested, erect, defile, indeed, prevail, aphorism, cobbler, points

100	Hrumachis, reproach, awaiting, according, deadlier, unicorn, tigers, love-chant, sunlight, furnace, enemy, create, crapulous, systems, little, brooding, chastise, stealthy, adorations, daughter, suited, queen, rabbit, plunges, enter, delights, encamp, floating
101	Mentu, thrice, memory, reaper, achieve, mystic, misery, absolute, desires, eyelids, creep, singing, divine, abrogate, seeker, vitriol, remains, eleven, debate, discover, yourself
102	Thelema, Eleusis, criest, supernal, desired, accept, simple, consume, unassuaged, constant, eyeless, entrap, ramparts, country, eighty, mingled, knowledge, tinges, fluidic, without, morning, adultery, mockery, refuse, theism, famine, afterward, death-star, utter, captain, leaping, severe, beauty, teeth
103	Thebes, tongues, reaching, lighten, deliver, cipher, abideth, defied, eternal, direful, averted, friends, alphabet, disposed, unite, bottom, sword-girt, profane, fashioned, atheism, progress, Hercules, seeing, opened, melted, ravishing, softness, asserted
104	Hoor-Pa-Kraat, stainless, nakedness, pelican, whereby, beside, conjure, mystical, return, incest, brother, mouthed, secret, overthrow, likened, victory, pyramid, insight, wonderful, melancholy, breaker
105	Buddhist, object, convert, drenched, steep, thence, hurting, daughters, exalted, running, confused, athlete, violent, androgyne, alembic, night-sky, became, chapter, blessing, jasmine, rending, stillness, idleness, defiled, changeless
106	Athenian, Mohammed, symbolic, lovelier, journey, ceaseless, wherein, because, figure, correct, tender, huntress, anything, concealed, colouring, centaur, counted, dissolving, starlight, diverse, upper, revealed, gargantuan, bearing, tidings,
107	seemed, successors, strife, thunders, wheeling, silence, splendid, captains, trouble, midmost, prime, magician, stirred, debated, languishes, lambent, profound, majesty, unclouded, sunshine, scorpion, matter, conquer, before
108	Stature, spelling, consumed, fingers, purple, wood-nymphs, ourselves, refuge, rebuke, pursued, gathered, mistake, crocodile, covenant, traitors, ablution, vintage, veiling, visible, garment, fortress, unstable, rustling, contract, resinous

109	Chinese, gropeth, secrets, grandsire, feather, beaten, profaned, inhabit, universal, pyramids, qliphoth, overmuch, number, hermit, wandering, feareth, possessed, solitude, peeled, atrocious, oversee, nonsense, obscene, infernal, strangely, brothers, compassed, establish, meaning, gemmed, regret, finest, darkeners
110	Buddhists, greater, stronger, writing, acquire, manliness, partaker, ordering, lapis-lazuli, penned, powerful, uplift, inflamed, ravening, tearing, pouring, quarter, goat-hoofed
111	Macedonia, Mexico, admiring, trample, atheists, division, affright, empty, cacique, thousand-fold, immortal, thereon, vineyards, breathe, beareth, people, overshadowed, poisonous, become, virtue, burning, corrupt, invoking
112	Belching, leering, ascending, unknowable, letter, lighting, eyebrows, magistry, beholding, sevenfold, vultures, revealer, triangle, further, essence, moment, seeking, certain, wretched
113	Bending, beneath, spirit, struggled, slipped, service, scourging, future, fulfilled, watering, garments, centre, pleasure, troubled, concourse, prince, weariness, cities, discourse, moonlight, either, horsemen
114	Redeem, blindness, desolation, translated, libation, ripple, transcend, hermits, devourer, mounted, meaneth, splendour, numbers, forties, malachite, ancient, bestrew, freedom, merchant, anointed, business, petty
115	Mercury, daytime, alienate, disguise, radiating, recesses, meanest, dominion, accomplish, thereof, priest, likewise, virtuous, provided, shrinking, quarters, unique, ninety, upraised, despise, thereat
116	Generous, corrupts, peoples, adulterous, fierce, devotion, totter, sprinkle, writest, tinted, bindeth, wineskin, summoned, sacrament, exceed
117	Purity, worshipful, mystery, burnest, encompass, embrace, letters, smoothness, unripe, defunct, pieces, upright, terraces, trampled, litanies, drinketh, triangles, stooping, expound, refine, breathed, inflict, support, rapture, fortify, seeketh
118	Ankh-af-na-khonsu, plunging, striding, pinnacle, seekest, confusion, spirits, commune, courtesan, purpose, miraculous, princes, fastened, torrent, attained, seventy, toucheth

119	Abramelin, ancients, splendours, painted, parricidal, creation, surpassing, deeper, encloseth, splendrous, incense, clerk-house, amethyst, emblems, moreover, negation, blasphemy, sweeter, utterly, poverty, yielding, strength, promise, desirable, explore, merchants, mastered, empress
120	RaHoorKhuit, star-fire, streets, dispelled, mistress, directly, staggered, especial, wilderness, fitted, ignorance, potent, sickened, celestial, plaything, overcome, eightfold, banquet, fashioning, opening, prophesy, priests, ill-ordered
121	Phoenix, rapturous, mountain, pondered, harmonized, elephant, beetle, secretly, brilliant, torture, stinted, nipples, content, despised, delicious, rejoice, glitter, sacraments, flapping
122	Magister, religions, worshipers, unchanging, compassion, ambiguous, sapphire, loneliness, instantly, scimitar, confusing, appeared, menacing, unveiled
123	Fountains, wherewith, yourselves, night-stars, revealing, fantastic, earnestly, understood, kneeling, temple, threefold, effect, combine, embraced, stinking, pinnacles
124	Eucharist, suffices, listened, promises, pierce, prophet, conquest, understand, sitting, minute, increased, trelliswork, sphinxes, unfledged
125	devouring, bartered, comment, enmeshed, destroyed, written, disappear, dimmest, descended, mediate, pointed, stricken, dropping, argument, expanded, thereby, circuit
126	Perdurabo, suffered, beetles, lightning, delighted, ignited, conqueror, strenuous, shattered, sensualists, setting, plastered, midnight, particle, mountains, companion, honeycomb
127	Encircle, therein, equinox, pitied, disperse, throughout, vertically, illumine, tortoise, rejoiced, formulate, deceive, torment, untouched, straining, neither, pregnant
128	Baphomet, Aphrodite, Besnamaut, bitter, offering, temples, otherwise, wickedness, emperor, bringing, trident, righteous, concealeth, precious, pendulum, fighting, inspire, disciples
129	spearmen, exhausted, quenchless, whispered, tremble, dipping, position, windswept, prophets, inviolate, bedecked, creature, happiness, sepulcher

130	Harpocrates, spinning, printed, sittest, sceptre, better, pierced, intense, attracted, princely, ambergris, gathereth, multiply, infallible, tremulous, equation, devoureth, refuseth, spectre, limitless, afflicted
131	Trickling, sweetness, forbidden, enthroned, merciless, exorcist, manifest, serpent, resistless, wherefore, sinister, passionate, universe, foundation, sleeping, supreme, protect, destroyer, brighter, present, entered, azure-lidded
132	Eyesight, ceremony, subtlety, together, delightful, sufferer, blue-lidded, double-wanded, distorted, voluptuous, exorcise, instruct
133	Deceived, adumbrated, sacrifice, prepared, tentacles, undesired, thundered, foursquare, receive, dissolution, expire, perchance, pitiful, butting, imperial, spiritual, formulated
134	Resounding, entwined, delivered, bloodthirst, despite, abominable, unattacked, inspired, vibration, pervert, elevenfold, venerable
135	Altogether, expect, returned, formidable, scattered, trinity, inscribe, trembled, brilliance
136	HeruPaKraath, between, solemnity, discoursing, serpents, abasement, crystalline, proclaimed, smitten, crystallized, conditions, selflessness, distressed, foundations
137	Neapolitan, worshipped, unfathomed, vermilion, fitting, journeyed, earthquake, ultimate, pretends, enterer, expansion, stridency, especially, stability
138	Ibis-headed, winepress, vengeance, conquered, stretched, enemies
139	Sacrificed, judgments, inverted, penniless, enginery, unveiling, servility, exposure, deceiver
140	Picture, enveloped, neophyte, hierophant, established, demiurge, eighties, instinct, realization
141	Continuous, terminus, victorious, uplifted, habitation, beauteous, elements, panpipe
142	Outermost, interplay, corrupted, prostrated, forgotten, magnitude
143	Transmute, informing, perfect, mightier, delighting, messenger, strenuously, complete, exempt, sustenance, terrible, worshipper, obstinate, mutilated, unthinkably

144	Capricorni, confident, irritate, dissipated, therewith, perfume, operations, rejoicing
145	Presiding, presence, consecrated, hierophants, unspeakable, transformed, treacherous, professional, invisible, innermost
146	Diffracted, dispersion, hereafter, nothingness, accomplished, themselves, drunkenness, shipmaster, incarnation, concerning, concubine, ineffable, quarrelsome
147	Hyperbolic, extended, enlightens, beautiful, bedchamber, stripped, abandonment, minister, exceeded
148	Conjuration, vehement, consummate, supremely, meetings, innocence, refulgent, presently, seductive, worshippers
149	Turquoise, thanksgiving, puppets, creeping, perfumes
150	Priestess, crucified, tempest, sentences, gentleness, incestuous, begotten
151	initiator, eighteen, certainty, chattering, lightening
152	Glistening, eventide, therefore, performed, tincture, intellect, thereunto, everlasting, appointed, excellent, self-knowledge, contented, directions, splitting, ointment, existeth
153	Ipsissimus, comprehend, consciousness, cemented, vestments, minutest, mischievous
154	Extreme, patiently, thereupon, infinity, identity
155	Meditated, conversation, alexandrite, fecundity, intolerable, mysteries, corruption, beginning, intimate, tenderness, conquering, thunderbolt, abomination
156	Fortified, self-luminous, generation, everywhere, fornication, cupbearers
157	Impossible, initiate, disruption, inevitably, butterfly, emphatically, quietness, philosophies
158	Continent, quicksilver, strengthen, mitigated, iniquity, cornerstone, centuries
159	Uttermost, multitude, marketplace, firmament
160	Beginnings, abominations, perfectly
161	Reverence, forcefulness, remember, impurity, sweetnesses, generations
162	Affirmation, profundity, eternity, imagination, manifested, enraptured
163	Everything, disposition, pretended, feminine, incantations

164	Tempered, infinite, exceeding, abstinence, concealments, extending, beautifully
165	Perceived, pernicious, beatitude, penetrant, perverted, fierceness
166	Obstruction, impressions, triumphant, expected, constellations
167	Reflecting, tribulation, redeemeth, projection, lengthening, consummation, discomforted, countenance, inebriate
168	Preserveth, reflections, meditation, emptiness, transcendest, forthspeaker
169	Glittering, inception, bewildereth, immediate, Hermeticus
170	Attribute, destruction, publication
171	Conceptions, attainment, disruptive, Trigrammaton
172	Understanding, hummingbird, reflecteth, inspiration, unimaginable
173	Innkeeper, contaminated, punishment, immortality
174	Indivisible, appetite, continuity, equivalence, regenerate
175	Determine, stabilities
176	Hierophantic, nevertheless, intoxicate, existence, penetrate, initiation
177	Expiration, understandeth, bitterness, transcendent, preciousness, serpent-woman
178	Thelemites, complement, inheritance
179	Protecting, difference, enchantment, never-ending, instrument, treasure-house
180	Initiating
181	Unutterable, existences, exceedingly, fingertips
182	Restriction, pestilence, viceregent, contemplate
183	Redemption, forgetfulness, expecting
184	Mother-of-pearl
185	Sweet-smelling, omnipotent
186	Reproduction, immediately, permitted
187	Imperfect, magnificent, perfection
191	
192	Remembered, perfections
194	Opium-poppy, intelligible, benediction, permutation
195	Intoxication, impatience
196	Persecutions, winebibbing

197	Sufficiently, trumpeting, peradventure, equilibrated
199	Extinguished, ever-weeping
200	Manifestation
201	Contemplation, intelligence, magnificence
202	Equilibrium, perpendicular
203	Weather-beaten, not-to-be-beheld
204	Putrefaction
208	Unrighteousness
210	Mother-of-emerald, omnipresence
211	Possibilities
216	Interpreted, infinitesimal
218	Impenetrable
225	Unintelligible
226	Enlightenment, light-transcending
228	Prince-priest
229	Unsubstantiality
230	Mighty-sweeping
231	Circumference, imperfection
272	Genitor-genetrix

Appendix B
A Qabalistic Analysis of Liber AL

Transliteration was applied in cases where nonstandard English words were used. The transliteration to English can be found in [brackets].

The number below each value of the letters indicates that a number appear in the text itself, and the number can also be found in [brackets].

Words that were connected together by a hyphen (-) were treated as whole words. For example: "blue-lidded" was counted as one word: "bluelidded."

All punctuation save the apostrophe (') and aspersand (&) has been omitted to prevent difficulty and confusion when reading the text and numbers. The aspersand (&) does not have a numerical value itself, and was ignored with the idea that the Prophet would have written "and" if there had been some significant enumeration.

The second number is the value of the letters and the numbers combined. The numbers on the right column indicates the number of the paragraph combined with the value of the entire paragraph. The verse numbers were added later, but may contain some significance.) The idea is that other Class A material analyzed in the same fashion may reveal some significance when deciphering and interpreting the Holy Books.

Chapter I

1.	Had! 11 The 53 manifestation 200 of 25 Nuit 78	367	368
2.	The 53 unveiling 139 of 25 the 53 company 97 of 25 heaven 79	471	473
3.	Every 87 man 36 and 21 every 87 woman 46 is 28 a 1 star 42	348	351
4.	Every 87 number 109 is 28 infinite 164 there 90 is 28 no 21 difference 179	706	710
5.	Help 57 me 46 o 7 warrior 70 lord 27 of 25 Thebes 103 in 37 my 36 unveiling 139 before 107 the 53 Children 99 of 25 men 60	891	896

6.	Be 45 thou 52 Hadit 58 my 36 secret 104 centre 113 my 36 heart 66 my 36 tongue 98	644	650
7.	Behold 64 it 47 is 28 revealed 106 by 35 Aiwass 38 the 53 minister 147 of 25 Hoor 30 paar 40 kraat 47	660	667
8.	The 53 Khabs 39 is 28 in 37 the 53 Khu 30 not 45 the 53 Khu 30 in 37 the 53 Khabs 39	497	505
9.	Worship 80 then 67 the 53 Khabs 39 and 21 behold 64 my 36 light 64 shed 40 over 54 you 39	557	566
10.	Let 51 my 36 servants 96 be 45 few 46 & secret 104 they 68 shall 14 rule 56 the 53 many 51 & the 53 known 47	720	730
11.	These 83 are 38 fools 39 that 53 men 60 adore 51 both 55 their 88 Gods 29 & their 88 men 60 are 38 fools 39	721	732
12.	Come 66 forth 65 o 7 children 99 under 74 the 53 stars 47 & take 59 your 51 fill 45 of 25 love 44	635	647
13.	I 23 am 22 above 63 you 39 and 21 in 37 you 39 My 36 ecstasy 88 is 28 in 37 yours 56 My 36 joy 38 is 28 to 31 See 55 your 51 joy 38	766	779
14.	Above 63 the 53 gemmed 109 azure 63 is 28 The 53 naked 55 splendour 114 of 25 Nuit 78 She 34 bends 70 in 37 ecstasy 88 to 31 kiss 42 The 53 secret 104 ardours 60 of 25 Hadit 58 The 53 winged 82 globe 65 the 53 starry 69 blue 64 Are 38 mine 83 O 7 Ankh-af-na-khonsu 118	1875	1889
15.	Now 24 ye 40 shall 14 know 33 that 53 the 53 chosen 68 priest 115 & apostle 90 of 25 infinite 164 space 70 is 28 the 53 prince 113 priest 115 the 53 Beast 75 and 21 in 37 his 32 woman 46 called 49 the 53 Scarlet 82 Woman 46 is 28 all 5 power 73 given 83 They 68 shall 14 gather 77 my 36 children 99 into 68 their 88 fold 33 they 68 shall 14 bring 80 the 53 glory 47 of 25 the 53 stars 47 into 68 the 53 hearts 71 of 25 men 60	2888	2903
16.	For 37 he 29 is 28 ever 72 a 1 sun 36 and 21 she 34 a 1 moon 49 But 61 to 31 him 48 is 28 the 53 winged 82 Secret 104 flame 67 and 21 to 31 her 41 the 53 stooping 117 starlight 106	1151	1167

17.	But 61 ye 40 are 38 not 45 so 12 chosen 68	264	281
18.	Burn 63 upon 64 their 88 brows 47 o 7 splendrous 119 serpent 131	519	537
19.	O 7 azure 63 lidded 68 woman 46 bend 65 upon 64 them 74	387	406
20.	The 53 key 49 of 25 the 53 rituals 84 is 28 in 37 the 53 secret 104 word 28 which 47 I 23 have 40 given 83 unto 62 him 48	817	837
21.	With 54 the 53 God 24 & the 53 Adorer 63 I 23 am 22 nothing 97 they 68 do 13 not 45 see 55 me 46 They 68 are 38 as 6 upon 64 the 53 earth 66 I 23 am 22 Heaven 79 and 21 there 90 is 28 no 21 other 72 God 24 than 43 me 46 and 21 my 36 lord 27 Hadit 58	1522	1543
22.	Now 24 therefore 152 I 23 am 22 known 47 to 31 ye 40 by 35 my 36 name 61 Nuit 78 and 21 to 31 him 48 by 35 a 1 secret 104 name 61 which 47 I 23 will 30 give 69 him 48 when 46 at 25 last 32 he 29 knoweth 86 me 46 Since 80 I 23 am 22 Infinite 164 Space 70 and 21 the 53 Infinite 164 Stars 47 thereof 115 do 13 ye 40 also 15 thus 50 Bind 63 nothing 97 Let 51 there 90 be 45 no 21 difference 179 made 53 among 54 you 39 between 136 any 30 one 46 thing 76 & any 30 other 72 thing 76 for 37 thereby 125 there 90 cometh 94 hurt 57	3769	3791
23.	But 61 whoso 26 availeth 90 in 37 this 56 let 51 him 48 be 45 the 53 chief 83 of 25 all 5	580	603
24.	I 23 am 22 Nuit 78 and 21 my 36 word 28 is 28 six 50 and 21 fifty98	405	429
25.	Divide 93 add 13 multiply 130 and 21 understand 124	381	406

26.	Then 67 saith 57 the 53 prophet 124 and 21 slave 43 of 25 the 53 beauteous 141 one 46 Who 14 am 22 I 23 and 21 what 32 shall 14 be 45 the 53 sign 53 So 12 she 34 answered 91 him 48 bending 113 down 30 a 1 lambent 107 flame 67 of 25 blue 64 all 5 touching 113 all 5 penetrant 165 her 41 lovely 61 hands 30 upon 64 the 53 black 45 earth 66 & her 41 lithe 78 body 48 arched 61 for 37 love 44 and 21 her 41 soft 54 feet 92 not 45 hurting 105 the 53 little 100 flowers 72 Thou 52 knowest 87 And 21 the 53 sign 53 shall 14 be 45 my 36 ecstasy 88 the 53 consciousness 153 of 25 the 53 continuity 174 of 25 existence 176 the 53 omnipresence 210 of 25 my 36 body 48	4519	4545
27.	Then 67 the 53 priest 115 answered 91 & said 35 unto 62 the 53 Queen 100 of 25 Space 70 kissing 90 her 41 lovely 61 brows 47 and 21 the 53 dew 34 of 25 her 41 light 64 bathing 97 his 32 whole 41 body 48 in 37 a 1 sweet 82 smelling 103 perfume 144 of 25 sweat 58 O 7 Nuit 78 continuous 141 one 46 of 25 Heaven 79 let 51 it 47 be 45 ever 72 thus 50 that 53 men 60 speak 66 not 45 of 25 Thee 78 as 6 One 46 but 61 as 6 None 60 and 21 let 51 them 74 speak 66 not 45 of 25 thee 78 at 25 all 5 since 80 thou 52 art 37 continuous 141	3663	3690
28.	None 60 breathed 117 the 53 light 64 faint 80 & faery 71 of 25 the 53 stars 47 and 21 two 34	625	653
29.	For 37 I 23 am 22 divided 99 for 37 loves 49 sake 40 for 37 the 53 chance 70 of 25 union 75	567	596
30.	This 56 is 28 the 53 creation 119 of 25 the 53 world 30 that 53 the 53 pain 64 of 25 division 111 is 28 as 6 nothing 97 and 21 the 53 joy 38 of 25 dissolution 133 all 5	1076	1106
31.	For 37 these 83 fools 39 of 25 men 60 and 21 their 88 woes 40 care 51 not 45 thou 52 at 25 all 5 They 68 feel 70 little 100 what 32 is 28 is 28 balanced 82 by 35 weak 38 joys 43 but 61 ye 40 are 38 my 36 chosen 68 ones 51	1389	1420

32.	Obey 67 my 36 prophet 124 follow 39 out 48 the 53 ordeals 58 of 25 my 36 knowledge 102 seek 64 me 46 only 38 Then 67 the 53 joys 43 of 25 my 36 love 44 will 30 redeem 114 ye 40 from 58 all 5 pain 64 This 56 is 28 so 12 I 23 swear 46 it 47 by 35 the 53 vault 54 of 25 my 36 body 48 by 35 my 36 sacred 62 heart 66 and 21 tongue 98 by 35 all 5 I 23 can 28 give 69 by 35 all 5 I 23 desire 96 of 25 ye 40 all 5	2485	2517
33.	Then 67 the 53 priest 115 fell 47 into 68 a 1 deep 82 trance 89 or 19 swoon 36 & said 35 unto 62 the 53 Queen 100 of 25 Heaven 79 Write 87 unto 62 us 22 the 53 ordeals 58 write 87 unto 62 us 22 the 53 rituals 84 write 87 unto 62 us 22 the 53 law 6	1751	1784
34.	But 61 she 34 said 35 the 53 ordeals 58 I 23 write 87 not 45 the 53 rituals 84 shall 14 be 45 half 25 known 47 and 21 half 25 concealed 106 the 53 Law 6 is 28 for 37 all 5	945	979
35.	This 56 that 53 thou 52 writest 116 is 28 the 53 threefold 123 book 43 of 25 Law 6	555	590
36.	My 36 scribe 98 Ankh-af-na-khonsu 118 the 53 priest 115 of 25 the 53 princes 118 shall 14 not 45 in 37 one 46 letter 112 change 68 this 56 book 43 but 61 lest 56 there 90 be 45 folly 44 he 29 shall 14 comment 125 thereupon 154 by 35 the 53 wisdom 65 of 25 Ra 13 Hoor 30 Khuit 77	1953	1989
37.	Also 15 the 53 mantras 78 and 21 spells 65 the 53 obeah 57 and 21 the 53 wanga 30 the 53 work 31 of 25 the 53 wand 24 and 21 the 53 work 31 of 25 the 53 sword 33 these 83 he 29 shall 14 learn 54 and 21 teach 67	1115	1152
38.	He 29 must 67 teach 67 but 61 he 29 may 37 make 56 severe 102 the 53 ordeals 58	559	597
39.	The 53 word 28 of 25 the 53 Law 6 is 28 [Thelema] 102	295	334

40.	Who 14 calls 23 us 22 Thelemites 178 will 30 do 13 no 21 wrong 47 if 41 he 29 look 25 but 61 close 52 into 68 the 53 word 28 For 37 there 90 are 38 therein 127 Three 90 Grades 60 the 53 Hermit 109 and 21 the 53 Lover 56 and 21 the 53 man 36 of 25 Earth 66 Do 13 what 32 thou 52 wilt 52 shall 14 be 45 the 53 whole 41 of 25 the 53 Law 6	2026	2066
41.	The 53 word 28 of 25 Sin 42 is 28 Restriction 182 O 7 man 36 refuse 102 not 45 thy 43 wife 69 if 41 she 34 will 30 O 7 lover 56 if 41 thou 52 wilt 52 de- part 94 There 90 is 28 no 21 bond 47 that 53 can 28 unite 103 the 53 divided 99 but 61 love 44 all 5 else 57 is 28 a 1 curse 72 Accursed 92 Accursed 92 be 45 it 47 to 31 the 53 aeons 52 Hell 33	2302	2343
42.	Let 51 it 47 be 45 that 53 state 79 of 25 manhood 75 bound 64 and 21 loathing 86 So 12 with 54 thy 43 all 5 thou 52 hast 34 no 21 right 74 but 61 to 31 do 13 thy 43 will 30	1019	1061
43.	Do 13 that 53 and 21 no 21 other 72 shall 14 say 21 nay 30	245	288
44.	For 37 pure 80 will 30 unassuaged 102 of 25 pur- pose 118 delivered 134 from 58 the 53 lust 48 of 25 result 85 is 28 every 87 way 19 perfect 143	1072	1116
45.	The 53 Perfect 143 and 21 the 53 Perfect 143 are 38 one 46 Perfect 143 and 21 not 45 two 34 nay 30 are 38 none 60	868	913
46.	Nothing 97 is 28 a 1 secret 104 key 49 of 25 this 56 law 6 Sixty 89 one 46 the 53 Jews 49 call 18 it 47 I 23 call 18 it 47 eight 87 eighty 102 four 54 hun- dred 84 & eighteen 151	1234	1280
47.	But 61 they 68 have 40 the 53 half 25 unite 103 by 35 thine 90 art 37 so 12 that 53 all 5 disappear 125	707	754
48.	My 36 prophet 124 is 28 a 1 fool 34 with 54 his 32 one 46 one 46 one 46 are 38 not 45 they 68 the 53 Ox 29 and 21 none 60 by 35 the 53 Book 43	892	940

49.	Abrogate 101 are 38 all 5 rituals 84 all 5 ordeals 58 all 5 words 33 and 21 signs 58 Ra-Hoor-Khuit 120 hath 33 taken 73 his 32 seat 55 in 37 the 53 East 55 at 25 the 53 Equinox 127 of 25 the 53 Gods 29 and 21 let 51 Asar 19 be 45 with 54 Isa 29 who 14 also 15 are 38 one 46 But 61 they 68 are 38 not 45 of 25 me 46 Let 51 Asar 19 be 45 the 53 adorant 65 Isa 29 the 53 sufferer 132 Hoor 30 in 37 his 32 secret 104 name 61 and 21 splendour114 is 28 the 53 Lord 27 initiating 180	2927	2976
50.	There 90 is 28 a 1 word 28 to 31 say 21 about 69 the 53 Hierophantic 176 task 39 Behold 64 there 90 are 38 three 90 ordeals 58 in 37 one 46 and 21 it 47 may 37 be 45 given 83 in 37 three 90 ways 24 The 53 gross 40 must 67 pass 37 through 79 fire 78 let 51 the 53 fine 80 be 45 tried 90 in 37 intellect 152 and 21 the 53 lofty 66 chosen 68 ones 51 in 37 the 53 highest 96 Thus 50 ye 40 have 40 star 42 & star 42 system 95 & system 95 let 51 not 45 one 46 know 33 well 32 the 53 other 72	3386	3436
51.	There 90 are 38 four 54 gates 66 to 31 one 46 palace 68 the 53 floor 46 of 25 that 53 palace 68 is 28 of 25 silver 77 and 21 gold 26 lapis 57 lazuli 53 & jasper 85 are 38 there 90 and 21 all 5 rare 50 scents 86 jasmine 105 & rose 49 and 21 the 53 emblems 119 of 25 death 60 Let 51 him 48 enter 100 in 37 turn 67 or 19 at 25 once 59 the 53 four 54 gates 66 let 51 him 48 stand 50 on 21 the 53 floor 46 of 25 the 53 palace 68 Will 30 he 29 not 45 sink 51 Amn 36 Ho 11 warrior 70 if 41 thy 43 servant 91 sink 51 But 61 there 90 are 38 means 66 and 21 means 66 Be 45 goodly 48 therefore 152 dress 53 ye 40 all 5 in 37 fine 80 apparel 93 eat 50 rich 52 foods 43 and 21 drink 64 sweet 82 wines 70 and 21 wines 70 that 53 foam 47 Also 15 take 59 your 51 fill 45 and 21 will 30 of 25 love 44 as 6 ye 40 will 30 when 46 where 69 and 21 with 54 whom 35 ye 40 will 30 But 61 always 27 unto 62 me 46	5549	5600

52.	If 41 this 56 be 45 not 45 aright 75 if 41 ye 40 con-found 96 the 53 space 70 marks 48 saying 69 They 68 are 38 one 46 or 19 saying 69 They 68 are 38 many 51 if 41 the 53 ritual 79 be 45 not 45 ever 72 unto 62 me 46 then 67 expect 135 the 53 direful 103 judgments 139 of 25 Ra 13 Hoor 30 Khuit 77	2161	2213
53.	This 56 shall 14 regenerate 174 the 53 world 30 the 53 little 100 world 30 my 36 sister 94 my 36 heart 66 & my 36 tongue 98 unto 62 whom 35 I 23 send 50 this 56 kiss 42 Also 15 o 7 scribe 98 and 21 prophet 124 though 67 thou 52 be 45 of 25 the 53 princes 118 it 47 shall 14 not 45 assuage 65 thee 78 nor 33 absolve 70 thee 78 But 61 ecstasy 88 be 45 thine 90 and 21 joy 38 of 25 earth 66 ever 72 To 31 me 46 To 31 me 46	2859	2912
54.	Change 68 not 45 as 6 much 55 as 6 the 53 style 71 of 25 a 1 letter 112 for 37 behold 64 thou 52 o 7 prophet 124 shalt 36 not 45 behold 64 all 5 these 83 mysteries 155 hidden 78 therein 127	1319	1373
55.	The 53 child 48 of 25 thy 43 bowels 62 he 29 shall 14 behold 64 them 74	412	467
56.	Expect 135 him 48 not 45 from 58 the 53 East 55 nor 33 from 58 the 53 West 57 for 37 from 58 no 21 expected 166 house 58 cometh 94 that 53 child 48 Aum 39 All 5 words 33 are 38 sacred 62 and 21 all 5 prophets 129 true 78 save 41 only 38 that 53 they 68 understand 124 a 1 little 100 solve 49 the 53 first 82 half 25 of 25 the 53 equation 130 leave 63 the 53 second 70 unattacked 134 But 61 thou 52 hast 34 all 5 in 37 the 53 clear 53 light 64 and 21 some 58 though 67 not 45 all 5 in 37 the 53 dark 28	3375	3431

57.	Invoke 88 me 46 under 74 my 36 stars 47 Love 44 is 28 the 53 law 6 love 44 under 74 will 30 Nor 33 let 51 the 53 fools 39 mistake 108 love 44 for 37 there 90 are 38 love 44 and 21 love 44 There 90 is 28 the 53 dove 48 and 21 there 90 is 28 the 53 serpent 131 Choose 61 ye 40 well 32 He 29 my 36 prophet 124 hath 33 chosen 68 knowing 81 the 53 law 6 of 25 the 53 fortress 108 and 21 the 53 great 73 mystery 117 of 25 the 53 House 58 of 25 God 24 All 5 these 83 old 15 letters 117 of 25 my 36 Book 43 are 38 aright 75 but 61 [Tzaddy] 60 is 28 not 45 the 53 Star 42 This 56 also 15 is 28 secret 104 my 36 prophet 124 shall 14 reveal 75 it 47 to 31 the 53 wise 56	4277	4334
58.	I 23 give 69 unimaginable 172 joys 43 on 21 earth 66 certainty 151 not 45 faith 70 while 57 in 37 life 68 upon 64 death 60 peace 90 unutterable 181 rest 66 ecstasy 88 nor 33 do 13 I 23 demand 73 aught 57 in 37 sacrifice 133	1740	1798
59.	My 36 incense 119 is 28 of 25 resinous 108 woods 28 & gums 54 and 21 there 90 is 28 no 21 blood 42 therein 127 because 106 of 25 my 36 hair 40 the 53 trees 91 of 25 Eternity 162	1265	1324
60.	My 36 number 109 is 28 [11] as 6 all 5 their 88 numbers 114 who 14 are 38 of 25 us 22 The 53 Five 76 Pointed 125 Star 42 with 54 a 1 Circle 88 in 37 the 53 Middle 83 & the 53 circle 88 is 28 Red 43 My 36 colour 58 is 28 black 45 to 31 the 53 blind 65 but 61 the 53 blue 64 & gold 26 are 38 seen 69 of 25 the 53 seeing 103 Also 15 I 23 have 40 a 1 secret 104 glory 47 for 37 them 74 that 53 love 44 me 46	2601 + 11 2612	2661 2672

61.	But 61 to 31 love 44 me 46 is 28 better 130 than 43 all 5 things 81 if 41 under 74 the 53 night 76 stars 47 in 37 the 53 desert 97 thou 52 presently 148 burnest 117 mine 83 incense 119 before 107 me 46 invoking 111 me 46 with 54 a 1 pure 80 heart 66 and 21 the 53 Serpent 131 flame 67 therein 127 thou 52 shalt 36 come 66 a 1 little 100 to 31 lie 50 in 37 my 36 bosom 60 For 37 one 46 kiss 42 wilt 52 thou 52 then 67 be 45 willing 78 to 31 give 69 all 5 but 61 whoso 26 gives 74 one 46 particle 126 of 25 dust 52 shall 14 lose 39 all 5 in 37 that 53 hour 40 Ye 40 shall 14 gather 77 goods 36 and 21 store 73 of 25 women 70 and 21 spices 97 ye 40 shall 14 wear 41 rich 52 jewels 76 ye 40 shall 14 exceed 116 the 53 nations 88 of 25 the 53 earth 66 in 37 spendour 112 & pride 92 but 61 always 27 in 37 the 53 love 44 of 25 me 46 and 21 so 12 shall 14 ye 40 come 66 to 31 my 36 joy 38 I 23 charge 66 you 39 earnestly 123 to 31 come 66 before 107 me 46 in 37 a 1 single 80 robe 64 and 21 covered 98 with 54 a 1 rich 52 headdress 89 I 23 love 44 you 39 I 23 yearn 67 to 31 you 39 Pale 54 or 19 purple 108 veiled 91 or 19 voluptuous 132 I 23 who 14 am 22 all 5 pleasure 113 and 21 purple 108 and 21 drunkenness 146 of 25 the 53 innermost 145 sense 74 desire 96 you 39 Put 67 on 21 the 53 wings 56 and 21 arouse 67 the 53 coiled 76 splendour 114 within 91 you 39 come 66 unto 62 me 46	9335	9396
62.	At 25 all 5 my 36 meetings 148 with 54 you 39 shall 14 the 53 priestess 150 say 21 and 21 her 41 eyes 70 shall 14 burn 63 with 54 desire 96 as 6 she 34 stands 55 bare 58 and 21 rejoicing 144 in 37 my 36 secret 104 temple 123 To 31 me 46 To 31 me 46 calling 66 forth 65 the 53 flame 67 of 25 the 53 hearts 71 of 25 all 5 in 37 her 41 love 44 chant 56	2284	2346

63.	Sing 53 the 53 rapturous 121 love 44 song 37 unto 62 me 46 Burn 63 to 31 me 46 perfumes 149 Wear 41 to 31 me 46 jewels 76 Drink 64 to 31 me 46 for 37 I 23 love 44 you 39 I 23 love 44 you 39	1289	1352
64.	I 23 am 22 the 53 blue-lidded 132 daughter 100 of 25 Sunset 90 I 23 am 22 the 53 naked 55 brilliance 135 of 25 the 53 voluptuous 132 night 76 sky 29	1048	1112
65.	To 31 me 46 To 31 me 46	154	219
66.	The 53 Manifestation 200 of 25 Nuit 78 is 28 at 25 an 15 end 45	469	535

Chapter II

1.	Nu 31 the 53 hiding 81 of 25 Hadit 58	248	249
2.	Come 66 all 5 ye 40 and 21 learn 54 the 53 secret 104 that 53 hath 33 not 45 yet 64 been 84 revealed 106 I 23 Hadit 58 am 22 the 53 complement 178 of 25 Nu 31 my 36 bride 86 I 23 am 22 not 45 extended 147 and 21 Khabs 39 is 28 the 53 name 61 of 25 my 36 House 58	1798	1800
3.	In 37 the 53 sphere 97 I 23 am 22 everywhere 156 the 53 centre 113 as 6 she 34 the 53 circumference 231 is 28 nowhere 90 found 62	1058	1061
4.	Yet 64 she 34 shall 14 be 45 known 47 & I 23 never 86	313	317
5.	Behold 64 the 53 rituals 84 of 25 the 53 old 15 time 93 are 38 black 45 Let 51 the 53 evil 60 ones 51 be 45 cast 43 away 20 let 51 the 53 good 31 ones 51 be 45 purged 97 by 35 the 53 prophet 124 Then 67 shall 14 this 56 Knowledge 102 go 18 aright 75	1665	1670
6.	I 23 am 22 the 53 flame 67 that 53 burns 68 in 37 every 87 heart 66 of 25 man 36 and 21 in 37 the 53 core 57 of 25 every 87 star 42 I 23 am 22 Life 68 and 21 the 53 giver 81 of 25 Life 68 yet 64 therefore 152 is 28 the 53 knowledge 102 of 25 me 46 the 53 knowledge 102 of 25 death 60	1930	1936

7.	I 23 am 22 the 53 Magician 107 and 21 the 53 Ex-orcist 131 I 23 am 22 the 53 axle 50 of 25 the 53 wheel 59 and 21 the 53 cube 75 in 37 the 53 circle 88 Come 66 unto 62 me 46 is 28 a 1 foolish 66 word 28 for 37 it 47 is 28 I 23 that 53 go 18	1525	1532
8.	Who 14 worshipped 137 Heru 58 pa 27 kraath 51 have 40 worshipped 137 me 46 ill 27 for 37 I 23 am 22 the 53 worshipper 143	815	823
9.	Remember 161 all 5 ye 40 that 53 existence 176 is 28 pure 80 joy 38 that 53 all 5 the 53 sorrows 51 are 38 but 61 as 6 shadows 31 they 68 pass 37 & are 38 done 52 but 61 there 90 is 28 that 53 which 47 remains 101	1454	1463
10.	O 7 prophet 124 thou 52 hast 34 ill 27 will 30 to 31 learn 54 this 56 writing 110	525	535
11.	I 23 see 55 thee 78 hate 54 the 53 hand 25 & the 53 pen 65 but 61 I 23 am 22 stronger 110	622	633
12.	Because 106 of 25 me 46 in 37 Thee 78 which 47 thou 52 knewest 105 not 45	541	553
13.	for 37 why 22 Because 106 thou 52 wast 33 the 53 knower 70 and 21 me 46	440	453
14.	Now 24 let 51 there 90 be 45 a 1 veiling 108 of 25 this 56 shrine 83 now 24 let 51 the 53 light 64 de-vour 77 men 60 and 21 eat 50 them 74 up 43 with 54 blindness 114	1168	1182
15.	For 37 I 23 am 22 perfect 143 being 93 Not 45 and 21 my 36 number 109 is 28 nine 76 by 35 the 53 fools 39 but 61 with 54 the 53 just 62 I 23 am 22 eight 87 and 21 one 46 in 37 eight 87 Which 47 is 28 vital 60 for 37 I 23 am 22 none 60 indeed 99 The 53 Empress 119 and 21 the 53 King 57 are 38 not 45 of 25 me 46 for 37 there 90 is 28 a 1 further 112 secret 104	2518	2533
16.	I 23 am 22 The 53 Empress 119 & the 53 Hiero-phant 140 Thus 50 eleven 101 as 6 my 36 bride 86 is 28 eleven 101	818	834

17.	Hear 42 me 46 ye 40 people 111 of 25 sighing 91 The 53 sorrows 51 of 25 pain 64 and 21 regret 109 Are 38 left 69 to 31 the 53 dead 38 and 21 the 53 dying 69 The 53 folk 36 that 53 not 45 know 33 me 46 as 6 yet 64	1386	1403
18.	These 83 are 38 dead 38 these 83 fellows 62 they 68 feel 70 not 45 We 28 are 38 not 45 for 37 the 53 poor 52 and 21 sad 12 the 53 lords 32 of 25 the 53 earth 66 are 38 our 36 kinsfolk 87	1163	1181
19.	Is 28 a 1 God 24 to 31 live 60 in 37 a 1 dog 24 No 21 but 61 the 53 highest 96 are 38 of 25 us 22 They 68 shall 14 rejoice 121 our 36 chosen 68 who 14 sorroweth 99 is 28 not 45 of 25 us 22	1062	1081
20.	Beauty 102 and 21 strength 119 leaping 102 laughter 96 and 21 delicious 121 languor 64 force 75 and 21 fire 78 are 38 of 25 us 22	905	925
21.	We 28 have 40 nothing 97 with 54 the 53 outcast 91 and 21 the 53 unfit 96 let 51 them 74 die 54 in 37 their 88 misery 101 For 37 they 68 feel 70 not 45 Compassion 122 is 28 the 53 vice 71 of 25 kings 62 stamp 77 down 30 the 53 wretched 112 & the 53 weak 38 this 56 is 28 the 53 law 6 of 25 the 53 strong 73 this 56 is 28 our 36 law 6 and 21 the 53 joy 38 of 25 the 53 world 30 Think 74 not 45 o 7 king 57 upon 64 that 53 lie 50 That 53 Thou 52 Must 67 Die 54 verily 87 thou 52 shalt 36 not 45 die 54 but 61 live 60 Now 24 let 51 it 47 be 45 understood 123 If 41 the 53 body 48 of 25 the 53 King 57 dissolve 83 he 29 shall 14 remain 96 in 37 pure 80 ecstasy 88 for 37 ever 72 Nuit 78 Hadit 58 Ra-Hoor-Khuit 120 The 53 Sun 36 Strength 119 Sight 67 Light 64 these 83 are 38 for 37 the 53 servants 96 of 25 the 53 Star 42 the 53 Snake 54	5725	5746

22.	I 23 am 22 the 53 Snake 54 that 53 giveth 97 Knowl-edge 102 & Delight 95 and 21 bright 94 glory 47 and 21 stir 64 the 53 hearts 71 of 25 men 60 with 54 drunkenness 146 To 31 worship 80 me 46 take 59 wine 65 and 21 strange 92 drugs 51 whereof 94 I 23 will 30 tell 53 my 36 prophet 124 & be 45 drunk 58 thereof 115 They 68 shall 14 not 45 harm 38 ye 40 at 25 all 5 It 47 is 28 a 1 lie 50 this 56 folly 44 against 79 self 50 The 53 exposure 139 of 25 innocence 148 is 28 a 1 lie 50 Be 45 strong 73 o 7 man 36 lust 48 enjoy 77 all 5 things 81 of 25 sense 74 and 21 rapture 117 fear 56 not 45 that 53 any 30 God 24 shall 14 deny 60 thee 78 for 37 this 56	4274	4296
23.	I 23 am 22 alone 49 there 90 is 28 no 21 God 24 where 69 I 23 am 22	371	394
24.	Behold 64 these 83 be 45 grave 59 mysteries 155 for 37 there 90 are 38 also 15 of 25 my 36 friends 103 who 14 be 45 hermits 114 Now 24 think 74 not 45 to 31 find 61 them 74 in 37 the 53 forest 91 or 19 on 21 the 53 mountain 121 but 61 in 37 beds 56 of 25 purple 108 caressed 92 by 35 magnificent 187 beasts 80 of 25 women 70 with 54 large 51 limbs 71 and 21 fire 78 and 21 light 64 in 37 their 88 eyes 70 and 21 masses 62 of 25 flaming 90 hair 40 about 69 them 74 there 90 shall 14 ye 40 find 61 them 74 Ye 40 shall 14 see 55 them 74 at 25 rule 56 at 25 victorious 141 armies 87 at 25 all 5 the 53 joy 38 and 21 there 90 shall 14 be 45 in 37 them 74 a 1 joy 38 a 1 million 92 times 98 greater 110 than 43 this 56 Beware 86 lest 56 any 30 force 75 another 87 King 57 against 79 King 57 Love 44 one 46 an-other 87 with 54 burning 111 hearts 71 on 21 the 53 low 12 men 60 trample 111 in 37 the 53 fierce 116 lust 48 of 25 your 51 pride 92 in 37 the 53 day 22 of 25 your 51 wrath 44	6827	6851
25.	Ye 40 are 38 against 79 the 53 people 111 O 7 my 36 chosen 68	432	457

26.	I 23 am 22 the 53 secret 104 Serpent 131 coiled 76 about 69 to 31 spring 91 in 37 my 36 coiling 93 there 90 is 28 joy 38 If 41 I 23 lift 67 up 43 my 36 head 36 I 23 and 21 my 36 Nuit 78 are 38 one 46 If 41 I 23 droop 58 down 30 mine 83 head 36 and 21 shoot 47 forth 65 venom 77 then 67 is 28 rapture 117 of 25 the 53 earth 66 and 21 I 23 and 21 the 53 earth 66 are 38 one 46	2515	2541
27.	There 90 is 28 great 73 danger 69 in 37 me 46 for 37 who 14 doth 41 not 45 understand 124 these 83 runes 73 shall 14 make 56 a 1 great 73 miss 54 He 29 shall 14 fall 23 down 30 into 68 the 53 pit 73 called 49 Because 106 and 21 there 90 he 29 shall 14 perish 95 with 54 the 53 dogs 29 of 25 Reason 64	1877	1904
28.	Now 24 a 1 curse 72 upon 64 Because 106 and 21 his 32 kin 46	366	394
29.	May 37 Because 106 be 45 accursed 92 for 37 ever 72	389	418
30.	If 41 Will 30 stops 67 and 21 cries 78 Why 22 invoking 111 Because 106 then 67 Will 30 stops 67 & does 43 nought 77	760	790
31.	If 41 Power 73 asks 20 why 22 then 67 is 28 Power 73 weakness 87	411	442
32.	Also 15 reason 64 is 28 a 1 lie 50 for 37 there 90 is 28 a 1 factor 75 infinite 164 unknown 78 & all 5 their 88 words 33 are 38 skew 42 wise 56	893	925
33.	Enough 78 of 25 Because 106 Be 45 he 29 damned 73 for 37 a 1 dog 24	418	451
34.	But 61 ye 40 o 7 my 36 people 111 rise 65 up 43 & awake 39	402	436
35.	Let 51 the 53 rituals 84 be 45 rightly 91 performed 152 with 54 joy 38 & beauty 102	670	705
36.	There 90 are 38 rituals 84 of 25 the 53 elements 141 and 21 feasts 78 of 25 the 53 times 98	706	742
37.	A 1 feast 73 for 37 the 53 first 82 night 76 of 25 the 53 Prophet 124 and 21 his 32 Bride 86	663	700

38.	A 1 feast 73 for 37 the 53 three 90 days 27 of 25 the 53 writing 110 of 25 the 53 Book 43 of 25 the 53 Law 6	674	712
39.	A 1 feast 73 for 37 Tahuti 93 and 21 the 53 child 48 of 25 the 53 Prophet 124 secret 104 O 7 Prophet 124	763	802
40.	A 1 feast 73 for 37 the 53 Supreme 131 Ritual 79 and 21 a 1 feast 73 for 37 the 53 Equinox 127 of 25 the 53 Gods 29	793	833
41.	A 1 feast 73 for 37 fire 78 and 21 a 1 feast 73 for 37 water 65 a 1 feast 73 for 37 life 68 and 21 a 1 greater 110 feast 73 for 37 death 60	867	908
42.	A 1 feast 73 every 87 day 22 in 37 your 51 hearts 71 in 37 the 53 joy 38 of 25 my 36 rapture 117	648	690
43.	A 1 feast 73 every 87 night 76 unto 62 Nu 31 and 21 the 53 pleasure 113 of 25 uttermost 159 delight 95	796	839
44.	Aye 41 feast 73 rejoice 121 there 90 is 28 no 21 dread 50 hereafter 146 There 90 is 28 the 53 dissolution 133 and 21 eternal 103 ecstasy 88 in 37 the 53 kisses 72 of 25 Nu 31	1304	1348
45.	There 90 is 28 death 60 for 37 the 53 dogs 29	297	342
46.	Dost 42 thou 52 fail 44 Art 37 thou 52 sorry 51 Is 28 fear 56 in 37 thine 90 heart 66	555	601
47.	Where 69 I 23 am 22 these 83 are 38 not 45	280	327
48.	Pity 88 not 45 the 53 fallen 62 I 23 never 86 knew 51 them 74 I 23 am 22 not 45 for 37 them 74 I 23 console 73 not 45 I 23 hate 54 the 53 consoled 79 & the 53 consoler 85	1171	1219
49.	I 23 am 22 unique 115 & conqueror 126 I 23 am 22 not 45 of 25 the 53 slaves 48 that 53 perish 95 Be 45 they 68 damned 73 & dead 38 Amen 61 (This 56 is 28 of 25 the 53 [4] there 90 is 28 a 1 fifth 87 who 14 is 28 invisible 145 & therein 127 am 22 I 23 as 6 a 1 babe 66 in 37 an 15 egg 47)	1834 +4 1838	1883 1887

50.	Blue 64 am 22 I 23 and 21 gold 26 in 37 the 53 light 64 of 25 my 36 bride 86 but 61 the 53 red 43 gleam 60 is 28 in 37 my 36 eyes 70 & my 36 spangles 89 are 38 purple 108 & green 87	1203	1253
51.	Purple 108 beyond 87 purple 108 it 47 is 28 the 53 light 64 higher 79 than 43 eyesight 132	749	800
52.	There 90 is 28 a 1 veil 60 that 53 veil 60 is 28 black 45 It 47 is 28 the 53 veil 60 of 25 the 53 modest 88 woman 46 it 47 is 28 the 53 veil 60 of 25 sorrow 46 & the 53 pall 31 of 25 death 60 this 56 is 28 none 60 of 25 me 46 Tear 62 down 30 that 53 lying 65 spectre 130 of 25 the 53 centuries 158 veil 60 not 45 your 51 vices 76 in 37 virtuous 115 words 33 these 83 vices 76 are 38 my 36 service 113 ye 40 do 13 well 32 & I 23 will 30 reward 59 you 39 here 66 and 21 hereafter 146	3216	3268
53.	Fear 56 not 45 o 7 prophet 124 when 46 these 83 words 33 are 38 said 35 thou 52 shalt 36 not 45 be 45 sorry 51 Thou 52 art 37 emphatically 157 my 36 chosen 68 and 21 blessed 88 are 38 the 53 eyes 70 that 53 thou 52 shalt 36 look 25 upon 64 with 54 gladness 69 But 61 I 23 will 30 hide 58 thee 78 in 37 a 1 mask 36 of 25 sorrow 46 they 68 that 53 see 55 thee 78 shall 14 fear 56 thou 52 art 37 fallen 62 but 61 I 23 lift 67 thee 78 up 43	2811	2864
54.	Nor 33 shall 14 they 68 who 14 cry 40 aloud 33 their 88 folly 44 that 53 thou 52 meanest 115 nought 77 avail 37 thou 52 shall 14 reveal 75 it 47 thou 52 availest 91 they 68 are 38 the 53 slaves 48 of 25 because 106 They 68 are 38 not 45 of 25 me 46 The 53 stops 67 as 6 thou 52 wilt 52 the 53 letters 117 change 68 them 74 not 45 in 37 style 71 or 19 value 55	2328	2382
55.	Thou 52 shalt 36 obtain 89 the 53 order 62 & value 55 of 25 the 53 English 84 Alphabet 103 thou 52 shalt 36 find 61 new 42 symbols 75 to 31 attribute 170 them 74 unto 62	1215	1270

56.	Begone 102 ye 40 mockers 92 even 74 though 67 ye 40 laugh 35 in 37 my 36 honour 61 ye 40 shall 14 laugh 35 not 45 long 34 then 67 when 46 ye 40 are 38 sad 12 know 33 that 53 I 23 have 40 forsaken 91 you 39	1234	1290
57.	He 29 that 53 is 28 righteous 128 shall 14 be 45 righteous 128 still 56 he 29 that 53 is 28 filthy 86 shall 14 be 45 filthy 86 still 56	878	935
58.	Yea 41 deem 77 not 45 of 25 change 68 ye 40 shall 14 be 45 as 6 ye 40 are 38 & not 45 other 72 Therefore 152 the 53 kings 62 of 25 the 53 earth 66 shall 14 be 45 Kings 62 for 37 ever 72 the 53 slaves 48 shall 14 serve 77 There 90 is 28 none 60 that 53 shall 14 be 45 cast 43 down 30 or 19 lifted 98 up 43 all 5 is 28 ever 72 as 6 it 47 was 9 Yet 64 there 90 are 38 masked 67 ones 51 my 36 servants 96 it 47 may 37 be 45 that 53 yonder 79 beggar 80 is 28 a 1 King 57 A 1 King 57 may 37 choose 61 his 32 garment 108 as 6 he 29 will 30 there 90 is 28 no 21 certain 112 test 78 but 61 a 1 beggar 80 cannot 73 hide 58 his 32 poverty 119	4062	4120
59.	Beware 86 therefore 152 Love 44 all 5 lest 56 perchance 133 is 28 a 1 King 57 concealed 106 Say 21 you 39 so 12 Fool 34 If 41 he 29 be 45 a 1 King 57 thou 52 canst 57 not 45 hurt 57 him 48	1206	1265
60.	Therefore 152 strike 98 hard 23 low 12 and 21 to 31 hell 33 with 54 them 74 master 88	586	646
61.	There 90 is 28 a 1 light 64 before 107 thine 90 eyes 70 o 7 prophet 124 a 1 light 64 undesired 133 most 57 desirable 119	955	1016
62.	I 23 am 22 uplifted 141 in 37 thine 90 heart 66 and 21 the 53 kisses 72 of 25 the 53 stars 47 rain 50 hard 23 upon 64 thy 43 body 48	878	940
63.	Thou 52 art 37 exhaust 98 in 37 the 53 voluptuous 132 fullness 88 of 25 the 53 inspiration 172 the 53 expiration 177 is 28 sweeter 119 than 43 death 60 more 65 rapid 68 and 21 laughterful 133 than 43 a 1 caress 61 of 25 Hells 38 own 24 worm 43	1749	1812

64.	Oh 11 thou 52 art 37 overcome 120 we 28 are 38 upon 64 thee 78 our 36 delight 95 is 28 all 5 over 54 thee 78 hail 30 hail 30 prophet 124 of 25 Nu 31 prophet 124 of 25 Had 11 prophet 124 of 25 Ra 13 Hoor 30 Khu 30 Now 24 rejoice 121 now 24 come 66 in 37 our 36 splendour 114 rapture 117 Come 66 in 37 our 36 passionate 131 peace 90 & write 87 sweet 82 words 33 for 37 the 53 Kings 62	2599	2663
65.	I 23 am 22 the 53 Master 88 thou 52 art 37 the 53 Holy 28 Chosen 68 One 46	470	535
66.	Write 87 & find 61 ecstasy 88 in 37 writing 110 Work 31 & be 45 our 36 bed 51 in 37 working 79 Thrill 67 with 54 the 53 joy 38 of 25 life 68 & death 60 Ah 5 thy 43 death 60 shall 14 be 45 lovely 61 whoso 26 seeth 83 it 47 shall 14 be 45 glad 20 Thy 43 death 60 shall 14 be 45 the 53 seal 33 of 25 the 53 promise 119 of 25 our 36 age 37 long 34 love 44 Come 66 lift 67 up 43 thine 90 heart 66 & rejoice 121 We 28 are 38 one 46 we 28 are 38 none 60	2802	2868
67.	Hold 19 Hold 19 Bear 58 up 43 in 37 thy 43 rap-ture 117 fall 23 not 45 in 37 swoon 36 of 25 the 53 excellent 152 kisses 72	779	846
68.	Harder 60 Hold 19 up 43 thyself 93 Lift 67 thine 90 head 36 breathe 111 not 45 so 12 deep 82 die 54	712	780
69.	Ah 5 Ah 5 What 32 do 13 I 23 feel 70 Is 28 the 53 word 28 exhausted 129	386	455
70.	There 90 is 28 help 57 & hope 62 in 37 other 72 spells 65 Wisdom 65 says 26 be 45 strong 73 Then 67 canst 57 thou 52 bear 58 more 65 joy 38 Be 45 not 45 animal 62 refine 117 thy 43 rapture 117 If 41 thou 52 drink 64 drink 64 by 35 the 53 eight 87 and 21 ninety 115 rules 61 of 25 art 37 if 41 thou 52 love 44 exceed 116 by 35 delicacy 98 and 21 if 41 thou 52 do 13 aught 57 joyous 67 let 51 there 90 be 45 subtlety 132 therein 127	3123	3193
71.	But 61 exceed 116 exceed 116	293	364

72.	Strive 99 ever 72 to 31 more 65 and 21 if 41 thou 52 art 37 truly 70 mine 83 and 21 doubt 74 it 47 not 45 an 15 if 41 thou 52 art 37 ever 72 joyous 67 death 60 is 28 the 53 crown 49 of 25 all 5	1262	1334
73.	Ah 5 Ah 5 Death 60 Death 60 thou 52 shalt 36 long 34 for 37 death 60 Death 60 is 28 forbidden 131 o 7 man 36 unto 62 thee 78	751	824
74.	The 53 length 80 of 25 thy 43 longing 82 shall 14 be 45 the 53 strength 119 of 25 its 52 glory 47 He 29 that 53 lives 65 long 34 desires 101 & death 60 much 55 is 28 ever 72 the 53 King 57 among 54 the 53 Kings 62	1414	1488
75.	Aye 41 listen 93 to 31 the 53 numbers 114 the 53 words 33	418	493
76.	A 1 B 20 K 9 A 1 L 2 G 11 M 21 O 7 R 12 Y 15 X 22 R 12 P 26 S 5 T 24 O 7 V 10 A 1 L 2 What 32 mean- eth 114 this 56 o 7 prophet 124 Thou 52 knowest 87 not 45 nor 33 shalt 36 thou 52 know 33 ever 72 There 90 cometh 94 one 46 to 31 follow 39 thee 78 he 29 shall 14 expound 117 it 47 But 61 remember 161 o 7 chosen 67 one 46 to 31 be 45 me 46 to 31 follow 39 the 53 love 44 of 25 Nu 31 in 37 the 53 star 42 lit 49 heaven 79 to 31 look 25 forth 65 upon 64 men 60 to 31 tell 53 them 74 this 56 glad 20 word 28	2991 +143 3134	3067 3210
77.	O 7 be 45 thou 52 proud 68 and 21 mighty 98 among 54 men 60	405	482
78.	Lift 67 up 43 thyself 93 for 37 there 90 is 28 none 60 like 59 unto 62 thee 78 among 54 men 60 or 19 among 54 Gods 29 Lift 67 up 43 thyself 93 o 7 my 36 prophet 124 thy 43 stature 108 shall 14 surpass 71 the 53 stars 47 They 68 shall 14 worship 80 thy 43 name 61 foursquare 133 mystic 101 wonderful 104 the 53 number 109 of 25 the 53 man 36 and 21 the 53 name 61 of 25 thy 43 house 58	2680 +418 3098	2758 3176
79.	The 53 end 45 of 25 the 53 hiding 81 of 25 Hadit 58 and 21 blessing 105 & worship 80 to 31 the 53 prophet 124 of 25 the 53 lovely 61 Star 42	935	1014

Chapter III

#	Text		
1.	Abrahadabra 79 the 53 reward 59 of 25 Ra 13 Hoor 30 Khut 54	313	314
2.	There 90 is 28 division 111 hither 92 homeward 79 there 90 is 28 a 1 word 28 not 45 known 47 Spelling 108 is 28 defunct 117 all 5 is 28 not 45 aught 57 Beware 86 Hold 19 Raise 66 the 53 spell 60 of 25 RaHoorKhuit 120	1456	1458
3.	Now 24 let 51 it 47 be 45 first 82 understood 123 that 53 I 23 am 22 a 1 god 24 of 25 War 16 and 21 of 25 Vengeance 138 I 23 shall 14 deal 34 hardly 40 with 54 them 74	959	962
4.	Choose 61 ye 40 an 15 island 51	167	171
5.	Fortify 117 it 47	164	169
6.	Dung 48 it 47 about 69 with 54 enginery 139 of 25 war 16	398	404
7.	I 23 will 30 give 69 you 39 a 1 war 16 engine 112	290	297
8.	With 54 it 47 ye 40 shall 14 smite 98 the 53 peoples 116 and 21 none 60 shall 14 stand 50 before 107 you 39	713	721
9.	Lurk 40 Withdraw 76 Upon 64 them 74 this 56 is 28 the 53 Law 6 of 25 the 53 Battle 96 of 25 Conquest 124 thus 50 shall 14 my 36 worship 80 be 45 about 69 my 36 secret 104 house 58	1212	1221
10.	Get 60 the 53 stele 81 of 25 revealing 123 itself 97 set 54 it 47 in 37 thy 43 secret 104 temple 123 and 21 that 53 temple 123 is 28 already 62 aright 75 disposed 103 & it 47 shall 14 be 45 your 51 Kiblah 59 for 37 ever 72 It 47 shall 14 not 45 fade 50 but 61 miraculous 118 colour 58 shall 14 come 66 back 43 to 31 it 47 day 22 after 80 day 22 Close 52 it 47 in 37 locked 62 glass 24 for 37 a 1 proof 70 to 31 the 53 world 30	2799	2809

11.	This 56 shall 14 be 45 your 51 only 38 proof 70 I 23 forbid 86 argument 125 Conquer 107 That 53 is 28 enough 78 I 23 will 30 make 56 easy 46 to 31 you 39 the 53 abstruction 160 from 58 the 53 ill 27 ordered 93 house 58 in 37 the 53 Victorious 141 City 75 Thou 52 shalt 36 thyself 93 convey 84 it 47 with 54 worship 80 o 7 prophet 124 though 67 thou 52 likest 88 it 47 not 45 Thou 52 shalt 36 have 40 danger 69 & trouble 107 Ra 13 Hoor 30 Khu 30 is 28 with 54 thee 78 Worship 80 me 46 with 54 fire 78 & blood 42 worship 80 me 46 with 54 swords 38 & with 54 spears 74 Let 51 the 53 woman 46 be 45 girt 70 with 54 a 1 sword 33 before 107 me 46 let 51 blood 42 flow 30 to 31 my 36 name 61 Trample 111 down 30 the 53 Heathen 97 be 45 upon 64 them 74 o 7 warrior 70 I 23 will 30 give 69 you 39 of 25 their 88 flesh 54 to 31 eat 50	2799	2810
12.	Sacrifice 133 cattle 89 little 100 and 21 big 54 after 80 a 1 child 48	526	538
13.	But 61 not 45 now 24	130	143
14.	Ye 40 shall 14 see 55 that 53 hour 40 o 7 blessed 88 Beast 75 and 21 thou 52 the 53 Scarlet 82 Concubine 146 of 25 his 32 desire 96	879	893
15.	Ye 40 shall 14 be 45 sad 12 thereof 115	226	241
16.	Deem 77 not 45 too 38 eagerly 91 to 31 catch 55 the 53 promises 124 fear 56 not 45 to 31 undergo 92 the 53 curses 77 Ye 40 even 74 ye 40 know 33 not 45 this 56 meaning 109 all 5	1270	1286
17.	Fear 56 not 45 at 25 all 5 fear 56 neither 127 men 60 nor 33 Fates 73 nor 33 gods 29 nor 33 anything 106 Money 82 fear 56 not 45 nor 33 laughter 96 of 25 the 53 folk 36 folly 44 nor 33 any 30 other 72 power 73 in 37 heaven 79 or 19 upon 64 the 53 earth 66 or 19 under 74 the 53 earth 66 Nu 31 is 28 your 51 refuge 108 as 6 Hadit 58 your 51 light 64 and 21 I 23 am 22 the 53 strength 119 force 75 vigour 80 of 25 your 51 arms 39	2794	2811

18.	Mercy 86 let 51 be 45 off 43 damn 42 them 74 who 14 pity 88 Kill 36 and 21 torture 121 spare 69 not 45 be 45 upon 64 them 74	918	936
19.	That 53 stele 81 they 68 shall 14 call 18 the 53 Abomination 155 of 25 Desolation 114 count 75 well 32 its 52 name 61 it 47 shall 14 be 45 to 31 you 39 as 6 [718].	983 +718 1701	1002 1720
20.	Why 22 Because 106 of 25 the 53 fall 23 of 25 Because 106 that 53 he 29 is 28 not 45 there 90 again 50	655	675
21.	Set 54 up 43 my 36 image 81 in 37 the 53 East 55 thou 52 shalt 36 buy 52 thee 78 an 15 image 81 which 47 I 23 will 30 show 19 thee 78 especial 120 not 45 unlike 90 the 53 one 46 thou 52 knowest 87 And 21 it 47 shall 14 be 45 suddenly 90 easy 46 for 37 thee 78 to 31 do 13 this 56	1841	1862
22.	The 53 other 72 images 86 group 73 around 57 me 46 to 31 support 117 me 46 let 51 all 5 be 45 worshipped 137 for 37 they 68 shall 14 cluster 98 to 31 exalt 74 me 46 I 23 am 22 the 53 visible 108 object 105 of 25 worship 80 the 53 others 77 are 38 secret 104 for 37 the 53 Beast 75 & his 32 Bride 86 are 38 they 68 and 21 for 37 the 53 winners 96 of 25 the 53 Ordeal 53 x 22 What 32 is 28 this 56 Thou 52 shalt 36 know 33	2861	2883
23.	For 37 perfume 144 mix 66 meal 49 & honey 65 & thick 73 leavings 91 of 25 red 43 wine 65 then 67 oil 32 of 25 Abramelin 119 and 21 olive 67 oil 32 and 21 afterward 102 soften 93 & smooth 68 down 30 with 54 rich 52 fresh 64 blood 42	1547	1570
24.	The 53 best 74 blood 42 is 28 of 25 the 53 moon 49 monthly 87 then 67 the 53 fresh 64 blood 42 of 25 a 1 child 48 or 19 dropping 125 from 58 the 53 host 40 of 25 heaven 79 then 67 of 25 enemies 138 then 67 of 25 the 53 priest 115 or 19 of 25 the 53 worshippers 148 last 32 of 25 some 58 beast 75 no 21 matter 107 what 32	2195	2219

25.	This 56 burn 63 of 25 this 56 make 56 cakes 53 & eat 50 unto 62 me 46 This 56 hath 33 also 15 another 87 use 47 let 51 it 47 be 45 laid 32 before 107 me 46 and 21 kept 84 thick 73 with 54 perfumes 149 of 25 your 51 orison 68 it 47 shall 14 become 111 full 39 of 25 beetles 126 as 6 it 47 were 65 and 21 creeping 149 things 81 sacred 62 unto 62 me 46	2459	2484
26.	These 83 slay 23 naming 84 your 51 enemies 138 & they 68 shall 14 fall 23 before 107 you 39	630	656
27.	Also 15 these 83 shall 14 breed 88 lust 48 & power 73 of 25 lust 48 in 37 you 39 at 25 the 53 eating 98 thereof 115	761	788
28.	Also 15 ye 40 shall 14 be 45 strong 73 in 37 war 16	240	268
29.	Moreover 119 be 45 they 68 long 34 kept 84 it 47 is 28 better 130 for 37 they 68 swell 37 with 54 my 36 force 75 All 5 before 107 me 46	1020	1049
30.	My 36 altar 40 is 28 of 25 open 72 brass 43 work 31 burn 63 thereon 111 in 37 silver 77 or 19 gold 26	608	638
31.	There 90 cometh 94 a 1 rich 52 man 36 from 58 the 53 West 57 who 14 shall 14 pour 62 his 32 gold 26 upon 64 thee 78	731	762
32.	From 58 gold 26 forge 73 steel 81	238	270
33.	Be 45 ready 59 to 31 fly 35 or 19 to 31 smite 98	318	351

34.	But 61 your 51 holy 28 place 67 shall 14 be 45 untouched 127 throughout 127 the 53 centuries 158 though 67 with 54 fire 78 and 21 sword 33 it 47 be 45 burnt 87 down 30 & shattered 126 yet 64 an 15 invisible 145 house 58 there 90 standeth 103 and 21 shall 14 stand 50 until 80 the 53 fall 23 of 25 the 53 Great 73 Equinox 127 when 46 Hrumachis 100 shall 14 arise 66 and 21 the 53 double 77 wanded 55 one 46 assume 74 my 36 throne 86 and 21 place 67 Another 87 prophet 124 shall 14 arise 66 and 21 bring 80 fresh 64 fever 90 from 58 the 53 skies 67 another 87 woman 46 shall 14 awake 39 the 53 lust 48 & worship 80 of 25 the 53 Snake 54 another 87 soul 31 of 25 God 24 and 21 beast 75 shall 14 mingle 96 in 37 the 53 globed 71 priest 115 another 87 sacrifice 133 shall 14 stain 67 the 53 tomb 72 another 87 king 57 shall 14 reign 85 and 21 blessing 105 no 21 longer 71 be 45 poured 93 To 31 the 53 Hawk-headed 84 mystical 104 Lord 27	6271	6305
35.	The 53 half 25 of 25 the 53 word 28 of 25 Heru-ra-ha 76 called 49 Hoor-pa-kraat 104 and 21 Ra-Hoor-Khut 97	556	591
36.	Then 67 said 35 the 53 prophet 124 unto 62 the 53 God 24	418	454

37.	I 23 adore 51 thee 78 in 37 the 53 song 37	5804	5841
	I 23 am 22 the 53 Lord 27 of 25 Thebes 103 and 21 I 23		
	The 53 inspired 134 forth 65 speaker 103 of 25 Mentu 101		
	For 37 me 46 unveils 96 the 53 veiled 91 sky 29		
	The 53 self-slain 95 Ankh-af-na-khonsu 118		
	Whose 44 words 33 are 38 truth 81 I 23 invoke 88		
	I 23 greet 97		
	Thy 43 presence 145 O 7 Ra-Hoor-Khuit 120		
	Unity 93 uttermost 159 showed 50		
	I 23 adore 51 the 53 might 83 of 25 Thy 43 breath 86		
	Supreme 131 and 21 terrible 143 God 24		
	Who 14 makest 85 the 53 gods 29 and 21 death 60		
	To 31 tremble 129 before 107 Thee 78		
	I 23 I 23 adore 51 thee 78		
	Appear 91 on 21 the 53 throne 86 of 25 Ra 13		
	Open 72 the 53 ways 24 of 25 the 53 Khu 30		
	Lighten 103 the 53 ways 24 of 25 the 53 Ka 10		
	The 53 ways 24 of 25 the 53 Khabs 39 run 43 through 79		
	To 31 stir 64 me 46 or 19 still 56 me 46		
	Aum 39 let 51 it 47 fill 45 me 46		

38.	So 12 that 53 thy 43 light 64 is 28 in 37 me 46 & its 52 red 43 flame 67 is 28 as 6 a 1 sword 33 in 37 my 36 hand 25 to 31 push 52 thy 43 order 62 There 90 is 28 a 1 secret 104 door 32 that 53 I 23 shall 14 make 56 to 31 establish 109 thy 43 way 19 in 37 all 5 the 53 quarters 115 these 83 are 38 the 53 adorations 100 as 6 thou 52 hast 34 written 125 as 6 it 47 is 28 said 35	6049 6087

The 53 light 64 is 28 mine 83 its 52 rays 33 consume 102
Me 46 I 23 have 40 made 53 a 1 secret 104 door 32
Into 68 the 53 House 58 of 25 Ra 13 and 21 Tum 62
Of 25 Khephra 81 and 21 of 25 Ahathoor 60
I 23 am 22 thy 43 Theban 88 O 7 Mentu 101
The 53 prophet 124 Ankh-af-na-khonsu 118

By 35 Bes-na-Maut 128 my 36 breast 87 I 23 beat 70
By 35 wise 56 Ta-Nech 81 I 23 weave 64 my 36 spell 60
Show 19 thy 43 star-splendour 156 O 7 Nuit 78
Bid 49 me 46 within 91 thine 90 House 58 to 31 dwell 38
O 7 winged 82 snake 54 of 25 light 64 Hadit 58
Abide 75 with 54 me 46 Ra-Hoor-Khuit 120

39.	All 5 this 56 and 21 a 1 book 43 to 31 say 21 how 14 thou 52 didst 64 come 66 hither 92 and 21 a 1 reproduction 186 of 25 this 56 ink 46 and 21 paper 90 for 37 ever 72 for 37 in 37 it 47 is 28 the 53 word 28 secret 104 & not 45 only 38 in 37 the 53 English 84 and 21 thy 43 comment 125 upon 64 this 56 the 53 Book 43 of 25 the 53 Law 6 shall 14 be 45 printed 130 beautifully 164 in 37 red 43 ink 46 and 21 black 45 upon 64 beautiful 147 paper 90 made 53 by 35 hand 25 and 21 to 31 each 43 man 36 and 21 woman 46 that 53 thou 52 meetest 149 were 65 it 47 but 61 to 31 dine 68 or 19 to 31 drink 64 at 25 them 74 it 47 is 28 the 53 Law 6 to 31 give 69 Then 67 they 68 shall 14 chance 70 to 31 abide 75 in 37 this 56 bliss 55 or 19 no 21 it 47 is 28 no 21 odds 24 Do 13 this 56 quickly 98	5031	5070
40.	But 61 the 53 work 31 of 25 the 53 comment 125 That 53 is 28 easy 46 and 21 Hadit 58 burning 111 in 37 thy 43 heart 66 shall 14 make 56 swift 73 and 21 secure 97 thy 43 pen 65	1180	1220
41.	Establish 109 at 25 thy 43 Kaaba 32 a 1 clerk-house 119 all 5 must 67 be 45 done 52 well 32 and 21 with 54 business 114 way 19	738	779

42.	The 53 ordeals 58 thou 52 shalt 36 oversee 109 thyself 93 save 41 only 38 the 53 blind 65 ones 51 Refuse 102 none 60 but 61 thou 52 shalt 36 know 33 & destroy 94 the 53 traitors 108 I 23 am 22 Ra-Hoor-Khuit 120 and 21 I 23 am 22 powerful 110 to 31 protect 131 my 36 servant 91 Success 83 is 28 thy 43 proof 70 argue 66 not 45 convert 105 not 45 talk 36 not 45 over 54 much 55 Them 74 that 53 seek 64 to 31 entrap 102 thee 78 to 31 overthrow 104 thee 78 them 74 attack 72 without 102 pity 88 or 19 quarter 110 & destroy 94 them 74 utterly 119 Swift 73 as 6 a 1 trodden 94 serpent 131 turn 67 and 21 strike 98 Be 45 thou 52 yet 64 deadlier 100 than 43 he 29 Drag 30 down 30 their 88 souls 36 to 31 awful 41 torment 127 laugh 35 at 25 their 88 fear 56 spit 78 upon 64 them 74	5547	5589
43.	Let 51 the 53 Scarlet 82 Woman 46 beware 86 If 41 pity 88 and 21 compassion 122 and 21 tenderness 155 visit 85 her 41 heart 66 if 41 she 34 leave 63 my 36 work 31 to 31 toy 46 with 54 old 15 sweet-nesses 161 then 67 shall 14 my 36 vengeance 138 be 45 known 47 I 23 will 30 slay 23 me 46 her 41 child 48 I 23 will 30 alienate 115 her 41 heart 66 I 23 will 30 cast 43 her 41 out 48 from 58 men 60 as 6 a 1 shrinking 115 and 21 despised 121 harlot 50 shall 14 she 34 crawl 31 through 79 dusk 37 wet 52 streets 120 and 21 die 54 cold 28 and 21 an-hungered 129	3540	3583
44.	But 61 let 51 her 41 raise 66 herself 91 in 37 pride 92 Let 51 her 41 follow 39 me 46 in 37 my 36 way 19 Let 51 her 41 work 31 the 53 work 31 of 25 wickedness 128 Let 51 her 41 kill 36 her 41 heart 66 Let 51 her 41 be 45 loud 32 and 21 adulterous 116 Let 51 her 41 be 45 covered 98 with 54 jewels 76 and 21 rich 52 garments 113 and 21 let 51 her 41 be 45 shameless 93 before 107 all 5 men 60	2583	2627

45.	Then 67 will 30 I 23 lift 67 her 41 to 31 pinnacles 123 of 25 power 73 then 67 will 30 I 23 breed 88 from 58 her 41 a 1 child 48 mightier 143 than 43 all 5 the 53 kings 62 of 25 the 53 earth 66 I 23 will 30 fill 45 her 41 with 54 joy 38 with 54 my 36 force 75 shall 14 she 34 see 55 & strike 98 at 25 the 53 worship 80 of 25 Nu 31 she 34 shall 14 achieve 101 Hadit 58	2304	2349
46.	I 23 am 22 the 53 warrior 70 Lord 27 of 25 the 53 Forties 114 the 53 Eighties 140 cower 60 before 107 me 46 & are 38 abased 58 I 23 will 30 bring 80 you 39 to 31 victory 104 & joy 38 I 23 will 30 be 45 at 25 your 51 arms 39 in 37 battle 96 & ye 40 shall 14 delight 95 to 31 slay 23 Success 83 is 28 your 51 proof 70 courage 86 is 28 your 51 armour 70 go 18 on 21 go 18 on 21 in 37 my 36 strength 119 & ye 40 shall 14 turn 67 not 45 back 43 for 37 any 30	2796	2842
47.	This 56 book 43 shall 14 be 45 translated 114 into 68 all 5 tongues 103 but 61 always 27 with 54 the 53 original 93 in 37 the 53 writing 110 of 25 the 53 Beast 75 for 37 in 37 the 53 chance 70 shape 61 of 25 the 53 letters 117 and 21 their 88 position 129 to 31 one 46 another 87 in 37 these 83 are 38 mysteries 155 that 53 no 21 Beast 75 shall 14 divine 101 Let 51 him 48 not 45 seek 64 to 31 try 51 but 61 one 46 cometh 94 after 80 him 48 whence 84 I 23 say 21 not 45 who 14 shall 14 discover 101 the 53 Key 49 of 25 it 47 all 5 Then 67 this 56 line 64 drawn 36 is 28 a 1 key 49 then 67 this 56 circle 88 squared 85 in 37 its 52 failure 98 is 28 a 1 key 49 also 15 And 21 Abrahadabra 79 It 47 shall 14 be 45 his 32 child 48 & that 53 strangely 109 Let 51 him 48 not 45 seek 64 after 80 this 56 for 37 thereby 125 alone 49 can 28 he 29 fall 23 from 58 it 47	5662	5709
48.	Now 24 this 56 mystery 117 of 25 the 53 letters 117 is 28 done 52 and 21 I 23 want 42 to 31 go 18 on 21 to 31 the 53 holier 73 place 67	852	900

49.	I 23 am 22 in 37 a 1 secret 104 fourfold 87 word 28 the 53 blasphemy 119 against 79 all 5 gods 29 of 25 men 60	672	721
50.	Curse 72 them 74 Curse 72 them 74 Curse 72 them 74	438	488
51.	With 54 my 36 Hawk's 22 head 36 I 23 peck 73 at 25 the 53 eyes 70 of 25 Jesus 68 as 6 he 29 hangs 35 upon 64 the 53 cross 42	714	765
52.	I 23 flap 47 my 36 wings 56 in 37 the 53 face 57 of 25 Mohammed 106 & blind 65 him 48	553	605
53.	With 54 my 36 claws 24 I 23 tear 62 out 48 the 53 flesh 54 of 25 the 53 Indian 81 and 21 the 53 Buddhist 105 Mongol 62 and 21 Din 43	818	871
54.	Bahlasti 80 Ompehda 90 I 23 spit 78 on 21 your 51 crapulous 100 creeds 86	529	583
55.	Let 51 Mary 49 inviolate 129 be 45 torn 57 upon 64 wheels 64 for 37 her 41 sake 40 let 51 all 5 chaste 72 women 70 be 45 utterly 119 despised 121 among 54 you 39	1153	1208
56.	Also 15 for 37 beauty's 107 sake 40 and 21 love's 49	269	325
57.	Despise 115 also 15 all 5 cowards 47 professional 145 soldiers 85 who 14 dare 44 not 45 fight 80 but 61 play 44 all 5 fools 39 despise 115	859	916
58.	But 61 the 53 keen 73 and 21 the 53 proud 68 the 53 royal 37 and 21 the 53 lofty 66 ye 40 are 38 brothers 109	746	804
59.	As 6 brothers 109 fight 80 ye 40	235	294
60.	There 90 is 28 no 21 law 6 beyond 87 Do 13 what 32 thou 52 wilt 52	381	441
61.	There 90 is 28 an 15 end 45 of 25 the 53 word 28 of 25 the 53 God 24 enthroned 131 in 37 Ras 18 seat 55 lightening 151 the 53 girders 94 of 25 the 53 soul 31	1034	1095
62.	To 31 Me 46 do 13 ye 40 reverence 161 to 31 me 46 come 66 ye 40 through 79 tribulation 167 of 25 ordeal 53 which 47 is 28 bliss 55	928	990

63.	The 53 fool 34 readeth 97 this 56 Book 43 of 25 the 53 Law 6 and 21 its 52 comment 125 & he 29 understandeth 177 it 47 not 45	863	926
64.	Let 51 him 48 come 66 through 79 the 53 first 82 ordeal 53 & it 47 will 30 be 45 to 31 him 48 as 6 silver 77	716	780
65.	Through 79 the 53 second 70 gold 26	228	293
66.	Through 79 the 53 third 69 stones 80 of 25 precious 128 water 65	499	565
67.	Through 79 the 53 fourth 82 ultimate 137 sparks 58 of 25 the 53 intimate 155 fire 78	720	787
68.	Yet 64 to 31 all 5 it 47 shall 14 seem 76 beautiful 147 Its 52 enemies 138 who 14 say 21 not 45 so 12 are 38 mere 83 liars 43	830	898
69.	There 90 is 28 success 83	201	270
70.	I 23 am 22 the 53 Hawk-Headed 84 Lord 27 of 25 Silence 107 & of 25 Strength 119 my 36 nemyss 85 shrouds 56 the 53 night-blue 140 sky 29	884	954
71.	Hail 30 ye 40 twin 64 warriors 75 about 69 the 53 pillars 71 of 25 the 53 world 30 for 37 your 51 time 93 is 28 nigh 52 at 25 hand 25	821	892
72.	I 23 am 22 the 53 Lord 27 of 25 the 53 Double 77 Wand 24 of 25 Power 73 the 53 wand 24 of 25 the 53 Force 75 of 25 Coph 50 Nia 38 but 61 my 36 left 69 hand 25 is 28 empty 111 for 37 I 23 have 40 crushed 82 an 15 Universe 131 & nought 77 remains 101	1581	1653
73.	Paste 81 the 53 sheets 88 from 58 right 74 to 31 left 69 and 21 from 58 top 57 to 31 bottom 103 then 67 behold 64	855	928
74.	There 90 is 28 a 1 splendour 114 in 37 my 36 name 61 hidden 78 and 21 glorious 84 as 6 the 53 sun 36 of 25 midnight 126 is 28 ever 72 the 53 son 26	975	1049
75.	The 53 ending 93 of 25 the 53 words 33 is 28 the 53 Word 28 Abrahadabra 79	445	520

The 53 Book 43 of 25 the 53 Law 6 is 28 Written 125 and 21 Concealed 106 Aum 39 Ha 5	504	

The 53 Comment 125 [*Total = 5393*]

Do 13 what 32 thou 52 wilt 52 shall 14 be 45 the 53 whole 41 of 25 the 53 Law 6

The 53 study 67 of 25 this 56 Book 43 is 28 forbidden 131 It 47 is 28 wise 56 to 31 destroy 94 this 56 copy 61 after 80 the 53 first 82 reading 92

Whosoever 98 disregards 106 this 56 does 43 so 12 at 25 his 32 own 24 risk 49 and 21 peril 88 These 83 are 38 most 57 dire 66

Those 65 who 14 discuss 74 the 53 contents 126 of 25 this 56 Book 43 are 38 to 31 be 45 shunned 85 by 35 all 5 as 6 centres 118 of 25 pestilence 182

All 5 questions 139 of 25 the 53 Law 6 are 38 to 31 be 45 decided 104 only 38 by 35 appeal 81 to 31 my 36 writings 115 each 43 for 37 himself 98

There 90 is 28 no 21 law 6 beyond 87 Do 13 what 32 thou 52 wilt 52

Love 44 is 28 the 53 law 6 love 44 under 74 will 30

The 53 priest 115 of 25 the 53 princes 118

Ankh-f-n-khonsu 116

Conclusion

There is work in other areas to discover the "key" implied in *Liber AL vel Legis*, in order to decipher the Thelemic Holy Books.

Even something as uncomplicated as Qabalah Simplex (A=1, B=2, C=3, D=4...) yields some results. Using this schema, for example, "Thelema" enumerates to 64, as does: Nuit, spell, chosen, and true. "Jesus" enumerates to 74, as do: cross, beauty, attained, and heavens. But these are small coincidences when compared to Cipher 6.

As stated at the very beginning of this work, the numerical schema presented here is only one in possibly hundreds. It could be argued that any numerical arrangement will yield results if one looks for meaning, but this has not been my experience with the Hermetic Qabalah, nor with New Aeon English Qaballa. In both cases, there seems to be an underlying intelligence dictating the process, by which those systems expose us to concepts previously unconsidered.

I define Gematria as the art of discovering the relationship that exists between words or phrases which share the same numerical value. It is based on the assumption that numerical equality may not be accidental, and that two words sharing the same value can reveal an internal meaning which corresponds to both. If I use this definition to determine the validity of Cipher 6 as a Gematria, then the answer is a resounding "yes."

I sincerely hope that I have accomplished what I intended with the writing of this book. My wish for you now is the same as it was when I wrote *New Aeon Magick*. It is my hope that this volume will encourage you to find your own path, so that you may open up a road not previously charted.

The Heretic's Guide to Thelema

Volume Three:

The Ethics of Thelema
by
Gerald del Campo

Issued by order of
The Grand Triumvirate
of the Order of Thelemic Knights

Concrescent Press

Introduction

The task of the excellent teacher is to stimulate "apparently ordinary" people to unusual effort. The tough problem is not in identifying winners: it is in making winners out of ordinary people.[*]
— K. Patricia Cross

It was hard to do this work. I haven't been compelled to sit on the sidelines to castigate others for their views on Thelema since I was a teen, and I decided I wouldn't do it now. Instead, I would simply show an opposing point of view collected from various writings which first appeared in *The Templar Cross* (The official communiqué for members of The Order of Thelemic Knights). This alternative point of view, in my opinion, is every bit as valid as the so-called accepted wisdom. I have always made my opinions known, regardless of how unpopular they might be within my own peer group, always keeping in mind that for Thelema to become a living tradition it must be lived like it matters to me. Eventually, one is going to have to put those beautiful leather-bound, first edition tomes down and get up from that comfy armchair and apply what they have learned in the real world. Test all things; hold fast to that which is good.

Many of today's magicians appear to have forgotten that they can use magick to change the world in which they live. This takes a lot of physical work, and so they many have learned to hide behind a lot of theory, philosophical argument, and critique of those very few magicians that have the vision and gumption to see the world they can have as opposed to settling for the world they have today.

Crowley may have unintentionally done the art of magick a great disservice by painting it with such a wide brush. In many ways the word *magick* has lost all meaning. It has been reduced to make people happy about the tedious mundane activities they feel imprisoned by as they live out miserably boring lives. It makes cowards feel at home in their self-made prisons, when magick should be the very thing that liberates people from going nowhere existences.

One could also make an equally valid argument that magick, as Crowley defined it, is actually really a good thing because it makes people feel good about doing some very unwholesome things, but

[*]   *Classroom Assessment Techniques: A Handbook for College Teachers*, 2nd ed., Jossey-Bass Inc Pub., 1993.

this isn't how I see it, and it isn't why I have dedicated my entire life to its study. I do agree with Crowley's basic premise, however: "Magick is the Art and Science of causing change to occur in conformity with Will."* What I disagree with is the idea that any 'willed act' can be a magical act. If this were true, then any trivial predetermined action (such as blowing ones nose) is classifiable as 'magical act'. One hardly needs to study magick, qabalah, and much less Crowley to do those things.

My pseudo-intellectual critics say my writings are "simple," or that I have "ghettoized Thelema" for having the audacity of writing in a plain English, but they think nothing of Crowley's painting magick with such a wide brush that the sheer act of wiping ones bottom after a bowel movement can be an act just as magical as Knowledge and Conversation with ones Holy Guardian Angel. While this might have helped him increase the market for the sales of his books, it also helped to devalue the Art of Magick by perpetuating the idea that it requires anything less than a lifetime of study.

My choice to write in plain English is a source of great pride for me for many reasons, one of which is the fact that English is my second language. When I decided to write about Thelema I wanted to do so in a way that I could reach the largest number of people – not to sell books, but because of the potential Thelema possesses to change the course of humanity. If one loves something they share it with others. Evidently, my books don't serve to keep Thelema confined to a few delusional individuals that actually believe they are the only worthy recipients of this paradigm. In response I just have to restate Crowley's sentiments: "The Law is for ALL!"†

Even Crowley wasn't able to make money selling his books to such a limited audience. He had to die before his material became valuable, not because his message is any more important today than it was during his own time, but because of the book collectors who believe that the magick is in the text itself. It is as if they believe that owning a first edition signed copy exempts them from doing the recommended work. What a sad commentary of Thelemic culture.

Furthermore, many of the folks that criticize my work appear to lack the courage to publish their own ideas, putting their own necks to the block for the unkind scrutiny that has become so popular

---

* *Magick: Liber Aba : Book 4.* 2nd Rev edition - January 1998, Weiser Books.
† *Liber AL vel Legis.* I:34

with many Thelemites. I was surprised to find that much of the criticism has come from people who haven't even read my books. They simply adopt the various assumptions made by someone else who thinks the message is more meaningful if one needs an encyclopedia and an eight-year college degree to understand it. And yet these superior minds often question my sincerity. I have been asked if that little red book will be at my side on my dying bed. This seems a rather strange question coming from a group of people that want Thelema to only be understood by a class of their own making. Wouldn't you expect a person to actually have some understanding of Thelema in order for The Book of The Law to be so meaningful to them that they'd want it with them when they died? I am more interested in living as a Thelemite. The dying part will take care of itself. But for what it is worth, that book has been my constant companion for more than half of my life. I sincerely hope it will be well within reach when I come to the end.

It is necessary to make some things perfectly clear from the very beginning. I will begin by making my standard disclaimer: The thoughts penned for this paper (yes, a pen and a paper were used) are my opinions. I am a Thelemite, and therefore my opinions will be colored by my understanding of Thelema. Just like anyone else, this understanding comes from my personal interpretation of various Thelemic holy books, comparative religion, and mythology; and from trying to live my life accordingly. Are these ideas biased in any way? Yes, of course they are. And for this reason, what you read here should not be misconstrued as an attempt to force my opinion on the masses. This should only serve as an example.

I have been very critical about many popular ideas. It is inevitable that my writing will once again be subject to much speculation and assumption, and therefore some clarification becomes a necessity. Generally speaking, in the pop-Thelemic culture there are three simplified categories of Thelemites: conservative, liberal (sounds like "Liber AL!"), and fundamental.

I find myself to be conservative with regard to policy. To me, accountability equals credibility, and I like it when people walk the talk. I wasn't always this way, but serving on various boards of Thelemic bodies has shaped my feelings about responsibility, devotion, and personal sacrifice.

When it comes to people's lives outside of their organizational duties and responsibilities I tend to be very liberal. *Do what thou wilt* and *Man has the right to live by his own law.*

How I feel about fundamentalism will become apparent as you read this book. But suffice it to say that I believe fundamentalism has no place in enlightened societies.

So there you have it: organizationally conservative, individually liberal, with a violent distaste for any form of fundamentalism. This doesn't mean that I will not approach some subject with unwavering determination and conviction. It is hard to get result without that discipline. I believe that one should approach organizational duties professionally, and conduct business within the organization like a soldier. Oaths, regardless of where they are made, are important because how one maintains them speaks volumes of that person's integrity. But more important than the oath one makes to an organization, is the integrity with which the organization requires those oaths from its members. If the leaders of an organization do not appear to take their roles and responsibilities seriously, then how can they expect their members to stick to their oaths? Remember this, because it is important.

These are my observations, and they are offered here as an example of my struggle to live my life as a Thelemite in the world. This is what Indian philosophy refers to as Karma Yoga. Karma implies movement and action. I abhor people who call themselves Thelemites but shrug the awesome responsibility that is implied by that a statement. In my opinion there are entirely too many soldiers that play and won't fight, and many of them have infiltrated organizations devoted to the Liberty of Man. To make matters worse, the people that run these organizations don't seem to mind since a toy soldier and a real one each pays the same dues.

When it comes to my criticism of democracy, patriotism, and capitalism you might feel compelled to think of me a communist, socialist, or anti-American. American politics is something I am most familiar with, because well...I live here. I am aware of many, many other countries whose governments lack any form of ethical conduct at all, torturing and killing their own people because no one strong enough will stand against them. So, yes...I am aware of the atrocities committed in other countries, but I do not have first hand experience of being a citizen there, and for this I am eternally grateful. I am an American by choice. I don't have to stay here, and yet I do. I believe that should speak volumes of my feelings for this country.

I have been called a lot of unkind things for holding these views. My motives are always questioned, and I have heard my share of 'love it or leave it.' As easy as that would be, I won't. I can't. If I complain about something it is because I love it. Why try to change something you don't care about? I am neither a coward nor a blind man. If you'd like to believe that Thelema has nothing to do with politics you probably won't care for many of the things in this book.

Having said all of this, it might surprise you to learn that I do not believe that all men are created equal. But I believe that all men, not just the privileged, should start with the same opportunities to exceed, for that is the only way that true valor, intelligence, virtue, and greatness can ever manifest on a national level. The people of this country have a lot to offer. They just need the opportunity to show what they are made off. As it is, only the privileged can afford a healthcare and good education. This from a government claiming to be the "richest country in the world." It may be naïve to think that these issues can be addressed today when capitalism has become the modern god. But I feel compelled to try because in my heart I believe ethical people must speak out against injustice everywhere. If ever there was a need for ethical conduct, it is today.

These are dangerous times for lovers of freedom and liberty, and anyone that speaks against oppression and tyranny does so at great personal risk. I imagine the Gnostics must have felt very much like lovers of freedom do today, and I reckon that if the oppression does not stop, then organizations dedicated to the preservation of democracy and freedom will be compelled to operate in secrecy, just as they have historically.

The basic premise of ethics is universal. It is the method – the art of distinguishing the differences between honor and dishonor, good and bad, commendable and appalling, just and unfair. We can see the application of ethics everywhere.

Ethics are important because they can provide a method to discovering a higher road, a path of honor and justice without having to resort to religious or superstitious justification. They are important because they help us learn to recognize why we do the things we do and how we justify them. After all, right action must by necessity begin with right thought. So let us shed the stinking thinking, the false pretences, excuses, and justifications that serve so well to pull us further and further away from our own Truth. Let us instead turn our attention to those things we already know to be in accordance with our own True Will and act accordingly to become agents of the Divine. Since we are destined to be remembered by our actions, then let us be remembered for being ethical soldiers in the battle against illusion. Since we are destined to make our mark, then let us collectively make that mark a testament of devotion to the Beloved whom we adore and serve. Let's begin setting the bar for those that will come after us.

Aleister Crowley briefly touches on the subject of ethics in "Duty," and his letters to students. While I am afraid that this book falls short for the reason that it is limited to one person's experience, it is my sincerest hope that it will cause you, the reader, to examine your own thoughts in light of the material contained in all metaphysical, philosophical, and religious material, whether they be explicitly Thelemic or not. It is my wish that others will be inspired to write about how Thelemic Gnosticism has influenced their own ethics and then share this information with others. This might in turn lead to a greater understanding of Thelema as a personal human experience rather than something that happened exclusively to Crowley, which will hopefully help to put Thelema into the lives of those people that The Prophet wanted to reach, as opposed to keeping it confined to the bookshelves of those individuals that wish to control the tremendous industry that Crowley's work has become.

If you are the sort of Thelemite that considers "going with the program" the proper course when the waters become choppy, or prefers to believe the lies we are told by our leaders, then you might want to reconsider going any further, what you read may do little more than insult you. I hope that you will keep reading, and if perchance the words you read here inspire you to take a different philosophical look at what Thelema might be, or makes you question your own beliefs and motives, then making these thoughts available to you has been worth it.

Once upon a time, all of us thought of Truth as indisputable. Our society and parents, seeking security, used those truths to justify the oppression of rules and regulations. When those rules restricted our passion, or attempted to extinguish our curiosity, we made the same mistake that humans have made since time immemorial: we rebelled against the Truth which appeared to be the source of restriction. In our youth we lacked the experience and skill to realize that rules and Truth are not one in the same thing, and so we veiled the source of our oppression instead of approaching the problem with the rules. By way of peer pressure we learned about the dangers of uncensored truth, and so we created socially acceptable loopholes to insulate ourselves against our own helplessness or the shortcomings of our loved ones, such as Oscar Wilde's concept of the 'casual lie' (the so called 'white lie' of politeness and tact). The 'noble lie' in Plato's Republic is a way of keeping people in their place by making them believe that their true nature has been crafted by some god or gods.

Convenience and financial advantage make it easy for us to adopt the idea that ethics were situational or subject to economics, or that truth might depend on status, social position, income, or degree; or that some are beyond secular law while others less fortunate are subject to it. Once upon the time, the Law was for ALL. The following thoughts are little more than my attempt to return to that time, and come to terms with my own hypocrisy.

The greatest human shame is that we hold the keys to greatness, the means to manifest our destiny and change the world, but instead choose a path less honorable for the sake of the same distractions that keep us from manifesting our own true purpose.

Gerald del Campo
May 25, 2004
Ashland, Oregon

Source of Ethics

A man's ethical behavior should be based effectually on sympathy, education, and social ties; no religious basis is necessary. Man would indeed be in a poor way if he had to be restrained by fear of punishment and hope of reward after death.

—Albert Einstein

The source of ethics is the subject of much controversy and debate, and I hope that it will always remain that way. The religionists say that ethics are divinely inspired, while the atheists insist that ethics come from being human, the ability to empathize, and a mindful recognition of the connection between himself and his fellow man. In other words, they claim being ethical is a human trait. While considering this, one might see this as a paradox: ethics as a uniquely human trait illustrate the divine nature of man on the one hand, and on the other we must question how human a quality can be when so very few humans seem to possess it. Perhaps this is what is meant by "let my servants be few and secret."* The Western Mystery Tradition has always been preoccupied with being more than human. If we look around, we can see why this is necessary.

The atheist blames religion for the world's woes because he generally feels that people should do the right thing out of humanity or principle, rather than fear, and yet this is a terribly unfair assessment. Not all religion is fear-based, nor are all religious people acting out of fear when they do the right thing. One must learn to take the bad with the good. Despite the many instances when evil men have used religion to justify killing and torture, a lot of good has been done and continues to be done in its name. The notable movie personality Martin Sheen once said, "We shouldn't be critical of Christianity, because it hasn't been tried."† If Christianity hasn't been tried, then how much less can we say of Thelema? Even more disturbing is the idea that 2,000 years can come and go with so very few people ever adhering to their chosen paradigm.

---

* Liber AL vel Legis – The Book of the Law. I:10

† It is a little absolutist to claim, "it hasn't been tried" without simultaneously discounting the work of some remarkable individuals, such as Mother Teresa, for example. But it is easy to agree since very few adherents of Christianity are actually doing the work of Christ.

Adherents of Christianity have, for the most part, only given lip service to the teachings of Jesus. It is true that people are healed, fed and taken care of in dire times, but at the cost of their soul: The motivation for this aid has always been to convert. This made me think of the hypocrisy inherent in so many religious zealots who insist on representing their sect because doing so gives them a feeling of superiority. They appear to be better than others, but their actions do their chosen paradigm a great disservice. In other words, it isn't the religious paradigm that has failed, but the adherents (if, after all this, we can still call them that) for not being sufficiently sincere to subject themselves to the inconveniences imposed by their chosen beliefs. They are only adherents when it serves them to reach their desired goals.

The religionists blame atheism for the world's problems, insinuating that a belief in God is necessary for ethical behavior. Again, this is misplaced blame. They believe that people are incapable of acting rightly or honorable unless they are motivated by fear. Atheists can have conviction. Neither Buddhism nor Taoism requires belief in a "god," and yet right action is a great preoccupation for adherents of both of these religious paradigms.

The ethical atheist may be more genuine than his religionist counterpart since the atheist is generally motivated by compassion, love, and/or 'enlightened self-interest,' while the other (at least if he subscribes to the concepts of hell and eternal damnation) is largely motivated by fear and 'selfish self-interest.' Perhaps the best way to explain the problem with religion-based ethics is to reference the 2004 US elections, where many people voted for the person that supposedly exemplified "Christian values" such as homophobia and a hatred for anything 'liberal.'* Crowley was clearly right about the shortcomings of so-called 'democracy.'†

While it is true that religion can advocate high ethical standards, we would err greatly if we were to identify ethics exclusively with religious conviction. If ethics were confined to religion, then we

---

* Such as affordable healthcare, education and scientifically based research.

† "The principle of popular election is a fatal folly; its results are visible in every so-called democracy. The elected man is always the mediocrity; he is the safe man, the sound man, the man who displeases the majority less than any other; and therefore never the genius, the man of progress and illumination." *Liber 194 – An Intimation with Reference to the Constitution of the Order*

would only see them in the actions of religious people. If this were true, then how do we explain the ethics of the atheist? Ethics are not synonymous with religion.

So what are ethics? I define ethics as a standard of right and wrong that dictates what humans should do in terms of rights, duty, and commitment to society, justice, or specific virtues, such as the Eleven Virtues of Thelemic Knighthood.*

Most importantly, however, are ethics as the development of one's personal standards. That is what an ethical person does. Feelings, laws, and social norms often stray from what is ethical, so we must constantly test our own standards to make sure that they are rational and well-founded. The study of ethics is the noble endeavor of scrutinizing our own beliefs and conduct, and the work of ensuring that the institutions we shape achieve the standards worthy of those chosen beliefs. This is an application of ethics that doesn't seem to be getting much attention today. To say it a different way: the study of ethics is important because it will guide us away from decision-making based on peer pressure and the desire for external validation, and help guide our lives in accordance with our own personal internal compass. It doesn't get any more Thelemic than that.

Nietzsche and many of his contemporaries went to great lengths to show that there was no such thing as altruism because all that we do, no matter how well-intentioned, benefits us in one way or another. In other words, there are no selfless acts. But we already know that. Perhaps the English journalist Gilbert Chesterton said it best when he wrote:

The modern world is not evil; in some ways the modern world is far too good. It is full of wild and wasted virtues[...] virtues gone mad because they have been isolated from each other and are wandering alone. Thus some scientists care for truth; and their truth is pitiless. Thus some humanitarians care only for pity; and their pity (I am sorry to say) is often untruthful.†

Nietzsche explains that any altruistic act creates weakness because compassion and charity are insults to the individual to whom they

---

* Valor, Nobility, Discernment, Pride, Compassion, Fidelity, Passion, Strength, Discipline, Self-Reliance, and Hospitality.
† Gilbert Chesterton, *Orthodoxy*, (Garden City, New York: Doubleday & Company, 1959), page 30.

are directed,* and that those actions, as well-intentioned as they may be, cause a sort of dependence rather than empowering the individual to rise up or fail on their own strength. Many Thelemites sincerely believe that this is what will cleanse the human race of all weakness of body and mind and create the ideal man, and that this sort of disregard to the suffering of one's fellows is to be credited for the greatness that humanity has already attained.

Crowley seemed to subscribe to this idea as well, and if one reads through his comments on *Liber AL,* this is how he has chosen to interpret some difficult passages of *The Book of the Law.* It is somewhat ironic that very few people seem to follow Nietzsche's or Crowley's advice of questioning all things.

1. Crowley was rather jaded toward the end of his life. His later comments reflect an attitude contradictory to what he wrote of the text when he was young and idealistic.

2. His views were, unfortunately, very biased against every idea associated with Christianity. Given his parents' strict, conservative household, one can hardly blame him for this, but the reader should keep in mind that he obviously had trouble with this and that it may have colored his interpretation of the message he was receiving.

3. Neither Crowley nor Nietzsche have considered that compassion might be a human trait† or that there may be a very good reason why people feel good when they do things for others. Nor have they considered how compassion, reverence, and empathy have contributed to human evolution. Humans help one another. As painful as it is for some to acknowledge, no man is an island, nor would we have developed communities, societies, or anything of lasting value without cooperating with others. Strength also comes in numbers.

4. It is illogical to demonize compassion, reverence, and empathy simply because of the selfish nature of altruism, since compassion, reverence, and empathy can come from other

---

* *The Antichrist.* Section 7. He uses the word "pity." Many wrongly (and conveniently) lump pity with compassion.

† Either as a natural occurring phenomena; something evolutionarily useful, or both. Current research may be on the verge of providing scientific data to support this view.

places. And as far as the 'weak' are concerned, without people like Einstein, who had trouble spelling his name until he was eight[*], without Stephen Hawking we may not have dared to venture beyond already known ideas about the nature of time and the universe. John Merrick[†] exemplified courage and inner strength. It is difficult to imagine never having heard a melody made by Chopin, or the teachings of Crowley himself, had they been allowed to die simply because of their debilitating illnesses. Strength comes in many forms, and often it only becomes apparent later in life. "Every man and every woman is a star."[‡] This is not to say that everyone has something worthwhile to contribute to human evolution, but in an ideal world, everyone would have the opportunity.

5. Christianity seems to imply that a person's primary ethical responsibility is to others first, while egoism holds that one's primary obligation is to one's self, and toward advancing one's own self interest. Nietzsche, Crowley and others have categorized altruism as a 'slave morality' without any redeeming qualities. I also concur. Both Nietzsche and Crowley have noted that what appears to be an altruistic act on the surface actually furthers one's self-interest, and they say it like it is a bad thing. A person's self-interest must come first, and there are many ways to further one's self-interest. For example, the Order of Thelemic Knights does not engage in charitable campaigns because its members are trying to learn to be altruistic; we do so because it furthers our own personal growth. That others benefit from our work began as a wonderful coincidence we'd like to keep.

---

[*]   According to his mother, didn't speak until he was three. Little Albert was terribly dyslexic.
[†]   The "Elephant Man."
[‡]   *Liber AL vel legis: The Book of the Law* - I:III

Different Ethical Paradigms, or Why Kant We Just Get Along?

The five examples listed below represent the most popular forms of ethics used today in everyday life. It will become apparent that each has its strength and weakness. There are numerous more which could not be included here due to the limited scope of this dissertation. There are approaches within approaches. To make matters more confusing, every method described below could be used to justify unethical behavior.

In the *Utilitarian* approach, for example, there is the Ethical Egoist, who concerns himself exclusively with his own benefit, while a Consequentialist Utilitarian works toward the good of all who are affected by an action or deliberation.* Both look for a positive outcome or opportunity, but they differ on who should benefit.

Frequently, Utilitarianism will require that one do what is best for the greatest number of people, rather than what is good for oneself, but that isn't to say that it cannot be used to justify something considered unethical by every other standard. For example, a Utilitarian could make the case that prisoners with life sentences should be used for medical experiments, arguing that discoveries could be made which would benefit millions of people of much higher character. This treatment of prisoners would not hurt the majority, and one could justify it by making the claim that the prisoners deserve to pay for their crimes in a way that would benefit society. If a prisoner should die in the experiments, then the scientists and doctors could endorse their experiments with the statement that, had they lived, they would be a burden to society since taxpayers have to pay to house, feed, and clothe them for life.

The bottom line is that whether we understand ethics or not, we still have the choice of doing the wrong thing or the right thing. Ultimately, we have to rely on our own self-knowledge, sense of self-worth, pride, integrity, and sincere effort to get us through tough decisions. You should also keep in mind, as you read this, that no one uses one method exclusively, but that they borrow what seems most comfortable to make their own ethical decisions.

---

* Always look for a way to benefit everyone... including one's self.

The Utilitarian Approach

Utilitarianism was conceived by the English philosopher and political radical Jeremy Bentham (1748-1832). Jeremy Bentham spent most of his life critiquing law and strongly advocating legal reform, and came up with the system to assist lawmakers in deciding which laws were the most ethical. In a nutshell, the Utilitarian approach dictates that the most ethical decisions are the ones that result in the least evil.*

United States politicians and lawmakers tend to be Utilitarian or Consequentialist† in their problem solving. The most important consideration is what effect the policy will have on the average citizen.

When using Utilitarianism to look for an ethical course of action, we might approach the issue by first asking ourselves a few questions. It might go something like this:

What are the options available to us?

Who will be affected by our decisions?

What benefit or harm will each course of action lead us to?

After those questions have been answered, we chose an option that will cause the least amount of harm and benefit the greatest number of people. In Utilitarianism, the most appropriate action provides the most benefit to the greatest number.

One of the clear shortcomings of the Utilitarian approach is that there is a tendency to ignore justice. Apartheid in South Africa comes as a good example in recent history, when South African whites decided that all South Africans, black and white, would be better served under white leadership. Those arguing in favor of this view claimed that social conditions declined in African nations that exchanged exclusively white governments for black or mixed governance. The proponents of apartheid predicted civil war, financial decline, food shortages, and social instability following the establishment of a black majority government. These predictions did not occur when apartheid ended. If it had, then the white government of South Africa would have been ethically justified by utilitarianism, in spite of its discrimination.

---

*   "Evil" is an emotionally loaded term, and this is why I have chosen to use it.

†   Consequentialism is a branch of Utilitarianism that dictates that we should do whatever increases the chances for good consequences. What one does to achieve these good consequences is irrelevant. What matters is that the good results are maximized.

The Rights Approach*

The *Rights Approach* is rooted in the philosophical works of Kant,†
whose focus was on the right to choose for oneself. This philosophy
supposes that humans have a moral right to choose freely, and that
this freedom of choice is what gives humans their dignity and separates us from objects that can or should be manipulated. In other
words, every human should be respected and given the choice to
live their life in accordance with that choice. To say it another way, it
is unethical to demand that a person act in a fashion that they have
not personally chosen.

> *Every action is right which in itself, or in the maxim on which it pro-
> ceeds, is such that it can coexist along with the freedom of the will of
> each and all in action, according to a universal law.‡*

Some of the rights listed below might remind you of Liber OZ. In
fact, Liber OZ is so close to the human rights dictated by this ethical
approach that it is entirely possible it might have come to Crowley
as a result of Kant's writings. See for yourself:

- *The right to truthful information.* The right to be told the truth
  about matters that may affect our lives.
- *The right of privacy.* The right to do, believe, and say whatever
  we choose, provided that we do not violate the rights of others.
- *The right not to be injured.* The right not to be harmed unless
  we knowingly do something that warrants retribution, or we
  choose to risk such injury of our own free will.
- *The right to what is agreed.* We are entitled to hold a reasonable
  expectation of what is promised to us by people with whom
  we have freely entered into a pact or covenant.

When using the Rights Approach to explore an ethical course of
action, we only need ask ourselves one question: does our decision/
action respect the rights of everyone?

We only need to look at the deceptively titled "Patriot Act"§ to see

---

* I have refrained from criticizing The Rights Approach by referencing *Liber
  OZ* to make this point because I felt it would be redundant. Most anyone that
  reads this will already have first hand experience of the tremendous potential
  for abuse in that document.
† Kant, Immanuel. *An Immanuel Kant Reader.* Trans. and Ed., with Commentary
  by Raymond B. Blakney. New York: Harper, 1960.
‡ *The Science of Right* by Immanuel Kant, 1790.
§ The Patriot Act was signed into law by President George W. Bush on October
  26, 2001. The name was carefully chosen in order to alienate those that disap-

how our rights are violated in the US. With the implementation of this act Americans lost the following freedoms and rights:

- *Freedom of association.* Government may now spy on religious and political institutions even if they are not suspected of criminal activity, discouraging individuals from pursuing their right to freedom of association. Specific groups have been branded 'terrorist organizations,' making membership in them illegal.
- *Freedom of information.* Government has closed immigration hearings and has held hundreds of people without charging them with criminal offense, and has applied pressure to public and civil servants to withhold once freely available information from the public.*
- *The freedom of speech.* Government may subpoena information from public librarians (such as individual patron records, listing books that were checked out), and may punish them if they alert individuals.†
- *The right to legal representation.* Government officials may monitor once protected attorney-client conversations in prisons, as well as denying legal assistance to Americans accused of crimes.
- *Freedom from unreasonable searches.* Government may search and seize property and papers without probable cause.
- *The right to a speedy and public trial.* Americans may be declared 'enemy combatants' and imprisoned indefinitely without a trial.
- *Right to confront accusers.* Not only can Americans be jailed without being charged of a crime, but also they do not have the right to confront their accusers.

In short, under the Rights Approach, it is clear that the provisions in the Patriot Act, which circumscribe citizens rights as described by Kant and enumerated in the U.S. Constitution, are unethical. Furthermore, the Patriot Act opens the door to future legislation

---

prove of the gross restrictions and violations of constitutional rights proposed by the act.
* The Freedom of Information Act.
† Librarians have rebelled against this act by changing the way they keep records.

further limiting or completely eliminating these and other rights. Government agencies are protected against accountability by way of increased secrecy and lack of judicial oversight, checks and balances.

The Fairness or Justice Approach

This method is very similar to the Rights Approach, but has its origins in the teachings of Aristotle, who states that favoritism and discrimination are unethical and unjust, because giving benefit to someone without a justifiable reason is unfair to those denied those benefits. He teaches that discrimination is unreasonable because it burdens people who are no different than those spared from the same burdens. The fundamental moral questions for using this method are:

How fair is an act?

Does it deal with everyone in a similar fashion?

Does it demonstrate preferential treatment or bias?

Consider ballot measure 36 in Oregon's Spring 2005 elections. This measure amended Oregon's constitution to define marriage as a union between one man and one woman. It is a reaction to Oregon's gay community in general (which rightly feels discriminated against), and specifically against Multnomah County's ruling that denying marriage licenses to homosexual couples was a discriminatory practice that denied homosexual couples the same benefits available to married heterosexual couples.* These people pay taxes, and should receive the same treatment and benefits as other socially responsible taxpayers, regardless of sexual orientation. If a true separation existed between Church and State, this wouldn't be an issue at all.

This political issue is a good example of a violation of The Fairness or Justice Approach AND the Rights Approach described above as well as the rights declared in *Liber OZ.*†

---

* These benefits include, but are not limited to medical benefits for their lovers, better opportunities for low interest home loans, the right to visit an ill partner in the hospital, the right to make end of life care decisions for partners, the right to inherit in cases of intestacy, the ability to adopt children, joint filing on income tax returns and other social benefits afforded to heterosexual couples.

† But the most important philosophical issue in this debate is whether or not the State can determine who can and cannot marry in a country where the separation of Church and State is guaranteed. If that separation truly existed,

Rules, such as the Equal Opportunity Act, the Fair Housing Act, and the like will always exist, no matter how well we evolve, so long as someone is denied the same opportunities as others. I realize that these laws are rather arbitrary, and oftentimes when misused they can be a source of reverse discrimination.* As a result, many shortsighted individuals have rallied to put an end to these protections, but if they succeed, we will never see the true geniuses rise up above the rest because they will not have an equal field on which to begin to prove themselves.

Consider this for a moment. On the one hand, we have the head of a corporation who had the best education money could buy, who never had to struggle with paying rent or putting food on the table, who inherited his father's fortune and who took over as the figurehead of the organization. On the other hand, we have a foreigner (or single mother) who comes to this country with little more than a dream, who lives in one of the many shanty towns, ghettos or 'projects,' who attends the overcrowded and under-funded public school systems and grows up to have his or her own tailor shop. Who is the superior being? Is the accumulation of wealth the sole genetic trait for strength, or are there others?

The Common Good Approach
This approach to ethical problems began some 2,000 years ago with the writings of Plato, Aristotle and Cicero. It suggests that a person's own good is inextricably connected to the good of the community. In other words, members of a community are duty-bound to the pursuit of common values and goals. In recent times, John Rawls has defined 'common good' as "certain general conditions that are...equally to everyone's advantage."†

This methodology approaches social problems by making certain that the policies, systems, institutions, and environments we so often take for granted are beneficial to all. Affordable health care,

---

then the argument would be between the heads of the churches, and not a matter for government.
* Reverse discrimination takes place any time that well-qualified native applicants are overlooked for employment in favor of people of color or a certain sex just to meet some arbitrary criteria.
† *A Theory of Justice* by John Rawls. Belknap Press; Revised edition (September 1, 1999)

public safety, world peace, justice, and environmental issues are all subject to consideration.*

Furthering the *common good* compels us to view ourselves as members of the same community; and questions regarding of the kind of society, order, fraternity or neighborhood we want to develop and how we are to achieve it are the dominant considerations. This does not mean that the Common Good Approach disregards the rights of individuals, but rather, it provides us with the opportunity to look for the things we have in common instead of the things that make us different.

For example, if you feel that the children and loved ones of politicians who start wars should not be exempt from fighting those wars, or that politicians should send their kids to public schools, or that politicians should live in the neighborhoods where they work while earning the same salaries of the average citizen living in the area, then you might be using the Common Good Approach.

The Virtue Approach

The presumption made by the *Virtue Approach* is that some ideals that will accelerate our own personal and universal evolution, because when one of us rises up above the norm, the whole of humanity benefits from the evolutionary leap. They make us better people by helping us to develop. We begin to develop a sense of the required virtues by reflecting on our own potential.

Virtues empower us to behave and act in a manner that leads us to our highest personal potential. Virtues, once embraced, become a characteristic trait. Additionally, an individual who has accepted virtues will be predisposed to act in a manner consistent with his or her ethical principles because virtue relates to ethics. A virtuous person is an ethical person, and those few that truly and sincerely embrace The Eleven Virtues of Thelemic Knighthood can inspire amazing changes in character.

Most of the questions one might consider while using the Virtue Approach deal with the compromises one is making to their character. For example:

What sort of person will this action make me?
Will I be compromising my character or betraying my beliefs or myself?
Will this action reflect badly on my chosen philosophical/religious paradigm?

* Marriage, as it is today, would be considered unethical in this approach.

126 The Ethics of Thelema

Will this choice of action promote, or interfere with, my development?
Is this behavior befitting of the sort of person I am trying to become?
Is this behavior and its consequences in line with my True Will?

The Virtue Approach concerns itself with self-worth. It holds that one's integrity and honor are reflections of the individual's true nature; therefore, there is an emphasis on action and works. This approach to ethics is a very popular substitute for rule-based (deontological) and results-based (consequentialist) ethics. In fact, the Virtue Approach to ethics was created out of frustration with ethical concepts of duty and obligation. It was a reactionary response to the use of convenient, but unbending and ineffective, moral rules and principles that are often used as standards to all moral situations.

How the Virtue Approach varies, from, say, the Utilitarian and Consequentialist Approach, becomes apparent when using the following classical ethical dilemma: A man's wife becomes very sick, and he spends an astonishing amount of money to attempt to save her life. In fact, with the amount of money he spent trying to save one woman, he could have saved ten women he didn't know. The utilitarian would say that the man should have used his money to save the greater number of people. A virtue ethicist would argue that placing the welfare of loved ones above the welfare of strangers is essentially good because it isn't natural for humans to make life-and-death decisions based on some mathematical moral calculation. They would also argue that few people would want to live in a world where we forsake our own spouses to save strangers.

Applied Ethics, or Ethical Problem Solving

Unfortunately, no templates or guaranteed methods provide nice, squeaky-clean solutions to ethical dilemmas. Wouldn't that be nice? Ultimately, we are all going to have to get our hands dirty, but maybe we can arm ourselves by looking at the facts, understanding ethics and choosing to be ethical so that we can minimize damage. First and foremost: cause no harm.

At the very least, ask yourself the following questions:

Do I have all the facts?
What are my options?
What option will lead to the most balanced end?
What benefits will my decision provide, and who will benefit?

Will my course of action violate anyone else's rights?
Will my action show unwarranted favoritism or discrimination?
Which decision increases the common good most?
Is my chosen course of action harmonious with my own ethics?

What is an Ethical Person?

Notice that in speaking of destruction of the intellect, nothing more is meant than recognition of the vanity of the intellect in relation to the absolute; so also for conscience. Twice two still makes four, and killing is still murder; but all this is relative, and relates to the individual in his limitations, not to the absolute. This very simple truth, that the planes are separate, is the greatest of all the discoveries of Fra. P. It is a complete key to life.
—Aleister Crowley, Equinox I:8, p. 23–4

Is a person that does the right thing due to fear of religious, judicial, or legislative repercussions ethical? What about people whose behavior is based on fear of loosing societal standing? Can ethics be a part of a person's genetic make up? Does a person WILL ethics, or can ethics be forced upon a person by society? Can ethics be used as a means to discover ones true nature?

Society can try to teach ethics (via education), and enforce laws by exacting penalties for failure to act ethically, but doesn't this sort of society risk becoming a fear based society because the motivation for right action will be based solely on self interest instead of a love for Light, Life, Love, and Liberty?* Furthermore, some laws require unethical behavior. Law is concerned with what is legal rather than what is right. Wouldn't you rather be a member of a society composed of ethical citizens? People who act ethically out of their own desire to be ethical, rather than motivated by fear? This doesn't mean that people acting out of fear are inherently ethical. Ethics concerns itself with action.

We have seen what occurs when unethical people use fear in order to make laws in our own society. Consider how in recent days Americans have given up freedom of association, freedom of information, freedom of speech, the right to legal representation, freedom from unreasonable searches, the right to a speedy and public trial, or the right to liberty.† The message those laws and regula-

---

*   Consider the motivation behind paying taxes in the absence of equal representation. Is it done as a sense of duty for ones country or social responsibility, or out of a desire to stay out of prison? If it is the later, then is it unreasonable to think of taxation as something akin to extortion?

†   If this seems fictional I would encourage the reader to examine the so-called

tions send is that it is okay to do the wrong thing, even when it violates the lofty ideals which founded this country, provided that it is legal or lawful.

Right thought leads into right action. Words mean nothing. So if we are to make intelligent decisions about other people then we must ignore what they say and pay attention to what they do. If a person complains, but makes no effort to correct a situation or condition, then it is clear that the issue is not really serious in that person's mind because it hasn't driven them into action.

What shall we say of a person that is aware of corruption and injustice in government but ignores political involvement such as voting? Is a person that ignores knowledge of unpleasant things, preferring instead to believe lies when the facts are in front of his face in order to justify inaction being ethical?

*Nevertheless have the greatest self-respect, and to that end sin not against thyself. The sin which is unpardonable is knowingly and willfully to reject truth, to fear knowledge lest that knowledge pander not to thy prejudices.**

Despise also all cowards; professional soldiers who dare not fight, but play; all fools despise!†

Ethics and laws are often times opposed to one another. This is clearly the case when we see people who sacrifice their own freedom for ones fellows, principles, ideals, or even ethics itself by breaking bad laws. Clearly, laws are not necessarily ethical, as when regulation and licensing prevent freedom of movement, speech, or making a living; when laws based purely on religious morality force non-adherents into compliance, or when government or big business (same thing, really) can make use of loopholes unavailable to all in order to avoid responsibility for wrongdoings. In fact, law is a bad model for ethics...unless, of course, *Love* happens to be the *Law*. What shall we say of a justice system that jails Martha Stewart whose only crime was to sell her company's stock when she heard that the market was about to crash, but criminals like Tom DeLay, who committed perjury, who smoked Cuban cigars during an embargo against Cuba, took bribes from casinos and funneled

---

"Patriot Act."

* *Liber Librae*, Paragraph 15.

† *Liber AL vel Legis: The Book of the Law* III:57

corporate contributions to state campaigns during the 2002 election cycle as well as the redistricting in 2003 to ensure a Republican victory will never see a day in prison? What pride can we have for our modernity with all of our medical breakthroughs in genetics if the best, most sophisticated bioethical solution for a woman on a feeding tube is to allow her to starve to death? Some times humans seem to get more excited by the possibility of cloning sheep than they are by advancing as an enlightened people.

The law should only be a marker for minimal standards for behavior necessary for a productive society. We must never forget the fact that laws are often created so as to have an unethical end, such as the laws justifying Apartheid in South Africa. Legislators that create and support laws like these create a social disrespect for them. It is not unlike the disservice that a zealot does his religion when he uses it to justify his own means. Nor should a law's popularity be a marker of ethical value since an unethical law can placate the majority of people as it did in Hitler's Germany. The absence of social agreement on many issues makes it impossible to link ethics with what is socially acceptable. The same is true of Thelema, but that shouldn't stop us from discovering our own, personal ethical standards.

Ethics, on the other hand, are something more than forced compliance. One cannot be forced into ethics. They must be willingly embraced, but today so-called 'ethics' tend to focus on rules, and this is simply another form of control. Furthermore, ethical values should be in compliance with ones True Will. This isn't to say that it is impossible for groups of people to adhere to a unified code, or agree on a codified set of ethics in order to accomplish a task which would be impossible without the assistance of others.

Aristotle tells us that the focus of ethics is on character, not rules.* In other words, how one tackles problems is a measure of a person's self-worth. It reflects an idea of ones value. According to Aristotle, the central question is what one should be, rather than what one should do, because if good character is in place then by necessity, good action will follow. Right thought leads into right action. Therefore, he tells us, we would do well by developing our character rather than trying to fit into some moral rule or law... unless, again, *Love* happens to be the *Law*.

* Aristotle's critique of Plato's Republic

Rabelais appears to have held similar beliefs. "Do as thou wilt" was the only rule of his Abbey of Thelema, for a person with good breeding will naturally do the right thing at the right time. Consequently, you won't find any clocks in this monk's Abbey, since according to him it seems ridiculous that man would regulate his life in accordance to a mechanical time-telling device, because the Thelemite (being possessed of the above mentioned good breeding) can only do things at the right time.

The Ego is a topic of both metaphysical and psychological concern, and in many instances the line that separates these two fields of human study becomes quite blurred and becomes important to the topic of ethics. This is especially true in present times where pseudo-intellectuals have reduced the spiritual reflex and the domain of the soul to simple but comfortable well-known psychological impulses without offering any real solutions to the problem of living a spiritual life in a world that demands selfishness and greed. 'God Is Dead.'

This following example is by no means all-inclusive. There are many paths that a person can travel to find spiritual freedom. The observation that follows is what I perceive as the ideal or best case scenario, and comes in part from watching people and reflecting on my own experiences on the path to self-discovery.

This piece necessitates an explanation of how the term "ego" is being used. For the religious creature, the ego signifies arrogance, self-importance, and unearned pride. For the psychologist, the ego is the function in the human psyche that organizes the different aspects of the Self* in order to create a facade of wholeness and integration: it is a function of deception that serves to affect the individual and those around them. It is a necessary tool for survival in the world. Both schools of thought are correct, but again, neither offers a clue as to how to use this information to create a true method for gaining access to the Higher Self.

There is a false assumption in the religious types that this ego must be destroyed. Individuals that have actually accomplished some success in this area find themselves having to go through years of therapy to get it back. In fact, the religious insistence of defining the ego as an enemy that must be destroyed at all cost may

---

* The archetype of personal totality; the governing nucleus of the psyche, and that influence that surpasses the ego.

be little more than the sinister strategy to control people. The ego questions everything and insists on individual freedom. It will not readily accept unjust or destructive demands of religious groups. It is an ally of the Will. Destroying the ego in order to achieve some resemblance of enlightenment is ludicrous because it is a component of the Self that was created by the Self to interact with all other aspects of the physical universe.

For the purposes of this book I choose to define 'ego' as the narcissistic, automatic, habitual desire to see one's self as separate from the universe in which one lives and those people within and without one's sphere of influence. It isn't anything evil, but it can be problematic when it is immature. In our present state of evolution, the ego is underdeveloped in most people. The ego can often be so successful in identifying the 'I' from the 'not I' that it can become self-centered and behave in ways detrimental to its own self interests as well as the interests of other individuals.*

The following stages have been oversimplified, but they serve to make the point.

1. The unrestrained articulation of the Ego. "I do whatever I want."

In the first stage, the individual envisions has been duped into seeing his ego as the whole of the self. He enthusiastically surrenders to every whim promising exaltation or pleasure, often times believing himself capable of indulging in destructive behavior without consequence. Here we may find people with an unhealthy obsession with drugs, alcohol, sex, material, and financial gain. They may have little regard for how their actions affect the lives of others. During this stage of development there is little hope for progress in the area of true love or understanding toward others, much less for one's self.

2. The awareness of the ego in relation to others. "Doing what I want causes unhappiness for those around me which may ultimately alienate me from others."

Here the Ego has come to realize others as intrinsic parts of its own existence and well-being. This realization usually comes as a result of trial and error and various failed attempts trying to act

---

* In many ways, the Gnostic Demiurge and the Ego are synonymous because both take credit for being, or having done something they aren't and haven't.

without consequences. This is the stage of most adults. The realization that they have hurt others frequently results in feelings of guilt that often leads to a backlash where the individual attempts to find redemption by immersing himself in religious or metaphysical practices. On the surface this appears to be a desirable step in the process of development, but in some cases an individual will develop a sort of psychopathology because he may (as a result of all that spiritual practice) begin to see himself as better than his fellows. In reality, at this stage, this is nothing more than another mask which the ego has spun out of arrogance. One vice has simply been replaced with another much more palatable vice since it pretends to espouse a higher loftier ideal. One may be capable of seeing the Holy City from this stage, but it is an illusion projected by the ego itself. Many religious people are inadvertently caught in this direful trap. Sometimes the use of drugs is employed to escape, or one may simply stop here, feel sorry for one's self and blame problems on everyone else rather than taking responsibility and moving on.

3. The subjugation of the Ego to the True Self. "I am more."

After various attempts to achieve some relationship with the Higher Self, or to connect with something outside of its own delusions the individual may actually begin to see his Ego at work and become conscious of its capacity to deceive. Here individual may safely offer up this false aspect of himself to some higher cause or deity. The emotional attachment to the ego provides the necessary fuel. This sacrifice cannot be offered as an act of faith, but rather as a modest, cognizant, and intentional undertaking that adheres to the magical paradigm embraced by the individual. In our particular case, this must be a sincere and total sacrifice: an act of love under will.

The ego experiences an inner struggle during this stage of development since it is only concerned with its own survival and fears its own demise more than anything else. This is where our mettle is most severely tested. Courage and perseverance are the most useful keys. Some people have associated this struggle with "The Dark Night of The Soul."* To succeed is to *embody the Law in the flesh* and

---

* Often encountered in magical work, this is a non-pathological condition marked by depression, lack of mental and physical energy. The energy that is not available to the conscious is re-routed and used in other areas of the

achieve an inner peace during tribulation that so many mystics have written about throughout the ages. One becomes a Lover in the Sufi sense, as the absence of the ego* makes it possible for the first time to see one's self in all things, and the way to the Higher Self is opened. The longer that one continues to hold this position, the greater the reward, and the clearer the road to the Holy Land. Many have tried to write about this experience but have failed from a lack of a suitable language.

This is important: The actual act of questioning something greater (as well as the actual act of sacrifice) does not originate with the Higher Self, or God, or whatever you choose to call it, because 'It' already knows. It is the Ego itself that is doing the questioning. Remember: The ego's function is to question, and now we are seeing it exert itself in order to become self-aware. In this stage, we can observe the ego actively progressing toward enlightenment.

4. Union with the Higher Self. In Western Hermeticism, "I who am most like himself" or "I am that I am" - in the Sufi tradition: "I am the Truth," "I am Love," or "I am the Law."

This may appear as a contradiction, or even a similar condition to what is explained in stage two. The difference is that the Ego (having been completely united with the totality of the Self) is in fact an integral part of that Truth which is the Higher Self. The deluded ego described in stage two can only make these statements while thumping his chest like a frightened gorilla. At this stage the individual makes these statements in humility, realizing that his Truth belongs to all.

> *Remember that this earth is but an atom in the universe, and that thou thyself art but an atom thereon, and that even couldst thou become the God of this earth whereon thou crawlest and grovellest, that thou wouldest, even then, be but an atom, and one amongst many.*†

---

mind: usually the imaginative functions of the brain. It is symbolic of the decent into Hades; an immersion in the unconscious. The experiences of Osiris, Christ, and Dante are examples describing this state. This condition is normal and even desirable, since it often leads the individual to a break in neurosis.

* The use of the word "absence" is misleading, since the Ego hasn't really gone anywhere, it has simply transcended its home in the lower places. Also, this stage is what the Sufi calls "mystical love."

† *Liber Librae,* paragraph 14.

To explain the differences between the ego and the Ego consider the following statements since they serve to illustrate the two stages very well.

"I am God." - One doesn't become one, or come to full realization of this in the Gnostic sense by simply saying it. It doesn't matter how often one repeats it. Whether "God" is really in there or not, the host will never really know it because he or she is trying to assume something without knowledge. This is faith.

"I am not God." - By beginning here, one is forced to separate those parts of his or her makeup which are made of "god stuff" in order to examine them objectively. After one has externalized the entire idea, one can go about assimilating it as one's own attributes. When one finds themselves one and indivisible from the Higher Self, the Ego sees no reason to cheapen the experience by broadcasting it.

Here we approach the gates and stand before the two pillars flanking the door to the Temple: Love and Law.

5. The Ego is assimilated by The Higher Self. "There is only Truth."

This stage marks Freedom in its ultimate sense. One is an agent of his own Divine Force and moves through the world confidently, without fear and completely trusting his newly found Divine guidance. The individual has been reborn* into an existence where every experience is an encounter with the Divine. Here, and only here, can a person say of himself: "There is no God but Man."

There is an idea that has become quite popular with pop-occultists which espouses the concept of absolute happiness once one reaches this stage. I believe that there is a tremendous joy which comes from being able to view the universe beyond the veil of illusion and deception. Suffering and sorrow, however, are still there, but you may now appreciate them (and isn't experience what Nuit calls us to do?) without the necessity of being emotionally involved with them because you will know that these experiences only have meaning in the duality of the physical universe. Existence is Existence, and tears of joy are no less salty than tears of sorrow.

---

* A process usually experienced following The Dark Night of The Soul whereby an alteration of the personality has occurred. Examples of rebirth appear in the world's mythology in the form of The Transmigration of the Soul, Resurrection, and Reincarnation.

Only Eleven?

The fact that man knows right from wrong proves his intellectual superiority to other creatures; but the fact that he can do wrong proves his moral inferiority to any creature that cannot.
—Mark Twain

Consider the *Eleven Virtues of Thelemic Knighthood* and what they mean. Some of them have a more obscure, deeper meaning. See if you can get a sense of how these qualities are necessary to our own personal mission of gaining knowledge of our true nature, or our world mission of promulgating the Law of Thelema through acts of charity and service.

Valor: Right-action in the face of any challenge.

Valor means to be valiant, brave, and strong, both mentally and physically. It is the ability to face danger with firmness* and courage. It is the power to do the right thing, stand up against wrong doings, and it is synonymous with courage; heroism; bravery; gallantry; boldness, and fearlessness. But its Latin root translates into 'value' and 'worth'.

Valor is the state when one does what must be done, understanding and accepting the consequences of one's actions, even if the consequences are painful. It means doing something with the foreknowledge that one may be hurt, lose, fail, or not make any difference at all and doing it anyway because it is the right thing to do. It is the ability to accept fear, and possessing the inner strength necessary to undergo trial.

Valor is not recklessness, however, and we must constantly consider the source of our courage to make sure it comes from a worthy place. Shakespeare once said of valor: "when valor preys on reason, it eats the sword it fights with." He was right.

The Rose Cross is a worthy symbol to explain the idea of valor. The Rose simultaneously symbolizes a sacrifice of our desires and the blooming of our True Will.†

---

*   This can be done with little to no thought when one knows his or her True Will. *Liber Tzaddi*, paragraph 16

†   Liber AL vel Legis: The Book of the Law II:77

Nobility: Poise and elegance in both word and deed.

This term is very misunderstood. Generally speaking, the word 'nobility' is used to describe a class of persons (the peerage of British society) distinguished by high birth or rank, such as dukes and duchesses, or barons and baronesses. The Order of Thelemic Knights prefers to reward members with titles for displaying a state or quality of being possessed by superiority of mind or of character and commanding excellence, rather than acknowledging individuals simply on the notion that nobility can be inherited. Therefore, the Order of Thelemic Knights defines nobility as a quality belonging to all individuals that possess these following virtues.

Discernment: Piercing all glamour to see the Truth in one's self and in others.

Synonymous with 'discrimination', discernment is the faculty of the mind which distinguishes one thing from another. It is the faculty of the mind which demonstrates acute insight and good judgment. It is a skill, that when developed enables us to view the differences in people and the relationship between us all. Discernment is the power of penetrative and discriminate mental vision that enables us to see things which escape others. A discerning person is not easily misled.

This shouldn't be confused with the nonsense that so many blathering idiots on the internet try to pass off as 'critical thinking'. In fact, discerning people will not waste their time educating individuals that already know everything.

Pride: Having a true sense of one's worth.

True pride is free of guilt and fear. It never second guesses. Many good, deserving people are generally incapable of feeling pride. The insistence of humility over pride by misguided Christian leaders has created a social neurosis where people are afraid to exceed or take credit for their hard work.

"O be thou proud and mighty among men!"* Pride is a wonderful thing. It is what one feels inside when they have triumphed in the

---

* AL II.77

face of adversity; created beauty; acted correctly and honorably, or faced their own illusions. Acting ethically leads to pride, and so we don't view pride as a vice but a virtue. Pride is not humble, and is often confused with arrogance,* which is indeed a vice because it is an attempt to deceive others, but most importantly, it is a great source of willful self-delusion. To say it another way, pride is the ability of deriving pleasure, self-respect, and confidence from knowing and accepting oneself without indulging in some delusion of adequacy that does not exist. It is the willingness to reveal something within or about oneself to others as an example to one's peers and taking joy in personal honorable achievement or the achievements of ones comrades.

The virtue of Pride leads to an accurate realization of one's self worth. Its vice is an over inflated impression which relies on the comparison of oneself with some other person perceived to be less worthy. A good example of malformed pride is clearly visible in today's so-called "intellectual Thelemites"† who take great pride in pointing out the faults of others and insist on the virtues of dialectic and critical thinking while they themselves appear to be completely clueless with regards to the 'scientific method' or the proper tools by which to measure a person's worth. This is the problem with individuals that are Thelemites and intellectuals in name only. They fail because they spend more time looking for faults in others rather than trying to understand their own. They are therefore unable to develop the tools and social skills necessary to make the criticism philosophically valuable. Their approach only serves to placate their petty needs for external validation. These 'misguided prophets' often congregate in small groups where there is always someone near by to pat their back and tell them just how great they are but also always on the lookout for some poor unsuspecting soul to add to their collection of followers. They often quote the great philosophers to prove their own limited view of the universe and are completely impotent when it comes to grasping more lofty meanings hidden in the writings of the philosophers they claim to know or coming up with something original.

---

* Unearned pride. Pride has no problems with humility, whereas vanity, on the other hand, avoids it at all cost.

† "Nietzschean Thelemite" might have been a better term, but it would have given Nietzsche a bad name.

When it materializes as a person's truth, Pride is a source of ethics, an elevation of character and dignified bearing and loathing for what is beneath or unworthy of one's self: A deep and uncompromising sense of self-respect and noble self-esteem. When a doctor puts his career* on hold to help the poor, he or she often does so because of a deep belief that they have the knowledge, know how, and gumption to do a job no one seems willing or able to do. It may be that the way a doctor is forced into conducting business may be at odds with the Hippocratic Oath he or she has taken upon their graduation from medical school. Perhaps pride allows them to hold the radical idea that sick people should be patients and not customers, or that hospitals should not be instituted for the generation of capital. Such actions and thoughts originate with pride.

Pride comes from a sense of purpose and a love of accomplishing the impossible. The more difficult the obstacle, the more lofty and ethical the mission may be, the greater the sense of pride. Just ask any soldier that is willing to sacrifice his life defending his kin or countrymen if he is proud.

It is pride that pushes and gives us a sense of accomplishment even when beginning a task that we can never hope to finish because there will always be someone dying from hunger or a lack of medical attention. *Liber Librae* tells us to work for its own sake.

"Do good unto others for its own sake, not for reward, not for gratitude from them, not for sympathy. If thou art generous, thou wilt not long for thine ears to be tickled by expressions of gratitude."†

We may become overwhelmed by this work, and we may often ask ourselves why we even bother when one person's contribution is so small in light of such huge problems. Support from a fellow soldier during those difficult times can provide light, encouragement and motivation in the darkest times. Working together, people can make a noticeable change in the world, and this is the position of the Order of Thelemic Knights.

A prideful person with a strong ego is not threatened by being a part of something larger than himself, because he is aware of the resources that they are able to provide for the greater good. A prideful person takes pleasure in the knowledge that while he is a necessary component to achieving a communal objective, he is no

---

* And financial goals.
† Paragraph 11.

more or less important than anyone else lending their talents to the accomplishment of the goal. People have pride in something they value highly. Pride is confidence stemming from the projection of one's personal values. Our communal values are the reason that members of the Order of Thelemic Knights are prideful.

Coincidently, a pride is a gathering of lions. A consciousness of power (and hence, responsibility); fullness of spirit, lust, and sexual desire. Interestingly, an excitement of sexual appetite in a female beast.[*]

Compassion: The vice of Kings!

Have you ever had a deep awareness of the suffering of another living thing and wished to relieve it for no other reason than wanting to relieve suffering? This is compassion: it is a human quality. Pity is not compassion. Compassion manifests as a sensation of sorrow provoked by the affliction or misfortunes of another. Pity, on the other hand, is the act of placing one's self above those less fortunate. Compassion is everywhere, it exists in nature, and therefore, we consider it a spiritual quality. It follows then, that it should be integrated as a spiritual practice.

Fidelity: Loyalty to one's self, one's comrades and to one's word.

Fidelity implies the unfailing execution of one's duties and obligations. It is a strict adherence or dedication to ones vows or pledges. Fidelity is synonymous with 'allegiance', and faithfulness considered as a duty; and 'loyalty', which implies a steadfast and devoted attachment that is not easily turned aside, such as a loyalty to an oath, one's family or ethics, country or Order.

It implies faithfulness. It is adherence to careful and exact observance of duty, truth, honesty, integrity or a discharge of ones obligations.

You cannot have an army without fidelity. Spiritual warriors must be faithful to their obligations, duties, or observances or they are little more than loose cannons. Mercenaries. They must stand fast by their allegiance with the principles they have embraced regard-

---

[*]   Members of the Squire degree will no doubt find this both fascinating and meaningful.

less of the circumstances.

Hamilton may have described our Order's approach best: "The best security for the fidelity of men is to make interest coincide with duty."

Passion: To do all with love under will.

Passion comes with boundless enthusiasm, ardent love, conviction and certainty. It is a powerful emotion. People who are unable to take a stand one way or another are not possessed of passion.

A passion can be ones desire, such as the passion for ones duties, art or lover. It is the fervor and zeal with which we approach our missions, the fire that burns within us, and the driving force behind any pursuit and the enthusiastic partiality for anything.

Strength: The body is the Temple of God.

In personal terms, strength is a source of mental, physical and ethical power to resist strain or stress. A form of control necessary to hold firmly to ones ethical or intellectual position firmly. It is an attribute or quality indicating worth or utility: an asset.

Organizationally, it is the embodiment of protective and supportive supremacy, the capacity to endure or resist attack: Impregnability. The gumption to carry out a mission in the face of opposition. The ability to work effectively, efficiently, and to produce an effect and secure results...or as Rudyard Kipling puts it: "Enough work to do, and strength enough to do the work."

Each of us is strong in our own areas, each according to his or her True Will. When we put all of our strength to the service of Our Order, we become an army. Force[*] is the application of strength.

Discipline: Perseverance, that the Work may be accomplished.

Discipline is the organization of behavior subject to will. It is any exercise that is expected to produce a specific character or pattern of behavior, especially training that produces ethical, physical, mental improvement or self-control. It is indicative of a branch of knowledge, such as the discipline of martial arts, yoga or psychol-

---

[*] Force and fire, are of us. AL II.20.

ogy. It also alludes to the rules regulating the practice of a church or religious order. It is synonymous with education, instruction and training.

When a man submits himself to a certain lifestyle or ethical code in order to remove badly formed habits and substitute them with good ones, he is exercising discipline.

Self-Reliance: Only a free man may walk our path.

Freedom begins with the recognition of a person's sovereignty. The following step is to use that freedom to self-govern: to choose ones course. Independence and freedom come from the reliance on one's own capabilities, judgment, and resources. When a man or woman is self-reliant he or she does not become a burden to his/ her Brothers and Sisters. On the contrary, such a person is an asset that can be counted on to do their own share of the work and contribute to the best of their ability...each and everyone in compliance with their own True Will. A self-reliant person will never need anything because they are self-contained.

Hospitality: To share what one has with others, especially those far from home.

Cordial and generous reception of or disposition toward guests is synonymous with Chivalry and Courtly Love. Hospitality is a lost art form. Few individuals really understand manners and a proper upbringing, preferring to lump it all in the rebellion of society and modern culture. It is a display of pride, generosity, and respect toward one's peers that is infectious. Unlike charity, hospitality is designed as a gesture of mutual recognition of ones autonomy. It can be best described by the Sanskrit word: "Namaste" - which is to say: "I respectfully greet the divine spirit within you."

Ethics in Government and Business

He who joyfully marches to music rank and file, has already earned my contempt. He has been given a large brain by mistake, since for him the spinal cord would surely suffice. This disgrace to civilization should be done away with at once. Heroism at command, how violently I hate all this, how despicable and ignoble war is; I would rather be torn to shreds than be a part of so base an action. It is my conviction that killing under the cloak of war is nothing but an act of murder.

—Albert Einstein

Initially, the ethics of government and business were to be examined under separate sections. I found it impossible, however, to speak of one without mentioning the other, and for good reason: government and business, at least in the US, are one and the same. It would not be unreasonable to think of US government as a Corporate Democracy.

I wish I could have come up with another country to serve as a better example of capitalism gone awry. It saddens me to no end to see the country I love, a country founded with such lofty ideals by such great minds, and whose government has been the object of poetry as an example for all other countries and freedom loving individuals, hijacked by corporate giants and special interest groups.

In the last few years alone, we have witnessed American intervention in El Salvador, Iran, Iraq, Afghanistan, the Philippines, Indonesia, Columbia, Panama, and South Africa. In Iran, our government overthrew a democratic government and replaced it with a dictatorship. The United States government funded Saddam Hussein for years, even before he came to power, and even stood by as he used chemical weapons against the Kurds, killing men, women and children alike. Panama did not exist as an independent country until the US decided it wanted to build a canal there. Then there is the matter of Manuel Noriega's ties to the CIA and the 'Company's' involvement in cocaine trafficking. In Chile, our government overthrew another popularly elected government, although it took two tries. And this doesn't even touch on American economic policies.

Even though most American citizens would rather not know these things, they are not secrets. No form of self-imposed ignorance such as blind patriotism or sentimentalism will change the fact that the horrible events, and the senseless disaster that occurred on 9/11 are (at least in part) in some way the result of American foreign policy. Our leaders know this. Those poor people did not deserve what happened to them on that fateful day, and the individuals that caused it should be hunted down like the animals that they are. Instead, government leaders have seized upon this opportunity to launch huge military campaigns for corporate interest groups. This is precisely why we must learn and use critical thinking skills and ethics, choosing freedom to deliberate rather than swallowing propaganda; logical thinking rather than sentimentalism, and individual pride in doing the right thing instead of blind patriotism if we are going to prevent this from ever happening again.

For many people,* the United States is a failed experiment. Americans are deeply divided; even the propaganda fails to cast a believable illusion of unity, and there appears to be little hope for reconciliation in the near future. The very government that pretends to be a champion of freedom has used the fear generated by the attacks of that fateful September day to convince its subjects to voluntarily surrender what is left of their freedoms. What little culture there is appears to be quickly fading under the military boots of America's so-called "religious right."† The liberals distrust the highest political practices and this will eventually erode whatever civility is holding this country together. Dialogue is useless because most people surrender like sheep to every lie fed to them by their religious leaders, such as the myth that America's Forefathers were champions of a Christian government. It is similarly useless to recommend that they read the works penned by the architects of this country, because they prefer a lie of their own making to the truth.

Men that loved freedom and were willing to die for it built up this country: Ethical men. Their voices can be heard while reading the founding documents, personal memoirs and the letters they wrote to their family and compatriots. The United States has not seen its greatest day, and that day is only delayed by greed, the lack of critical thinking and ethics, blind patriotism and sentimentality. We must be capable of thinking beyond our own needs to observe the impact that these lies are having on our families and friends, government,

---

* Many of them Native Americans.

† Must we wonder why religion is so repulsive to so many people?

and ultimately the relationship and responsibility that you share with every other human on this planet. In corporate democracies, people vote with their money. Every dollar is a vote. Think of money as a talisman, and learn to use the power it affords you wisely.

So why apply ethics to business? The Libertarian will tell you that corporations are, by definition, designed solely to make money for their stockholders. In other words, a corporation's 'True Will' is to make money, and it should not be subject to same penalties or restrictions as regular people. The stockholders, lacking ethics, lobby to make a world where their corporations rule supreme. In such a world, they can do business without any mandatory compliance with regard to environmental restrictions, worker's rights, and unions; without paying corporate taxes, and without shame for exploiting people at home and abroad. Consider the benefits afforded to HMO's, oil companies, energy brokers, and the like. The Food and Drug Administration, which was instituted to protect consumers from harm caused by snake oil salesmen, takes donations from the very pharmaceutical companies that manufacture the drugs it is supposed to regulate. This is a conflict of interest at best, and accepting bribes at worst. Is this ethical?

Was it ethical for the Fox Network to persuade the court that they were not obligated to report the truth in their news broadcasts? Fox thereby avoided paying damages in a lawsuit awarded to a former reporter wrongfully terminated for trying to report the truth. Where were the ethics of this company? Where were the ethics of the judge that ruled in their favor? Knowing this, what can be said of people that still tune in to get their news there?

Is a company, fined for polluting in one country, ethical when it relocates its plants to other countries too poor to demand environmental compliance? What of a rancher that introduces a cow displaying symptoms of mad cow disease into the food chain rather than lose a few bucks? Is the sole purpose of business to make money, without concerning itself with ethics? Can a business justify its disregard for public or ecological responsibility because their primary objective is to make money for their stockholders? If a business creates an environmental disaster affecting people everywhere, should that company be responsible for cleaning up its own messes, or should the taxpayers foot the bill? Is it ethical when government forces the taxpayer to pay for the logging roads that will be utilized exclusively by logging companies in harvesting our forests?*

Consider capitalism† and how governments embracing this paradigm conduct their affairs as businesses. Capitalism, in its present
form, is concerned with the accumulation of wealth to no particular
end. When the few benefiting from the money-grab have milked
their own country dry, capitalism must, by necessity, spread its domain to other cultures in order to continue feeding their addiction.
This is why countries go to war. It isn't for freedom or liberty. It isn't
for a love of justice, but a love for more and more things.

Reflect on the present conundrum in the Middle East. In recent
memory, we can trace this problem to an Iranian 'bad guy' that
wouldn't play ball with the US government. The US government
replaced this leader with someone they could exploit. This led to
the American hostage crisis, where the radical Iranians kidnapped
American citizens. Back then, Saddam was a 'good guy'‡, and Rea-
gan armed him to fight against the Ayatollah who was a 'bad guy.'
When Saddam wouldn't play ball with the US, President Bush Sr.
dubbed him a 'bad guy' and carpet-bombed his country. Later,
when now Vice President Cheney wanted to do business with him,
he was once again a 'good guy' —until, of course President Bush
Jr. needed a diversion for not being able to find Bin Laden— who
in turn was a 'good guy' when we armed him to fight the Russian
invasion of Afghanistan in the 70's and 80's, but a 'bad guy' for having the US bombed in 2001. In short, people who do what we want
are 'good guys' —but they are 'bad guys' when they resist exploitation. Government can get away with these things time and time
again when citizens suffer from historical amnesia and intellectual
laziness.

The simplest way to make this point is to compare capitalist or
corporate governments to ancient Rome. Much like today, Roman
soldiers were deployed to other countries in order to feed some
emperor's hunger for gold and other luxuries. There is an obvious
difference between Rome and our present world: Roman citizens
benefited from Rome's conquests, and the Roman government

---

* The same forest taxpayers pay to protect?
† Capitalism is not unethical in and of itself. There are ethical ways of doing
  business. It is what is been passed off as "capitalism" today which is without
  ethics.
‡ Even though he was using chemical agents to genocide the Kurds.

only catered to the greed of the emperor rather than business interests. Like those of yesteryears, today's emperors remind us to be 'patriotic' and 'support our troops' while they send our boys and girls to fight—not to liberate some country from an intolerable despot, but to 'capitalize' the country and exploit its resources. It is surprising that more people don't protest these maneuvers, but it is even more astounding that they can find people to fight these wars in the first place.

At the same time, well-meaning soldiers that enlisted for a love of their country, or because joining the military provides them the only opportunity to have an education,* spill their blood and the blood of the occupied people so that the friends of the commander-in-chief can enlarge their coffers. Presently, concurrent with the call for patriotism and support, senators plot the end of military medical benefits for those very same soldiers they sent to the desert, in order to pass those savings on to the hungry corporations (HMO's and other medical insurance corporations). Some support.

It is typical to blame human nature for our own individual failures or our inability to exchange the things we *want* to do for the things we *should* do. Killing others over resources is often justified as human nature. It is romanticized by religion, portrayed as some lofty spiritual goal. We force ourselves into the social acceptance of war when we accept it as a form of 'patriotism'. To posit that true human nature is driven by a desire for universal brotherhood is to invoke the wrath of individuals who find it easier to watch the atrocities of war than to stand against it. To categorize war as human nature without a second thought is to deny the possibility that we may one day evolve beyond our own self-destructive behavior. It denies the existence of the True Will, making all of us slaves, unable to choose our own course.

It is a good scam, if you think about it. Taxpayers foot the bill for a military occupation to benefit their business interests. Soldiers are exploited and are stripped of their benefits so that they will either have to pay to for the emotional and physical injuries that they incurred while fighting for the same companies that are now discarding them like broken tools, or else join the thousands of mentally and physically handicapped vets - a large majority of whom are homeless.

---

* How fortunate for the military.

Elsewhere, genocide and ethnic cleansing occurs on our little blue planet, but since there is no economic benefit to corporate interests there, 'the powers that be' turn a blind eye to the slaughter. To prove this point, we must simply consider how the US has imposed trade embargoes on Cuba and Vietnam because they are communist* while China, which is also communist, and a country with a horrible record and long history of human rights violations can be awarded "most favored trade status." The answer is quite simple. Capitalism has spread to China, and its emperor is willing to play the capitalist game to cash in on its resources of slave labor so that huge corporate interests in the US can benefit by the cheap manufacturing that slave labor provides. American government turns a blind eye to the fact that the Chinese government regularly harvests the organs of living prisoners against their will for profit, even when the overwhelming majority of Chinese prisoners have been imprisoned solely for having spoken against an oppressive government.

Again, this form of capitalism has to spread abroad, once all resources in the homeland are exhausted. The relationship between the US and China is tenuous at best, and dangerous at worst, since once each of these countries have exploited one another they will once again have to compete with one another for resources, and today is a much more dangerous world that it was during the Cold War. And all the while, people in Vietnam, North Korea and Cuba die every day from hunger and lack of medical supplies because they refuse to cave in to capitalist pressure. This is what we can expect to see from ethically bankrupt governments (and businesses).

---

* The "red threat" is still an effective boogieman for fear-based societies.

Ethics of Consumerism and Global Will

Theoretically, the True Will dictates what one has. Having more than one is intended means that someone else is forced to live with less than they are intended. This leads to suffering. One must ponder: how much is enough? Or, at the very least one must consider if that new house, car, or computer that one desires so much is worth having when one understands the effect that pursuing those things will have on oneself, as well as those who already have too little to eat. The goofs* abhor this idea, for the entire economic well-being in modern times depends on people's greed and the disregard of their humanity for the convenience of more hings. In a way, it is painful for most people to admit that their consumerism may be indirectly responsible for the 20,000 people that die from hunger in this world every day.†

Keeping up with the Joneses and identifying with one's things or income is the result of an illusion that corporate interests perpetuate. Presently, we can see the rewards of following such rotten advice, as the ever increasing number of unemployed in the U.S. find very little comfort in the fact that their jobs are being outsourced to overseas companies so that corporate interests can exploit workers by paying them less, or because the laws in those impoverished countries do not require American corporate giants to provide workers with medical benefits. How nice for them. We are expected to rejoice because now those exploited workers abroad can be consumers and buy Nikes. And when people abroad can buy Nikes, then that is good for America. But what happens when Americans can't afford to buy shoes, much less Nikes?

Greed is and always has been responsible for most of the world's woes, and an ethical person will not perpetuate an evil that causes war, pestilence, hunger, and misery to billions of his fellow humans. Instead, he or she will conceive a way to conduct business that is more in line with his or her beliefs, and will refuse to buy into that form of

---

*   Noun - From the Hebrew "Goph" —a reference to the physical body. A derogatory term to explain humans that refuse to acknowledge their spiritual nature or humanity because doing so would mean they'd have to inconvenience themselves with the ethics such beliefs would imply.

†   In the time it would have taken the average person to finish reading this book, 40,000 people will have died. Tomorrow, 20,000 more will die.

legalized theft and exploitation we have come to accept as 'capitalism'.

Consider how modern society seems to de-emphasize cooperation. Cooperation is dangerous, and the demiurge likes to perpetuate the myth of 'rugged individualism' or the idea that every man is an island. Consider to what extent we have bought into this illusion: that we would warehouse our children, leaving them to be raised by total strangers in order to free ourselves to pursue some 'dream' that seems more and more like a nightmare. How did it get this far—that two adults would consider having children in the first place, knowing that they wouldn't have time to raise them because of the fixation with material things. Again, we must ask ourselves: *how much is enough?* How much of the violence, racial and religious hatred, and other increasing social ills could have been avoided by raising and educating our own children rather than putting them away like a book we intend to read later? The excuse has always been that we are working hard for their future so that they can have more of those material things we use as a measure of success (and doesn't this seem to vindicate us?)when what they really need is the love and attention of a parent.

Our neighbors are subjected to human rights violations. Their doors are kicked in and we watch them from the illusory safety of our homes, thanking our gods it isn't us. We must "look out for number one." We mustn't rock the boat by holding an unpopular thought, because that might interfere with our ability to collect more *things*. We stand by and do nothing because we are supposed to "mind our own business."

We are worker bees, all of us. If we learned to cooperate, got to know our neighbors, and protested when injustices were committed against them, then we might come to realize that we control our own flow of honey, and that the demiurge cannot exist without its honey.

In the U.S., we like to think of ourselves as free. We like to think of Lady Liberty, in New York, as a symbol of that altruistic ideal. Yet, we seem to be collectively unable or unwilling to extend that benefit to others. China does not claim it was founded as a country of the free, but America does, and it resorts to hypocrisy of the worst kind by trading with countries like China. Many Americans don't seem to give buying goods made by forced prison labor a second thought, since they individually benefit from the exploitation of those people. The less they pay for one toy, the more they have left to buy other toys.

On a very mundane level, we exploit others when we purchase items made by prison labor, occupied territories or the underprivileged because we expect to get these items at a much better price than we would if they were not being exploited. We benefit from their poverty. We even do it to our own countrymen when we patronize stores that exploit their workers by cheating them out of reasonable pay, hours, medical benefits, or when we employ businesses that promote, or pass up, individuals based on color, race or religious beliefs rather than a good work ethic.

This planet has a Will. It is the Little Sister of Nuit. Should we patronize organizations, special interest groups, or individual wills when their actions violate global wellness? Of course, we could argue (and often have) that since we are all global creatures, any action we make, even actions that destroy our home, are in accordance with the global will. Crowley didn't think so, and neither do I.

Apparent, and sometimes even real, conflict between interests will frequently arise. Such cases are to be decided by the general value of the contending parties in the scale of Nature. Thus, a tree has a right to its life; but a man being more than a tree, he may cut it down for fuel or shelter when need arises. Even so, let him remember that the Law never fails to avenge infractions: as when wanton deforestation has ruined a climate or a soil, or as when the importation of rabbits for a cheap supply of food has created a plague.

Observe that the violation of the Law of Thelema produces cumulative ills. The drain of the agricultural population to big cities, due chiefly to persuading them to abandon their natural ideals, has not only made the country less tolerable to the peasant, but debauched the town. And the error tends to increase in geometrical progression, until a remedy has become almost inconceivable and the whole structure of society is threatened with ruin.

The wise application based on observation and experience of the Law of Thelema is to work in conscious harmony with Evolution. Experiments in creation, involving variation from existing types, are lawful and necessary. Their value is to be judged by their fertility as bearing witness to their harmony with the course of nature towards perfection.

– Aleister Crowley, Duty

Remember: every dollar is a vote. Money is a talisman.

The Ethics of Liberty and Organizational Will

Next to greed, Liberty is the second reason that man seems to be willing to kill and die for. What did Patrick Henry mean when he said, "Give me liberty or give me death?" Are both of these human experiences a means to the same end? What does it mean to be free?

If one is greedy, one might feel free to exploit others by insisting that they behave in a matter inconsistent with their own true nature* in order to benefit from them. Again, no matter what the subject, greed always seems to rear its ugly head.

"Thou hast no right but to do thy will." **No right.** This is a profound statement, and yet how many of us have ever contemplated what this means? Does it mean that one does their will automatically, or instinctively? If so, then what would be the point of spending our lives (as many of us have sworn) to discover our True Will? Furthermore, we are told, "the slaves shall serve." What does this mean? How do we reconcile this with "Every man and every woman is a star?" Who are the "lofty ones" or the few secret servants that "shall rule the many and the known?"

Every adherent of Thelema should strive to answer these questions for themselves, each according to their ability to grasp these complex answers. I trust that there is no right answer, and perhaps the benefit from this exercise lies in the search for the Truth.

For me, it appears we are all connected. All of us are pieces of some tremendously large puzzle that we cannot comprehend. When we attempt to discover our True Will, we are seeking our place in the puzzle. When all the pieces are in their place, one piece informs the other piece next to it until they achieve universal balance. We restore Liberty because all of us are acting in accordance with our own True Will. It makes me think of the mechanism inside of a pocket watch and the beautiful ballet of the gear movements.

On the other hand, it is entirely possible that a person's True Will is to be a slave. In fact, when it comes down to it, aren't we all slaves to 'something?' Who among us does not consider serving Nuit a tremendous privilege?

When we perform our charitable events, aren't we in the role of servant? It is difficult to think of one's True Will, Liberty, or Truth

---

* Against their will.

when one is hungry. Liberty becomes a more complex matter when approached this way. Some Gnostic, Buddhist, Taoist, and Catholic sects believe that Liberty comes with a detachment (not disinterest) of the physical world. One can be detached and yet concerned with the suffering of others.

According to the Gnostics, this world was the domain of the demiurge. In Gnostic cosmology, Jehovah* did not create the world at all, but he has told the lie for so long even he has come to believe it. This will be discussed in detail in another chapter. Suffice it to say, they liken the god of this world to a small child that enjoys torturing little animals.

The Buddhists have their Maya, or 'illusion'. The idea is that suffering come from identifying with things, and that the more that one has the more one is imprisoned by his possessions.

These two positions are extreme reactions to greed, since it is the source of all suffering.

Self-interest threatens Liberty because personal gain justifies the annulment of fairness, even when a person is ethical. For example, there is a church in Oregon that grew to a sizeable number. The pastor of that church built an entire wing to house a huge screen so that his parishioners could better see him. On the surface, this appears to be a very normal thing to do, but later one begins to ask oneself how that expense could have served many homeless people or orphans.

The CEO of a corporation, whose only purpose is making money, could have the same idea, and spend twice the amount that the church spent on something equally frivolous. People do not question the ethics because the corporation is not broadcasting a message of love and requiring stockholders to donate a percentage of their earnings to relieve suffering, as the church does. The church has violated its own ethics by being dishonest about its mission. The pastor has forced the church to act in a manner inconsistent with its mission† by causing it to act against its true nature and design. He has gone against the collective will of the church's founders and it is no longer free to pursue its mission.

In short, an organization, tribe, or social unit that has a mission statement has a Will, an egregor. The ethical person will not inter-

---

*   Or "Samael" - "blind god."

†   Egregor

fere with the organization regardless of how much he is at odds with its stated purpose because he knows that "success is your proof" implies that unhealthy social constructs are doomed to fail on their own accord. On the other hand, all organizations (especially fraternal or religious organs that enjoy tax-exempt status) have mission statements, which define their goals and service to their members. The mission statement is how they draw in support to obtain their goals. If the organization's mission has changed from its original design as defined by the organization's founding documents, then it has an ethical responsibility to inform that every member that pays dues, or financially supports the organization in any way, of its new or modified mission or modus operandi. Any effort to cover up its new direction or hesitation to inform should make one suspect of the organization's emphasis on the ethical conduct of its officers.

One mustn't abuse Liberty. Is it ethical for a person to force his or her will upon the organizational will? For example, it is ethical for the parents of a young girl to file a lawsuit against the Boy Scouts, forcing them to spend thousands of dollars that would normally have been allocated for the education and pleasure of their members rather than legal fees because they refused the little girl membership? Why couldn't her parents have sought membership for her in the Girl Scouts? Were her parents being ethical?

Recently, a woman serializing her experiences as an airline attendant was fired* from her job for posting a picture of herself on her online journal in uniform. What is most disturbing is a comment made by the company's attorney: "You have to remember that as an employee, you don't have total free speech anymore." What he is really saying is that corporate interests override the individual's rights to free speech. What is worse is that this applies to all working class people so that only those lucky few who are able to refrain from work can exercise free speech. This excludes all but the wealthiest. That this does not enrage people suggest that people have accepted the philosophy that corporate interests should prohibit free speech.

What makes this interesting from an ethical studies point-of-view is that the US Constitution reads: ...congress shall make no law..."† Doesn't this suggest that by chartering corporations Congress is ipso facto making laws that prohibit free speech? To put this an-

* Delta Airlines. Remember this when you buy your airline tickets.
† The Bill of Rights of the United States of America. First Amendment.

other way: Congress needs to take a hard look at this issue to make sure that it isn't violating the Constitution by chartering corporations that prohibit free speech.

Ethics in Love

Now a lot of us are preachers, and all of us have our moral convictions and concerns, and so often have problems with power. There is nothing wrong with power if power is used correctly. You see, what happened is that some of our philosophers got off base. And one of the great problems of history is that the concepts of love and power have usually been contrasted as opposites - polar opposites - so that love is identified with a resignation of power, and power with a denial of love.

It was this misinterpretation that caused Nietzsche, who was a philosopher of the will to power, to reject the Christian concept of love. It was this same misinterpretation which induced Christian theologians to reject the Nietzschean philosophy of the will to power in the name of the Christian idea of love. Now, we've got to get this thing right. What is needed is a realization that power without love is reckless and abusive, and love without power is sentimental and anemic. Power at its best is love implementing the demands of justice, and justice at its best is power correcting everything that stands against love. And this is what we must see as we move on.

—Dr. Martin Luther King, *Where Do We Go from Here?*

If we love, we empathize. How then, can an ethical person relish in their freedom while others are enslaved against their will? Ethics are impossible without compassion and love. But "there are love and love."* In my reading of *Liber AL*, Nuit wants Agape from us; Eros from Hadit; and Philio from the Earth. In other words, the mysteries of love are revealed to us in our own holy books.

People have been obsessed with love since time immemorial. So much so that the Greeks have approached the mystery by dividing love into different categories and types, as well as explaining its influence by assigning it godly offices in their mythos. Why should we bother ourselves with the definition of love? Ethical behavior is connected to love in a very profound way, as we shall soon see. Furthermore, if we are ever to understand the whole of the Law, we will need to know what is meant by Love; it must be important. In other words, we must endeavor to determine what love means so that we

* Liber AL I:57

might develop a greater understanding of Thelema in general. This should be pretty obvious, but love is often overlooked because "doing what one wills" sounds much more butch and Nietzschean than learning how to love.

For our purposes, we will examine three components of love corresponding to intimacy, passion and commitment. These components can be associated or attributed to three states: general, individual, and personal.* It isn't unusual for a person to experience one or two facets of love toward the object of one's attention, but "Godly Love" requires all three forms to be in place. This is so difficult to do, and so very rare since, for the most part, love is generally considered in terms of romance in today's world.

How shall members of a TRUE Fraternity love one another? As Brothers and Sisters sharing the same struggle to understand the deity that resides within every man and every woman: as soldiers in the trenches in a battle to liberate the human spirit.

How shall we love our partners? As the object of our desires, with the same love and respect we show our Brothers and Sisters, but also as reflections of our Beloved worthy of our reverence.

So, how shall we love our God? This work isn't for the lazy or half-dedicated. Approach your God as a lover and friend, but also as a disciple willing to sacrifice everything to accept Its Will as yours until you develop the Gnosis of God's Will being synonymous with your own. To this end: Godspeed.

EROS

In Greek mythology, Eros is the god of love, son of Aphrodite. Eros can represent creativity, sexual yearning, or desire evoked by physical attraction or an expression of physical love. It is that 'pull' that people feel when they are sexually attracted to one another. He excited erotic love in gods and mortals with his arrows. Eros love, however, represents a new, disorienting sort of passion. His influence was often conceived as an attack of undesirable yearning.

In psychiatry, Eros represents the sexual drive, the libido. The sum of life-preserving instincts that are manifested as impulses to

---

*   They correspond rather nicely to The Man of Earth, The Lovers, and The Hermits mentioned in The Book of The Law, as well as the three outer Grades of the Order of Thelemic Knights: The Squire, The Knight, and The Peer.

gratify basic needs (as sex[*]); as sublimated impulses motivated by the same needs, and as impulses to protect and preserve the body and mind called also 'life instinct'.

So much so-called brainpower has been spent debating whether or not polyamory[†] is more Thelemic than monogamy that I refuse to waste ink going over this insignificant argument here. Suffice it to say, man has the right to love as he will, and doing what is most rightful to one's true nature is as Thelemic as it gets. Making promises that one can't keep, or forcing someone into oaths contradicting their own nature is not love, isn't Thelemic, and certainly isn't ethical. Misrepresenting one's self is not only dishonest, but will eventually lead you to taking oaths you are unable of keeping. As my friend likes to say: *Don't write any checks you can't cash.*

Having said that, I have heard more than one critic of Thelema imply that *Liber OZ* condones rape.[‡] Some people are unable to hold two seemingly opposing thoughts until they are either reconciled or utterly destroyed. *Liber OZ* is applicable to all humans, not just Thelemites. Therefore, a rapist is in violation of his victim's rights by forcing himself on her.[§] The text reads: 'love as he will', and rape is hardly an act of love. Love is a God... and Love is the Law.

PHILIO

To the Greeks, Philio is brotherly love and represents the affection that one feels toward one's comrades when a common bond is shared. It is a love that is manifested when we are united and/or supporting one another as we are working toward achieving a common goal. We are under its influence when we are being affectionate, welcoming or kindly to our mates. The city of Philadelphia in the United States gets its name from Philio. It is called "the city of brotherly love."

Ironically, in psychiatry, Philio is synonymous with phobia. It represents an obsession with a particular thing or subject.

---

[*]   Sex can lead to offspring, which is a form of preserving ones genes. Immortality through one's children.

[†]   A new trendy name for a relationship in which there are multiple lovers.

[‡]   "Man has the right to love as he will...when, where, and with whom he will."

[§]   Or visa versa.

AGAPE

Agape is synonymous with compassion, caritas, charity, affection, altruism, amity, attachment, benevolence, benignity, bountifulness, clemency, generosity, goodness, goodwill, grace, humaneness, kindliness, magnanimity, and mercy. It is a love of a spiritual nature, not concerned with sexual fulfillment. Agape denotes a divine, self-sacrificing love. It is an altruistic love, and we are under its influence when we do things for another person or god without the expectation of reward.

Agape indicates action. A willful act of doing and caring for someone as deeply as one cares for one's self. It is considered a *godly love* because it manifests in the absence of the desire to personally benefit of Lust of Result. It is said that only God is capable of Agape. What does this mean today, when "there is no god but man?" Are we capable of it? More than that: "Love is the law." Are we required to do it?

How can we understand of Agape without discussing Charity?

Charity comes from empathy and a direct knowledge of the thread that holds us all together. It often originates from some unconscious understanding that others are at the heart of one's own universe, and therefore linked to the Self. Charity is a form of love* that flows out from this realization.

Charity, no matter how well intentioned it may be, can also be used as a way to avoid work. The recipient may begin to feel they are getting something for nothing, while the bourgeois feels good about charity because they can throw money at the problem of homelessness without having to experience the desperation of the poor directly. This does not mean that cash contributions are unnecessary, unwanted or unwelcome, but the people that want to get their hands dirty in the trenches and physically help are a breed apart. They see themselves as the 'magical link.'

Charity has to be regulated and monitored since it can lead to dependence. We must learn to view poverty (and wealth, for that matter) as cycles. Always remember that the ultimate goal is to liberate people from the affliction of hunger and poverty, not make

---

*   Inseparable from Agape.

them dependent on anyone for relief. Also, we must be vigilant that the same people aren't there to take advantage of our charity time and time again. This does not benefit anyone, even if at the time they might feel as though they have gotten something for nothing. Charity should be given with the idea in mind that the playing field is being leveled so that the needy will have the basic resources to do what is necessary to improve their condition. All men are not created equal, but everyone deserves opportunity. Charity is the way to help improve the starting point.

Even with such precautions in place, people will naturally gravitate toward dependence or abuse of charity. When confronted with the prospect of a 'free ride', very few people possess the necessary ethics to avoid abuse. And by 'abuse', I mean self-abuse. Some people will gladly manipulate the consequences of their lives in order to constantly qualify for assistance.

In his book *Cultural Anthropology*, Daniel Bates tells us of a tribe in Northern Kenya that has, until recently, survived quite well in the desert by raising animals and trading with other tribes for items like grains, tea and sugar. The recent introduction of Christian missionaries has resulted in the loss of tribal identity. Before this event, the tribe survived quite well as a result of their hard work. The government wants members this nomadic tribe to set up house in towns so that it can control them. The missionaries, on the other hand, can only benefit from separating these individuals from their tribe so that they can more easily convert them to Christianity. Bates' message is simple: people will naturally give up their independence, and often times their own cultural identity,[*] in exchange for some free trinkets or provisions. This is the sort of welfare that enslaves.

On the opposite extreme, we find strong, ethical, and self-contained individuals who will not compromise their dreams or self-reliance in order to protect some source of income.

So how does one address this problem? The Order of Thelemic Knights serves as a good example, since it is the first Thelemic Organization to be instituted to provide a public benefit. Whenever possible, charitable campaigns will contain employment support such as resume writing assistance, clean clothing for work searches, and a place to pick up mail. Charity, given without expectation, as noble as it sounds on the surface, undermines autonomy and con-

---

[*] And soul!

ditions individuals to seek the reliance on others.

Of course, it may also be entirely possible for a person's True Will to require them to live in poverty. It is said that a King may choose his own garments.* But in these cases one has learned to live in their poverty without having to rely on others, or burden charitable organizations for their survival. The exception to the rule is in the monastic, esthetic life. A good example would be the Buddhist, Catholic, and Coptic monks who are supported by the community for the spiritual benefit their presence bestows.

We don't have to look hard or far to see what occurs to charitable organizations when collecting money is the focus of their work. In light of sizeable coffers, the organization's officers often begin by paying themselves unreasonable salaries rather than using the funds to further its mission. The more money they collect, the larger the salaries they pay themselves. It would be tacky to mention names, but suffice it to say that one of the largest 'green' organizations dedicated to environmental stewardship is now largely ineffective in its stated goals as a result of this. Only a small percentage of donations actually go toward environmental protection, the largest percentage being spent on 'operating costs'.

But what of the socially responsible individual? How much is enough, and when is one shrugging their responsibility to their fellow man? Obviously, donating until one is poor is a self-defeating enterprise.† The best thing that we can do to be part of the solution is not to be an inconvenience on the already overburdened charitable groups.

---

*   Liber AL 2:58
†   This is likely the objection that Crowley appeared to have with the Christian sort of compassion which suggest that we put others first.

Charity as a Magical Sacrifice

People are generally mesmerized with what the richest people in the world give to charitable causes. These donors should indeed be applauded for the remarkable amounts they have given, but they are not the most generous charitable people in America. Giving from surplus is painless. The most charitable donors are those individuals that donate small amounts out of what they need to survive. Their contributions are great sacrifices made to organizations that represent their values. Their numbers are in the millions but their names are largely unknown and their sacrifices go, for the most part, unappreciated. The impact they make, however, can be felt and seen everywhere.

A donation can be used as a sacrifice when one is working magick. But a sacrifice must be just that. A sacrifice, to be effective, must inconvenience in some way. If I do not smoke cigarettes and ceremonially claim cigarettes to be my sacrifice then how effectual can I reasonably expect it to be? To explain this, the writers of the Old Testament devised a little understood story in the parable of 'The Widow's Mite'. In short, it goes to illustrate the donation by the poor widow is more valuable* than the donation that a rich man makes because the widow is making a bigger sacrifice than the man for whom money is no object. Is she more sincere than he? If he were to inconvenience himself more than she, would he be equally ethical or sincere? To put it in a way that hits home: should we be inconvenienced by our charity? I don't believe that it is necessary, provided it isn't being used as a magical sacrifice of some sort. Nor would we ever need to inconvenience ourselves if everyone did his or her share. As it is now, the few carry the burden, while the majority could care less. In a magical context, the biblical parable makes perfect sense, but not so much in the practical sense, however. Unfortunately, many people have come to misinterpret this parable's message. The recipients of the charity we provide have, on more than one occasion, benefited from the donations of various well-to-do supporters. This is how they support us. In Christianity, we are told that the rule is 'others first'. However, one cannot help others if they have used up their resources to the point that now they need help themselves. It defeats the entire purpose.

* At least on some magical level.

Furthermore, charity must be freely given without expectation; otherwise it is little more than a bribe. Christian missionaries have done more to destroy cultures around the globe than the war machine. They teach, feed, and comfort the sick with the expectation that they will embrace Christianity. The motivation is often times less than altruistic. In contrast, organizations like the Order of Thelemic Knights performs its charity work because it benefits our members in a profound way: the act of helping others is a noble end onto itself. Like the Christian churches, we also promulgate our chosen paradigm, but we do so by example.

Think about this. What if every employed human being on the planet donated $5.00 per month to feed the hungry at home and abroad? Provided that the officers of the organization did not spend the money on their own salaries, it is quite possible that with this $5.00, and the donations in food and supplies from corporate giants seeking tax breaks, we might feed the world's starving population or use the money to teach and enable these people to survive on their own.

A Personal Story

When I first arrived in Portland on December 31st, 1992, I became horribly ill with a life-threatening illness.* Having no money, I was driven to a Catholic hospital where I was first processed through the financial department and asked about my financial situation. I gave them all the data I had and was rushed into the emergency room for treatment. I couldn't stop thinking about the financial burden I was about to encounter. I went home and recovered. Two weeks later I received a letter from the hospital that impressed me so much that I have kept it ever since:

> *Dear Gerald. After evaluating your financial situation we have concluded that you are unable to pay for the medical care you received on January 18th, 1993, and we will not be seeking compensation. What we would ask, however, is for you to make donations to the hospital once your financial situation has improved so that we could continue to offer people such as yourself the sort of medical care this organization is known for.*

---

*   Ecoli from tainted fast-food.

I kept this because this as a reminder of the kind of organization I want to have. This letter displays the sorts of ethics that should dictate how the leaders of the organization conduct business.

TEACH YOUR CHILDREN WELL

Another true story, which is worth telling, begins with the clothing drive that the Order of Thelemic Knights held for the Lakota Indian reservation at Wounded Knee. We had donation receptacles in various place. The Ecclesia Gnostica Catholica Hermetica joined us in this drive and as a result we had a donation bin in a smoke shop in Kenosha Wisconsin. A little girl and her mother walked into the store and walked up to the shopkeeper. The little girl said to him: "Here you go. This is the $20.00 I collected in my lemonade stand to help pay for the shipping of these clothes."

Out of the mouth of babes. If children get it, why do such few adults? How odd it is to begin our lives with this outlook on life, only to loose it in the bustle of today's world, looking out for number one, minding ones own business, and then to have to spend the rest of our adult lives trying to get it back? The irony could kill.

COMPASSION IN THELEMA?

Many people question whether or not Thelemites can be compassionate. I usually answer with another question: "Can a person's True Nature be to show compassion?"

The following is the content of an email exchange which occurred between an unknown interested party and Tau Apollonius from The Thelemic Gnostic Church of Alexandria. We have decided to include this since it is yet another example for how the Order of Thelemic Knights approaches the subject of Gnosticism and Thelema.

Them: Do you believe that compassion has a place in Thelema? Could you define 'compassion' in your own experience?

Tau Apollonius: Compassion is the vice of Kings. We are told indulge our vices. Compassion has a place everywhere...or, I should say: I find compassion everywhere and in everyone. If we believe that compassion is spiritual, then it follows that it should be an integrated part of our spiritual practice.

Them: But Crowley was hardly compassionate!

Tau Apollonius: This isn't a very logical thing to say.* Does it follow that we should all be like Crowley? It may not be in everyone's True Nature to be compassionate. Shouldn't we be most concerned with doing OUR True Will? One of the many problems that people have with Crowley was that he would give uncompassionate instructions. It is hard to find compassion in much of Crowley's work if one does not understand his sense of humor or commitment to his spiritual discipline.

For Crowley, promoting Scientific Illuminism was his priority, feeling that once a person accomplished Knowledge and Conversation with his own Guardian Angel his newly discovered True Nature would dictate the moral/ethical code most appropriate to the that individual, and that any externally adopted morality could interfere with the process of Knowledge and Conversation. In other words, he wasn't teaching that morality was 'wrong' but that it should come from ones' self once one has discovered their true nature. How we should conduct ourselves until that moment occurs is, in my opinion, hidden in plain sight in the two statements that define the entirety of the Thelemic paradigm most succinctly: "Do what thou wilt shall be the whole of the Law" and "Love is the law, love under will". Let's look at these critically. On the surface we can begin to see that perhaps Love must come before Will—or more than that: That Love IS before Will. Or if you'd like to take it a step further, that one must first learn how to Love before learning to Will.

The use of "shall be" in "Do what thou wilt shall be the whole of the Law" implies that some other thing must first occur in order to manifest this "Law". It doesn't say "Do what thou wilt is the whole of the Law." When we look at the second part of this puzzle we see the word "is" to define what the Law is. Love. If by Law we mean Thelema, and by Love we mean Agape,† then it seems pretty obvious what one's modus operandi should be as they strive to discover

---

* A perfect example of a syllogism: Crowley was a Thelemite. Crowley was not a compassionate man. Therefore to be compassionate is not Thelemic.
† Both of which enumerate to 93 in Hebrew Qabalah.

their own True Will. Agape and Charity are synonymous. Remember, Crowley didn't come to his own Will by chance. He worked at it. Much of that work included devotional practices he picked up from the world's religions.

As to his 'bad boy' persona is concerned, much of what people dislike about him is either bad publicity, (something he preferred over no publicity at all), slander from his contemporaries or the second-hand accounts of people who haven't read his material either. He is often referred to as a fascist. How one can be a fascist and simultaneously insist everyone discover and manifest ones own True Will is something that still escapes me today.

One of the many problems facing the young Aeon of Hours is that most humans in this early transition period compare all prophets against the mythical Jesus while Thelemites compare them against Crowley. This is very unfortunate, but we can consider the Jesus problem as 'residue'. But what about the issue with the Crowleyites? What we know from the life of Jesus is that he was a man,* and not nearly as perfect as most people think he was. What we know about Crowley is that he wasn't nearly as imperfect as most people think he was. If we keep comparing our prophets against some unattainable and mythological state the words of our Prophets will fall on deaf ears.

Them: I am curious about your take on human suffering. Do Thelemites have a role or responsibility to relieve suffering?

Tau Apollonius: I often look at Thelema, in my limited understanding to see if it addresses this problem. I think it does. For example, for humans ignorance is the root of suffering. By ignorance, I mean a reactionary state where one abscessed by material gain, recognition, or passion rather than being focused on self-knowledge. I am not saying that one should renounce those things as the Gnostics of the past did. We can have it all, but self-knowledge must come first. That Gnosis can only occur with sincerity and truthfulness about ones motivations. Remove ignorance, and everyone is living their own truth. That Truth transcends death, or at least that is what I feel.

---

* Indeed, a man whose message was that God is in Man.

Them: You said the "D" word. How does a Thelemite transcend death?

Tau Apollonius: Beats me. No one has been able to answer that question—ever...so I am flattered that you think I may have. How does a Christian, Buddhist, Taoist, Jew, Gnostic, Muslim, transcend death? There is a song that goes "all roads lead to disaster. Only God knows what comes after." The answer is unknowable because we can't ask anyone what it is like to die. I suspect that a salvation comes from Gnosis. All we can do is to interpret the Holy Books and the internal voice that will occur for each one of us as a result. If I shut up for a while, I hear a lot of things that I trust. The reason that death is such a preoccupation with humans is that the ego is unable to come to terms with its own demise. We all know that the physical body begins breaking down when we are young and doesn't stop until we finally die. Identification with the physical body may sound like fun when one sweats testosterone or estrogen, but generally speaking one outgrows that, and then... we begin to look for something more. In my opinion, some parts of *Liber AL* seem to address a *BIGGER* problem than death: *the problem of living*. We should hasten the process of achieving self-knowledge so that we can get on with the joy of existence. The dying part will take care of itself.

Them: But why work at all? Most of what I have read in Thelema seems to lead people away from accomplishing anything of value.

Tau Apollonius: That is an unfair assessment. The same thing could be said from any religious movement. It isn't the prophet/religion/ Order's fault if the majority of its adherents are insincere. It is a matter of ones priorities. If one wants to play and hang out with people of like mind that is fine. Others will do that, and prioritize their lives to include a quest for self-knowledge, or in Thelemic terms, coming to the knowledge of ones True Will.

Them: I didn't mean to offend. It just seems that I hear people saying, "There is no god but man" as if there is no reason to work anymore. Like it is a done deal.

Tau Apollonius: Okay. We are told, "There is no god but man." Sounds nice, and this would solve the problem of suffering, but saying it doesn't make it so. Many people will take that phrase for granted to the extent that it will justify their laziness. So what? Others will understand that the knowledge of this is meaningless unless it is understood in a Gnostic sense and put into practice. This self-knowledge that I keep talking about is different than mundane knowledge that preoccupies scholars and mental masturbationists. I am referring to the ability to know the difference between physical and spiritual matters. While these two overlap, there are areas where they (in my limited understanding) appear incompatible. If you want to know who is sincere about their godhood, observe them for a while. How much control do they exercise over their own lives, and how much does this godhood mean to them? How much of themselves do they give to help others discover their own immortality? In other words, what do they do with this gift?

So How Much is Enough?

The question of "how much is enough?" can never really be addressed. One is either charitable or they are not. Giving out of pressure or guilt is not true Charity, and no self-respecting Thelemic organization will ever resort to such tactics to get support from its members outside of what they might pay in regular dues.

Other churches have, however, come up with a way to get the needed funds out of parishioners by asking for a tiding. A tiding is generally an amount based on a percentage of one's income, often times as high as 10% of gross. It works very well since someone who is well off will end up paying more than one who is not. Everyone pays the same percentage. And at least in the US, those donations are tax deductible, which appeals to people's self-interest to be charitable. One of the nice things about charity is that we do not have to concern ourselves with the reason behind donation. The important thing is that we receive them in order to continue helping others get on their feet.

Are Monetary Donations the Only Way to be Charitable?

Charity does not always come in the form of money. Doctors Without Borders send badly needed medical supplies and assistance to some of the most dangerous places in the world, putting themselves as great risk for the benefit of others they don't even know. They are fighting the battle for freedom in their own way according to their own talents.

Ethical people that are unable to serve their elected cause by throwing money at the problem can join with others according to their strengths and talents to achieve their chosen directive. This is what the Battle for Freedom is really about. Each of us should fight in whatever way is natural for us, according to our own True Nature. As already has been said, for a doctor, disease might be his foe; for a teacher, ignorance. And this is how it goes for soldiers when they have come to realize their own True Nature: they can now choose their battles according to their own True Wills, thereby maximizing their chances of causing change in conformity with that Will. This is the mark of a true soldier who MUST fight as opposed to those that play and will not.

Members of the Order of Thelemic Knights and the Thelemic Gnostic Church of Alexandria often contribute above and beyond his or her annual dues. All contributions are equally important regardless of how insignificant it may appear on the surface. Sewing altar cloths, making icons for the Church, writing for the curriculum or newsletter, illustrating, building, cooking, publishing, phoning possible contributors, fundraising, etc.

I posit that every individual possesses at least one skill that has charitable value and can be used by one's Order, Church, or chosen charity to achieve their stated goals. If one has a special talent for oration and reading, the Order of Thelemic Knights will endeavor to place them at a children's hospital so they can volunteer to help a child through a difficult and frightening time, or we can place them in an adult learning program where they might help adults to learn how to read. If you are charitable, you will never stop thinking how to use your talents to exercise charity. Our Order and Church are both vehicles. Use them and support them.

Ethics and the Scientific Method

TRUTH

The experimental method of inquiry aims at establishing regular events which can be repeated. Consequently, unique or rare events are ruled out of account. Moreover, the experiment imposes limiting conditions on nature, for its aim is to force her to give answers to questions devised by man. Every answer of nature is therefore more or less influenced by the kind of questions asked, and the result is always a hybrid product. The so-called "cientific view of the world" based on this can hardly be anything more than a psychologically biased partial view which misses out all those by no means unimportant aspects that cannot be grasped statistically.
—Carl G. Jung, *Synchronicity*

The obvious problem with moving Magick out of the sphere of personal understanding and into scientific scrutiny is the absence of a technology that will allow man to measure magical force and/or energy. Until then, we should learn to observe phenomena instead of ignoring things that lack explanation. Until then we should refrain from attempting to reduce the entire Art of Magick to simple psychological terms that can be easily understood.

Scientific Illuminism is the application of the scientific method to apparently supernatural phenomena. For this, one needs an open mind capable of holding two or more opposing ideas. For this, the scientific illuminist must be able to put aside his own ideology and opinions in order to carefully consider opposing views with the same consideration to detail he or she gives.

One should not discount the effectiveness or existence of magick because we lack scientific evidence to corroborate many of its postulates. Keep in mind that not all things considered 'scientific' can be confirmed. Until recently, the existence of black holes could not be established or observed, and yet scientists postulated and created models supporting their existence for many years. Quantum physics says it is possible for a solid to pass thorough a solid: that two objects can occupy the same space and time. This cannot be demonstrated either, and yet there are entire branches of scientific study dedicated to proving these things mathematically. One of the

obvious problems with fundamentalism in Thelema is that by limiting our studies to Crowley's observations, we will only constrain our
understanding to scientific knowledge of his own time. Remember:
the thing that sets Thelema most apart from other religions is that
it does not conflict with science. What can be said then, of so-called
'scientific illuminists' that are unable to fathom a Thelema which
transcends the work of its Prophet?

We can't really say much of Truth…but we can sure ask questions.
Nietzsche and many of his contemporaries dedicated a lot of time
to questioning truth. And indeed, this is a worthy endeavor if what
we are trying to prove is that truth exists independently of ethics or
morals. But for those of us that already knew this, the entire exercise seems to be redundant. So what do we do with that knowledge?

There is a very small but extremely loud group of Thelemites that
spend most of their waking hours trying to prove that other Thelemites do not possess gnosis. If you find this idea offensive, you are
not alone. This is how they work:

In order to maintain the appearance of adhering to the "scientific
method," they create some badly-calibrated rules in the form of some
arbitrary criteria they already meet. This way, no matter what happens, they appear to win…well, at least in their own minds. Usually
these rulers are composed of some illogical assumptions or values
that have nothing to do with gnosis in the first place. This in itself indicates *agnoia.* On more than one occasion, these good scientists and
pseudo-intellectuals* have insinuated that a person's gnosis can be
measured by how much money they have in their pockets. Again, this
shows a complete ignorance in the area of gnosis and only a superficial understanding of the philosophers they claim to admire. If, according to the ruler, one is successful in one area, and they measure
for strength in a completely different area with the same instrument,
then this is not scientific nor can one expect reasonable results. This
is like trying to measure specific gravity with a thermometer.

People are successful in various different areas according to their
talents. Making money is one of them. Some people are terrible in
this regard, and yet this is not a sign of agnosia. If one steps back
and looks at the big picture with the idea in mind that one's gnosis
will manifest itself according to one's natural talents, then we can
begin to appreciate what True Will is all about.

---

* Please note the sarcasm.

I suspect that if their finances didn't look so well, they might use some other rule, calibrated for something they exceed at to illustrate how much better they are then the rest. Another double standard is that they rarely use the same badly calibrated instruments to measure the worth of the same philosophers whose teachings they use to justify the use of their flawed criteria in the first place. Take Nietzsche and Crowley, for example. What were their lives like?

Nietzsche was driven mad, either by syphilis or his own thoughts. Now his writings are used to justify the work of Nazi sympathizers who think of themselves as the *Ubermensch*. Crowley spent his inherited fortune publishing books and traveling abroad, trying to get his students to think for themselves but ended up with a majority of unquestioningly followers and ultimately, died financially destitute.

So what have we learned from this? We have two choices. We can either disregard the work of Crowley and Nietzsche, claiming them to have been poor magicians, or we can conclude that the way their followers measure the worth of an individual's gnosis is flawed. Bring this up, and these intellectuals will come up with a variety of very creative excuses to dismiss the personal shortcomings of these philosophers. It is true that Crowley left an incredible legacy, and all Thelemites owe him something. It is equally true that Nietzsche wasn't insane all the time, but the point is that one must have use of the proper tools. Scientific Illuminists are not exempt, nor can they make up the rules as they go.

These same people adhere to Darwinism as a universal truth. I am not here to argue against that. I actually agree with it.* But I do want to point out a flaw in how it is presently used in various Thelemic circles. What invalidates Social Darwinism in most people's minds is that the folks that cling on to it and use it as the end-all tool for measuring success espouse the idea that it only works to thin out others. Rarely do they see themselves in danger of becoming dinosaurs because they tend to be fixated on *one idea* or *one area* where they excel. They rarely share how their own weaknesses are working against them because in their minds —*they are the poop*—at least according to their incestuous, limited scope. They measure up just fine against their own ruler because they are calibrated according to the cycles of their own success. As a result of this flawed logic, many end up darwinizing themselves out of certain social sit-

* Success is your proof, after all.

uations, and the result is to complain about how 'lame' those other social circles are in the first place.*

Furthermore, Darwinism is a poor tool for measuring gnosis. To use the faulty argument that 'gnosis = money' as an example:

I might have all the money in the world, but might loose it all in a Tsunami. This doesn't mean that I didn't posses knowledge in the area of accumulating wealth, only that circumstances outside of my control resulted in the loss of the capital, NOT in the loss of my gnosis.

In short, for most of these people, 'Darwinism' is really little more than some crazy expression indicating an inferiority complex at best, and simple bashing at worst. It is where a small but vocal group of people gathers for the purpose of condemning another social group that doesn't meet whatever criteria they feel isn't being met. That isn't what Darwinism is all about. That's just a group of bullies trying to show off at the expense of some poor guy who doesn't fit into their preconceived notions of success. This can hardly be called 'social darwinism'. It is more like *Lord of The Flies*. Flawed logic aside, Reason is an inadequate tool for transmitting Truth because the Truth is not always reasonable. Gnosis equals Certainty: Reason does not necessarily equal gnosis.

> *Since Truth is supra-rational, it is incommunicable in the language of Reason.*
> —*Aleister Crowley, p. 197, Equinox Vol. I, No. 2.*

It would be different if we were, say auto mechanics, and we were arguing over the right carburetor to use to achieve performance - but we are not doing that. The topic of Gnostic accomplishments is highly subjective and therefore, immeasurable. These topics are far beyond the scope of physics and logic.

Furthermore, people that say they have gnosis when they don't are only fooling and cheating themselves. Besides, we should be so vested in our own gnosis that we wouldn't have the time to care about whether or not someone else has it.

What is Truth? Can it be articulated and communicated as the ancients tell us, in any human language such as ritual or parable? Is there an absolute Truth? Or is it objective, varying from one individual to the next based on the sum of ones direct experiences, perceptions, and observations? Is 'scientific truth' absolute? Or does

---

* The "I have been kicked out of better places than this" syndrome.

that form of truth also depend on our perspective?* Does it rely on human logic? If there is absolute Truth, is it directly knowable or understood? Or is it our perceptions of it, which are necessarily subjective? That being said, is truth temporal or situational?

Is religious or philosophical truth absolute, or is it a feeble attempt on the part of humans to explain the unknowable by using already accepted knowledge? If scientific truth is fragile at best, with its logic, fact and experimental methods, then how much more fragile is philosophical truth? Is gnosis Truth? Is it reasonable to expect a seeker of truth maintain an open mind? How else should it be?

Truth hurts. How many times have we heard this and shaken our heads in agreement without really understanding what this really means? Truth destroys every false assumption and belief regardless of how dear we may hold them. It can be described as a sense of sincerity and honesty. People generally run away from the Truth, and like most things, man may use the Truth to justify the things he likes while ignoring the components of the Truth he dislikes or does not serve his end.† What can we expect from a person that is willing to lie to himself?

I believe that there are universal truths that affect all of us regardless of what we may believe. But generally speaking, those are ignored due to the ethical inconvenience that they present us with. In many ways, modern man has collectively learned to look at Truth and Justice as games. The object is to look for loopholes and make up exceptions to the rule in order to continue with the status quo while dodging any appearance of dishonesty or insincerity. It is logical then, that so many of us have become so desensitized to this unethical mindset when we consider how corrupt our judicial system and government have become. The secular courts are clear in the message they send: "Don't do what is right. Do what is legal." Leaders have not set good examples for the rest to follow.

Truth involves responsibility. To say that "There is no god but man," for example, is to imply that we are all responsible for every problem that man has created. With knowledge and acceptance of this Truth‡, we can no longer blame some absentee father god for

---

* Consider the number of scientific "truths" that were considered infallible a half-century ago that have gone the way of the flat earth today.

† See *Liber Librae*, paragraph 15.

‡ If we are Thelemites, we have already accepted the divine nature of man in

world hunger, the environmental disaster that awaits our children, or war for corporate economic gain. We are all collectively and personally responsible, and every ethical man and woman that holds the divinity of man as Truth will do his or her share to put an end to injustice, greed and the suffering that they cause to countless of his fellows all over the world.

Intellectual prowess is a part of the process. Gods know what happens when people begin dabbling with poorly understood magical concepts. The intellect should be well developed, and critical thinking skills should be cultivated. The word 'metaphysics' is composed of two words in Greek: Meta and Physics. The Greek prefix Meta means 'beyond', while Physics, is, well… 'nature'. So when it comes to metaphysical matters it should be pretty obvious that the intellect will only get you so far. Also, intellectualism is no different than magick: they are both means to an end, rather than the end itself. This is very hard to remember, especially if we should become adept in any one of these areas. Crowley himself warns of the traps of specializing in any one area when certain practices yield spiritual gifts. We must always move forward, and we shouldn't let ego get in the way of achieving the ultimate goal of magic: Union with God. Those that are wise beyond the confines of their own opinions and insecurities will know when to move on.

The changing of aeons corresponds with the evolution of the human spirit, which (coincidently) corresponds to planetary rotations, and it is our perception of the same unchanging Truth that appears to evolve. This is why the study of religion and mythology are so important to our Work. If you want to know where we are going as a species, then we have better learn where we have been, because there are many places not worth revisiting.

For the ethical man, Truth is the object of desire…a carrot, if you will, that will ultimately lead him to freedom by making it possible for him to act in accordance with his own true nature. The benefits of embracing the truth are overwhelming. It presents us with the opportunity to overcome obstacles; it is the source of Beauty and its influence on humans is liberating. It fortifies the soldier with courage and a sense of righteousness during dangerous times to know that he is an agent of Truth and Justice.

---

which is God.

To Gnow or Not to Gnow

An intellectual is someone whose mind watches itself.
—Albert Camus

Gnosis is about Personal Salvation. This Salvation is the freedom from the bonds of illusion, and the vision and experience of those things that are real, and those things that exist beyond reality. To get Gnosis, we don't count on someone else to open our eyes or to show us the way. While initiation is a very potent method of enlightenment, it is the candidate that must take the tools received at the event, and use them to pry his sleepy eyes open.

What is Gnosis?

Crowley summed it up with an expression: "Aha!" It is the blinding light that had such a profound effect on Saul that he changed his name to Paul. It is a realization that all things are connected, and ones place in the grand scheme of things. The laughter that comes when one understands all the world's problems. The unmistakable feeling that comes from transcending obstacles. The Inspiration you receive when the Creative Genius flows through you. The surprise of opening your mouth and hearing the Wisdom of The Beloved unexpectedly roll through your lips. This is the moment of being born again and the Freedom from which you can never return to slavery. It is all of these things…and much, much more.

Not everyone wants to wake up. Some people are quite happy with their illusions. Nor is there anything wrong with that: some people go to great lengths to create them. Take a look at The Devil trump, for example. There you will see the Master of Illusions ruling supreme, its subjects shackled loosely to the altar. Close inspection of the irons will reveal that these restraints must be voluntarily. Hidden in the symbolism of this card is a very powerful magical formula. The trick is not to forget that you are there by choice: don't forget the goal, which must ultimately always lead to absolute freedom. Why would anyone want to be voluntarily shackled to illusion? Think about it. What is a paradigm if not some useful tool to accomplish one's goals?

Tarot isn't the focus of this little treatise. Its purpose is to encourage you to pull away the fabric of your own creation, and peer into the unknown. It's okay. You can always draw the curtains tighter than before, if you so will. But if you begin to understand what is beyond the curtain, you will never be the same again, and your illusion will not work anymore to hide you from the unknown. You will have to create a different illusion to shield you, until you are able to peer through that tapestry once again. And the cycle repeats itself an infinite number of times, until the illusion you create begins to look and feel more and more like reality. As above, so below. It's a long road from Atziluth to Assiah.

The differences between the Magi and the Mystic are numerous. One of the most important is that the Magi is in a more advantageous position to receive Gnosis than the Mystic is. Why? Because the Mystic counts exclusively on the methods from others that have come before him: the same prayers, same meditations, same Bhakti. The Magi, on the other hand, spends his life learning from his predecessors, but doesn't really earn the right to use the title until he has stood on the shoulders of the Magi before him, and has jumped off. This is where the fun really begins.

Personal Revelation is the only path to a true understanding. You can't rely on the inspiration from the past. Are you a Magician? Can you draw inspiration from The Beloved, or do you rely on someone else's experience with the Divine? Do you simply trust what others have said about the journey, or do you make your own way, knowing that The Path has changed? The Mystery of what is, and the Mystery of what you are, your Hadit (called *Pneuma* by the ancient Gnostics), is the goal. There is great danger in this. How will you respond when you see yourself in your naked splendor? Will you like yourself once the persona you fancy yourself to be disintegrates before you? How will you interact with the Infinite?

Once the vault to your Gnosis has been thrown open, it can never be closed again. There is great danger and great reward. The proverbial Pandora's Box. You can open the way to your Gnosis, or you can take your chances with 'destiny.' Consider the following warning from The Gospel of Thomas: "Let one who seeks continue seeking until one finds. When one finds, one will be disturbed. When one is disturbed, one will be amazed, and will rule over all."

It is like being on a roller coaster ride. Some will open their eyes, throw their hands in the air to get the full experience of the moment, to come off the other side feeling as though the ride has been conquered and looking forward to the next, more intimidating ride. Others will grip their restraints, clenching their eyes, and the fuel for the scream that comes out of the throat is the desire for the ride to end. Don't worry, you can always make another curtain…but you will never be the same again. The fear is understandable. As 'modern' humans, we are completely at odds with our own true nature.

As a result, we live in troubled times. How can we be true to who we are without compromise, when all around is despair, poverty, violence, corruption, and war? It is hard to think about exposing one's self to all of this Darkness without one's self-made armor. But that is exactly what the Gnostic teachings say we must do. The ancient Gnostics were able to do this because they surrounded themselves with other Gnostics who were devoted to the same goal and vision. They assisted each other, and every time the individual's True Self peered out, his or her comrades encouraged them to let go and allow it to rule supreme. This is difficult to do in today's world. Probably much harder than it was back in those days, and yet we cannot call ourselves Gnostics until our True Self shines through us for the world to see.

Don't fear Darkness or Death. They are your friends. If your eyes are closed, you might think of Darkness as something that hides things, and makes everything appear imperfect and flawed. Once your eyes have been opened, you won't see imperfection, but beautiful and unique one-of-a-kind things. Darkness is a playful child, and if you are lucky, it will, from time to time, engage you in a game of hide-and-go-seek. Its only purpose is to make the journey more rewarding. The greater the obstacle, the sweeter the reward.

Death makes everything perishable, limited by time and space. The body you now occupy will never be here again, once it is gone. It is there for one moment, in the next it is not. Even though there are millions of other bodies that have not yet been made, ready to replace the one you will eventually leave behind, this particular one will never be here again. Nor will there ever be a moment exactly like this one, or another you, and you only get one chance to make your mark or to manifest what you want into Reality. Even if we postulate reincarnation, you only get this time to experience this body, to use it to accomplish your True Will. Death is what gives everything around us meaning. It is what makes us mortal and immortal at the same time. It is what makes us all unique Stars: it gives our lives value and meaning.

So, how do we get Gnosis?

Well, that is the only question worth asking. Sometimes it happens to us without our awareness. It often occurs as a result of some tragic event or trauma. Those are the easy ways.

For most of us, it involves work...a lot of work. We have created shells to hide behind, shields to protect us from an unfriendly world. These trappings must come off. To do this, one must be brutally honest with one's Self. There is no place for egoism here, for the only person you will deceive is yourself. Arrogance is the enemy of Gnosis. Liber AL tells us to be proud, but shouldn't one have something real to be proud of?

Pride without substance is arrogance.

To get Gnosis, one has to begin by being true to one's own Self. The Self can't be fooled, despite our best efforts. When antagonism is chosen or preferred over harmony; when oaths or the little principles we have proclaimed dear to our hearts are willingly violated, when we betray the trust of a Brother or Sister when we stand to gain a political advantage; these things prevent Gnosis. How so? Because in doing these things, regardless of our justification, we betray our Self, The Watcher, and our Internal Integrity. The Self cannot be lied to even if we manage to convince ourselves that we are doing these things for some greater good.

No. Gnosis only occurs to rare individuals for a reason. It surrenders itself readily when one is honest with one's Self. It withdraws itself just as readily the minute it is betrayed. You want Gnosis? Inquire within. This is an invitation. I invite you to take a peek: to try looking behind that tired old mask. Who knows...you could like who you really are a lot better.

At the end of each day we are faced with one important question: Did I give in to 'human nature' or did I choose to reach for something greater. Because more times than not, the things we do and the things we should have done are not one in the same.

It seems that the conventional wisdom has given up on humanity being able to attain any higher plane than the one for which we are genetically destined. I for one do not think it is that simple. Like it or not, we HAVE evolved, and we ARE thinking creatures with CHOICE. We CAN and DO determine our course. Whether that course leads to our liberation and the liberation of every person on the planet, or whether it leads to our own destruction remains yet to be seen. But wherever we end up, it will be the place we CHOSE, for better or for worse. You can blame it on 'human nature', however, if it makes you feel better about yourself. You may even get the 'scientific' data to back it up.

Spiritual Ethics: Calling a Spade

Thelema as a social phenomenon is interesting to people that don't necessarily consider themselves Thelemites. Like it or not many view it as a cultural phenomena, and as such Thelemites tend to get the attention of forward thinking individuals looking to see how we differ from 'regular people', and if we match the profile that they have created based on what they have read about us from our own Holy Books. I know that the idea that someone might judge us based on the claims we make about our beliefs seems atrocious to many individuals who'd like to continue to have license to do what they want, but discrimination is a human trait that cannot be shaken. For better or for worse people are going to see what makes us unique for any number of reasons beginning with idle curiosity all the way to looking to see if Thelema is for them.

It might have occurred to you that those of us that call ourselves Thelemites are subject to much more scrutiny than those fortunate individuals that live Thelemic lives without ever having heard of Thelema.*

Most people use the 'duck test' to determine what something is. If it looks, smells, walks, swims, and flies like a duck, it must be a duck. So, what sort of question might a social anthropologist or comparative religion student look for to further ascertain the nature of Thelema while observing its adherents? They obvious answer is to look at our Holy Books and see if we walk the talk.

THERE IS NO GOD BUT MAN? REALLY?

Whether you believe in god or not, this simple statement explains the challenges that humans face in the New Aeon. Nietzsche was the first to proclaim the observation that mankind has killed God with the advent of science:

> Whither is God?" he cried; "I will tell you. We have killed him—you and I. All of us are his murderers. But how did we do this? How could

---

* Some people believe that one can only be a Thelemite by having been exposed to Crowley's work. This does not account for those individuals that do their Will in the world never having heard of Thelema. We therefore define a Thelemite as a person that lives their life in accordance with their own True Will.

we drink up the sea? Who gave us the sponge to wipe away the entire horizon? What were we doing when we unchained this earth from its sun? Whither is it moving now? Whither are we moving? Away from all suns? Are we not plunging continually? Backward, sideward, forward, in all directions? Is there still any up or down? Are we not straying, as through an infinite nothing? Do we not feel the breath of empty space? Has it not become colder? Is not night continually closing in on us? Do we not need to light lanterns in the morning? Do we hear nothing as yet of the noise of the gravediggers who are burying God? Do we smell nothing as yet of the divine decomposition? Gods, too, decompose. God is dead. God remains dead. And we have killed him.

– Frederick Nietzsche, The Gay Science

In other words: we are responsible. We are responsible for world hunger; we are responsible for what is being done to the planet in the name of capitalism and economic growth. We are responsible for health care becoming a commodity for those that can afford it, and we are responsible for imperialism. We will be held accountable in the end. To put it in Gnostic terms, we will not be punished for our sins, but by our sins.

Yes, we are responsible. But what do we do with that responsibility? This is the horrible truth all humans have to face.*

Neither the atheist or deist has 'God' to kick around any more. The deist has always known that God helps those who help themselves, and has noticed that help usually comes by way of humans. The lights are on, and it seems that the humans are caught with their pants down. Every body knows and for the most part, we are all in denial.

So what does this have to do with Thelemites?

Can one simultaneously hold the belief that there is no other god than man (whatever that may mean to you) and close his or her eyes to the problems that plague today's world? Of course, one can simply choose to ignore the entire issue...but what does that say about us as Thelemites? An excellent bit of old aeon advice is "by their fruit ye shall know them," and so for the casual observer or social anthropologist (or anyone else that is sufficiently interested), it be-

---
*   Especially Thelemites!

comes very simple to tell the posers from the real deal. Some of the questions they might ask themselves are how seriously concerned Thelemites seem to be with current events? Do we get involved; try to be a part of the solution, or are we simply ignoring the problem? How do we view human suffering? Do we instinctively quote OZ, or snap back with "the slaves shall serve" when asked what we are doing about the predicament humans are in? Do we appear to labor under the false assumption that to oppose religion we must also oppose responsibility and charity?* Do we justify apathy by trying to prove involvement is 'dumb' or 'Old Aeon'? What will they say about the actions of the self-proclaimed Thelemites who appear to find no joy in Thelema save that of arguing trivialities such as whether the monogamous or polyamorous† are most Thelemic.

We would do well not tolerate the hypocrisy that exists in many other philosophical circles. Perhaps one day all Thelemites will rise out of their ivory towers of their computers and lazy-boy couches and wake up to the fact that the desecration of the spirit of Thelema has gone on long enough, and that Thelema is about doing ones True Will, not trying to figure out creative ways of getting out of it.

How do our stated beliefs make us responsible in the real world?

Everything in Crowley's work could generally be taken to be 'god training'. It is said that Nuit is "divided for love's sake for the chance of union." I postulate that the thing we call 'god' is the totality of the human experience, and that each of us carries a small spark in us (Hadit) so that It can experience reality in human bodies. If we can accept this as a hypothesis, then "god" is in everyone. The little boy on the news who has died from hunger is god dying from hunger. And the same holds true of the well-to-do, financially flush men and women that walked past him ignoring his pleas for food.

Anyone with loose pocket change (being gods themselves) could have helped to prevent the young man's death, and yet they chose not to concern themselves with the boy's problems. The little boy had no choice due to the limitations imposed upon him by his

---

* Doesn't that sound a little "old aeon" too?
† Q: How many Thelemites does it take to screw in a lightbulb? A: Twelve. One to actually do it and 11 to argue how Crowley would have done it.

country of birth, social circumstances, or caste. These are the sorts of moral issues that the study of ethics attempts to address. Suffice it to say that freewill and the ability to choose is what makes us gods. Freewill is power.[*]

We can take this example a bit further: "make no difference between one thing and any other thing for thereby there cometh hurt." We could use this declaration, if we chose to, to argue against the lack of concern in part of those individuals that walked by the boy without helping, because by not acknowledging the deity in themselves or the young boy they failed to see the connection they shared with him that ultimately ended in his death. In short, they caused hurt when it could have been prevented. They chose to make a difference between himself and the boy.

The same quotation in *Liber AL* might serve us to justify this indifference, but we shouldn't be like those that justify inappropriate action with their Holy Books. Rather, we should endeavor to give our Holy Books more thought than the unconcerned crowd gave the poor boy. We may also question how it may be possible to "make no difference between one thing and any other thing" when freewill implies choosing one thing over another.

Compassion is the key.[†] It is impossible to reconcile those (apparently) opposing concepts without it. Perhaps the idea isn't to discard the concept of connectedness, but to see ourselves simultaneously as individuals and as connected to others.[‡] Choosing to make a difference in the world is different than using division to set one apart and above others. It would be silly to take the quote above literally: I know the difference between the pen that writes these words and the paper they are written on[§] and I assure you that this knowledge has not caused me any pain. It is how these objects are related that is important.

"As above, so below" is another, more ancient dictum of the same thing. If we do not recognize the difference between 'heaven and earth' then we are destined to end up in a godless earth, unworthy of His magnificent presence, or a sterile 'heaven' devoid of any earthly pleasures. We have had 2,000 years to see the effects of this thinking.

---

[*]   And this is reason enough for governments to impose limits upon it.
[†]   The vice of Kings.
[‡]   Much like contemplating the infinitely large and infinitely small.
[§]   Though the relationship between them is obvious.

The members of The Order of Thelemic Knights do not believe that our charitable work is an exclusively spiritual endeavor, for if there is one thing that we should never do is to make any difference between the spiritual and the mundane. By doing that, those uncaring individuals could simply forgive themselves for ignoring the boy's pleas for help by doing something as trivial as attending church on Sunday, or making a donation at some event. We should hardly call our charitable work 'spiritual' if doing so makes us feel as though we are better in some way than the people we help. Our inspiration should be love, for as it has already been said: Love is a God.

To say that one must be religious, or believe in some exterior force in order to engage in charitable activity cheapens the tremendous contributions made by the atheists of the world. In many ways the atheist has most readily embraced the idea of "no god but man".

Ethics in Religion

Much is gained once the feeling [reverence - Ehrfurcht] *has finally been cultivated in the masses...that they are not to touch everything; that there are holy experiences before which they have to take off their shoes and keep away their unclean hands - this is almost their greatest advance toward humanity. Conversely, there is nothing about so called educated people and believers in "modern ideas" that is as nauseous as their lack of modesty and the comfortable insolence of their eyes and hands with which they touch, lick, and finger everything; and it is possible that even among the common people, among the less educated, especially among peasants, one finds today more relative nobility of taste and tactful reverence than among the newspaper reading demimonde of the spirit, the educated.*
—Nietzsche, Beyond Good and Evil, section 263,
translated by Kaufmann.

How do we know the difference between a myth and a religion? It is easy. Simply observe and ask yourself how seriously self-proclaimed adherents take the paradigm? This will determine if the philosophical model is the source of a living religion or a myth. If the outspoken adherents of religious sects do not live their life in accordance to their own principles, then why should anyone think that the paradigm is worth a second look?

Religion is nothing less than the divine, organized rebellion against the forces of the Demiurge. On another level it is the celebration of the life of the Spirit. It brings out the best of what is in man.

Is a religious person being ethical when he twists the message of his chosen paradigm to further his agenda? If Jesus loves you, but hates homosexuals...what does that say, exactly?

In the biblical story, we are told that Jesus saved a prostitute from being stoned, not for prostitution, but for working on the Sabbath. So why is this example of compassion twisted to support some fundamentalists gripe against prostitution? Furthermore, if the prostitute had been male, would Jesus have walked away from him?

Is it ethical for religious fundamentalists to ignore unwanted pregnancy and disease by adhering to the ill-conceived idea that adolescents can be forced into refraining from sex by making sex education or birth control impossible to obtain? Are they not responsible for the hundreds of teens that will contract AIDS, unwanted pregnancy and the abortions that will occur as a result?

Fundamentalism has infiltrated every aspect of our government as well. Why should a woman be denied the freedom of making decisions involving her body, while corporations are free to make decisions which affect all humans without regulation? Why is global warming considered 'junk science' at the same time that we are told that the schools must teach our children creationism?

They have forgotten that Christianity itself is an eclectic mixture of various religious and mythological notions. Coincidently, the loss of devotion we are experiencing everywhere around the globe presently is not unlike what occurred in the course of the Greco-Roman era. This spiritual dryness appears to have been crucial to the birth of Christianity. The present spiritual dryness may be crucial to Thelema. Perhaps we are also approaching a spiritual renewal, and maybe this will in turn lead to a new renaissance. The New Religion should not only exhibit the greatest wisdom of all preceding paradigms, but must be adoptable to our present psychological development as well as our present understanding of the universe. People are beginning to wake up...one by one.

The Portal of human evolution is unfolding before us. We care only that the adherents of the old religions choose to be active participants of this coming age rather than throwing it all away to fulfill some ill-gotten prophecy they do not understand. Presently, however, there is so much resistance to change from the entrenched so-called 'Christian' elements in this country, and such a great desire to have the prophesy manifest as they understand it that they gladly adopt unethical means in their Master's name in order to infiltrate and force their misguided beliefs into just about every governmental or educational institution,* there to ensure that the 'end of the world' occurs just as they think they should. To this end they unknowingly† assume the role of 'Anti-Christ.' The second Inquisition

---

* Doing away with every form of environmental protection policies in favor of more "corporate friendly approach" which will ensure the end of what is left of the American Rain Forest, the salmon and thousands of other species struggling to survive with man.

† Perhaps, unknowingly.

could well be on its way, and the mark we might have to begrudgingly accept is a Christian one.

The irony is that today's 'religious right' wouldn't know their Jesus if he DID come as prophesized. If he preached that all people deserve health care they'd call him a socialist or a communist. If he said that they shouldn't judge homosexuals they might call him a 'fruit' or a gay sympathizer. Or perhaps he'd say that the earth is God's creation and should therefore be protected from pollution, and they'd call him a hippie. Maybe he would stand up against corruption in the government of what is supposed to be the fairest nation in the world and they'd call him an 'enemy combatant' and lock him up in Guantanamo Bay. In many ways, these people and the charlatans that lead them have become the Antichrist they fear so much.

The old aeon is indeed in its death throws and the proof is in the fundamentalist leaders in the US that appear to be trying to bring about the apocalyptic end prophesized in the New Testament. Never has it occurred to their flock that the books were written in a language different than their own, and that the original passages contain hundreds of hidden references and secret teachings which are lost in the translation. Not one of them seems sufficiently vested or sincere enough to read the original text. Such arrogance. So much suffering has been caused simply because they prefer the doom of the entire human race rather than face the possibility that they might have been wrong or misled, not by the teachings of their Master, but by their priests, pastors, and reverends. They question nothing that their supposed leaders tell them, exhibit no curiosity regarding the nature or source of the material they are fed and become hostile when others point out logical inconsistencies or use their own holy book to disprove their position. The method that they seem to hold on to most dearly is to cling so some supposed absolute truth even when discredited by evidence to the contrary, or with little regard of how actions based on such false beliefs causes needless suffering.

Religion is a language. A cage, if you will, in which we can observe and experience truth. We must always be vigilant to remember that we cannot capture Truth in any vessel without restricting it to the limits imposed upon us by our understanding. Religion is a complex symbol set which adherents of the paradigm can use to discover and communicate the spiritual truths they share with others. A wonderful by-product of religion is an Egregore. This is why all religion must, by necessity, eventually become orthodoxy.

Religion can provide the experience of truth to its adherents but the rituals and celebrations must be performed exactly and deliberately in order to deliver the desired result or message. The reason that so many people have distaste for religion or orthodoxy in general is that many of the prominent religions have softened their own guiding principles in order to be more inclusive.* This means that more people must understand the symbol set than originally intended. The language is watered down to be all-inclusive.† We can see what has happened to Christianity, after 2,000 years of manipulation and distortion. Its language has become the Spanglish – the Ebonics of the spiritual world, its original message being lost to all except its most sincere scholars who have no choice to preserve the original meaning of the Sacred Law in their hearts for fear of being blackballed by their own colleagues.

Are Thelemites being any more ethical when they use their Holy Books to validate socially unacceptable behavior? Such as referring to the drug of choice as a 'sacrament' even when they overindulge to the extent that it negatively affects their brethren?‡ Or using some passage in OZ to condone murder, theft, or guilt others into sexual activity? If Thelemites don't think any better of Thelema, then how can we expect others to embrace it?

Karma Yoga is ethics in action. As such it is of great importance to the work with which the Order of Thelemic Knights is involved in the outside world. It isn't enough to understand ethics. One must become ethical by putting what he has learned of his own ethical code into action. We must understand how our chosen religious/ philosophical paradigm effects the way we look at ethics. Clearly, holding the opinion that the human race entered a new aeon in 1904 while continuing to perpetuate the corrupt ideals of the old aeon isn't working for us.§ Just look around. Are the Thelemites you

---

*   Some do it to be more exclusive.

†   Or too incestual to be inclusive.

‡   Drugs can indeed be considered sacraments provided they are used in ritualistic or ceremonial context. But can we consider them "sacraments" when they are done while watching television.

§   The old rituals are black, after all.

know the sort of people the Book of The Law indicates we should be? Are they powerful? Do they 'rule the many and the known'? Are they really the 'chosen ones'? Perhaps it takes a little more than what most people think to be a Thelemite. If Thelemites had as much political pull as the fanatical Christians presently do, would this country look any better?

Most religions are personality cults. This is what makes them fail. For Christianity, Jesus is the hero, and his message of love and compassion is largely overlooked while his name is used to justify things he would have abhorred. In short, it has become easier for many Christians to worship Jesus rather than do the work he did. Many Thelemites face the same problem by adopting Crowley's bad-boy persona and ignoring what is prescribed in the Holy Books. Crowley was many things. He was human first and foremost. But he was also one of the hardest working people on the planet, devoting his life to the liberation of the human spirit and promulgating the Law of Thelema to ALL people. Is it ethical to dishonor him by embracing his vices while ignoring his virtues altogether? Is it ethical for Thelemites to enjoy the freedoms without at least trying to liberate his fellows from the tyranny that prevents his fellows from having the same opportunities to live freely?

What do you think Crowley meant when he said to avoid "the demon Crowley"? Maybe the 'demon Crowley' refers to his own lifestyle and perhaps this was an endeavor to appeal to people's common sense. It is likely that he saw the tendency for people to emulate religious leaders and teachers and he was simply warning people against doing the Will of their guru and concentrate instead on discovering their own. In my opinion, Crowley's lifestyle and personal rituals could only have been beneficial to Crowley and no one else.

To put it another way, how can we avoid the hypocrisy of criticizing any system if we continue to perpetuate it in our own behavior? There was a time when the Roman Catholic Church controlled the Holy Scriptures of the old aeon. The leaders of that organization were so afraid of men finding their own salvation in the Scriptures without intervention from a Priest, that the Bible was written in Latin and it became a crime for 'regular folks' to read it. Was it ethical to take the message of their prophet and interpret his desires to serve their own greed and lust for power?

So, what is a Thelemic fundamentalist? I have said on more than one occasion that I believe *Liber OZ* to contain the seeds for world peace. Do I think claims like this make me a fundamentalist? I certainly hope not. A person who believes that the whole of Thelema is contained exclusively within the body of Crowley's work or insists that all good ideas or ethics should be disregarded because they are 'old aeon' is, in my opinion, a Thelemic fundamentalist.

To make my point, one only need look at the list of lofty individuals (real or mythical) sainted by Crowley in his Gnostic Catholic Mass. The list is immense, and the lives of these individuals are testaments of their character, integrity and honor. There is a small group of Thelemites that only see in their Saints the elements of phallicism. I do not argue this point, but to stop there would be to diminish the greatness of the lives and sacrifices these people made, and I am not willing to do that. It is unconscionable for anyone to completely disregard the contributions they have made to humanity because they'd like to think of themselves as being just as worthy, but are not much interested in acquiring similar virtues. But when one of the Saints* lives or writings gives weight to some argument with regards to race, or might being right, then you can bet that the topic of phallicism isn't even considered. Simply stated, it is a double standard.

And while on the subject of phallicism. To me, the entire concept seems suspect and rather Osirian in light of the Aeon of The Child. Perhaps this just goes to further prove the point that Crowley did not simply disregard something useful just because its source is 'old aeon'. Perhaps Truth endures after all.

A paradigm as complex as Thelema could not begin and end with Crowley† anymore than Freud's work could contain all there is to know of psychoanalysis. Furthermore, to say that Thelema couldn't exist without Crowley is as absurd as claiming that gravity wouldn't exist had Newton not discovered it. Fundamentalism of any kind should be despised regardless of how benign it appears on the surface. I have a propensity to view Thelema as a link in a very long chain. I have noticed that many of the ideas and virtues contained in Crowley's body of work are compatible or originate with Christianity, Buddhism, Taoism, Islam, Hinduism, and other

---

*   Usually Nietzsche.

†   I'd like to see what he would have called Thelema if he hadn't read Rabelais.

long forgotten paradigms which existed before it. Crowley was too wise a man to throw the baby out with the bathwater, and we should work hard to prevent being any less intelligent. By incorporating all the truths of other paradigms into his own, Crowley ensured that all roads would lead to Thelema.

Ethics in Religion begins with giving credit where credit is due.

Is Thelema a Religion, Philosophy or Yoga?

Yes, to all three. In his Karma Yoga, Vivekenanda states that a religion must possess three things: Philosophy, mythology, and ritual. Some groups will form treating it as a religion, others will come together to explore it as a philosophy, and yet others will see it as a personal yoga. Some groups (such as the Order of Thelemic Knights) may even explore all three concepts together.

Defining something like Thelema is problematic for the very reason that it is too large for any one interpretation/experience. It is too big for a person to grasp entirely. Perhaps all we are entitled to is a snapshot. Each snapshot being highly personal image and proportionate to ones relation to the entire thing. Each snapshot, then is its own sort of sect.

Every Thelemite must try to define it in his/her own terms in order to make it useful. This will lead to a greater understanding of what Thelemites are and what we are doing. It isn't necessary that all Thelemites agree, and calling people stupid for disagreeing with our point will never help us come to at least a fraction of the cohesion we need to make Thelema anything more than a fringe movement for eccentric, anti-social individuals. Thelema is definitely too large for that.

Whether or not it conflicts with Science is the thing that really sets Thelema apart from other religions. Not only must it not conflict with scientific facts, but if we call it a religion it must also provide possible solutions to the unknowable or lend itself toward explaining new phenomena which we cannot yet explain in scientific terms. These metaphysical explanations must in turn provide the direction for scientific scrutiny and discovery. Also, adherents of such a religion must be willing and able to adjust their own definition of the paradigm to accommodate recent scientific discovery (regardless of sectarianism). Otherwise Thelema will end up being little more than personality cult or superstition.

Call Thelema a religion, and the non-religious Thelemites who fear loosing some sort of status crawl out of the woodwork to protest. It is rather silly to think that something as benign as religion* would exclude those individuals that see it as something else. And in a way, they are quite correct in saying that Thelema is too big to be confined by religion. What we are seeing presently are groups of people with a mutual interpretation of Thelema and rites to celebrate those unique interpretations. In other words: Sectarianism.

Some Thelemites liken Thelema to Taoism for no other reason than most Westerners with a dislike for religion do not see it as one, and it might surprise those individuals to know that Taoism was and is indeed a religion that thrived from the second century until 1949. Perhaps the reason for so many people seeking Taoism as a form of spirituality devoid from religion is that its religious elements were removed as Communism spread over China, making ALL religion illegal, so its most recent expression has been devoid of any organized dogma.

Because of this vast interruption in popularity as a religion Taoism does not appear explicitly dogmatic like Islam or Christianity, and therefore many see it as a model to compare against our own Thelema, or wish to use it as a template for a Thelemic Priesthood.

Taoism coexists with Buddhism and Confucianism, and the three religions have mixed so greatly it is difficult to say which one inspired the other. Some Taoist rituals were borrowed from Buddhism, and vice-versa. Many Thelemites have seen how these philosophical paradigms influenced Crowley and how many of those elements flowed into Crowley's work. Those individuals seeking a greater understanding of Thelema have taken note of all this borrowing† and have undertaken the study of comparative religion, which proves an indispensable tool toward the understanding of our own Thelema. During ones studies it will become increasingly impossible to ignore just how much Crowley borrows from Taoism, Gnosticism, Christianity, Hinduism, Buddhism, and Islam and other less known religious paradigms. It is for this reason that part of the recommended work of the Squire is to study Liber AL and compare it to other religious texts. Crowley was a lot more pragmatic than most

---

*   As I define it.
†   This is something that brings many Thelemic fundamentalists who think Crowley came up with Thelema without any outside influence much grief.

Thelemic fundamentalists give him credit for. After all, a good idea is a good idea regardless of where it comes from.

In China, the practice of Taoism varies from province to province, even from village to village. There is no church to go to, no specific creed to follow. Because of this, Taoism encompasses a wide variety of beliefs and practices and there are many different Taoist sects. Among the varied interests encompassed by Taoism are alchemy, yoga, magic, meditation, and religious ritual. Also, discipline is the way to learn how to control spirits which cause sickness and suffering, come to the realization of one's immortality, and eventually to enter heaven. The Taoist priest shares these benefits with his community through the performance of public ritual and liturgy.

In other words, the practice of Taoism is a social celebration of one's beliefs, and as such qualifies as a religion complete with sectarianism. My apologies if you thought otherwise.

It follows that the same fate awaits Thelema, and sectarianism will occur,* as one would expect by observing what occurred with Taoism.

There are, in fact, three classes of Taoist, and curiously they correspond to the "three grades" mentioned in Liber AL. The layman, the priest, and the ascetic: The Man of Earth, The Lover, and The Hermit.†

The layman may include not only those people who believe specifically in Taoism, but also those who perform its rituals unthinkingly, for no other reason that it is part of their tradition and their history. Performing the rituals, however, does not make the layman a Priest. Nor should any Thelemite that performs Mass think of himself as a Priest.

The Taoist priest seems to share the same function as all other religions. He is a priest because he serves his community, and is available in times of need. They cure sickness, expel demons, perform rituals for the benefit of their congregation, officiate in marriages and funerals, and assist the congregation to live their lives in accordance with their chosen dogma by educating them.

There is an ascetic class that lives in the mountains, or somewhere far away from the distractions of others, and will contemplate his or

---

* It is evident that this has already occurred with the advent of various Thelemic religious Orders.

† Or, if you prefer, The Squire, The Knight, and The Peer degrees of OTK.

her religion in monasteries in the wilderness. This does not make the ascetic a priest because he has removed himself from a community. He serves only himself.

If one refrains from taking dogma and dress into account, and focuses primarily on function, a Taoist priest and the Catholic priest are virtually indistinguishable.

All this to say that Taoism is a religion: A religion that shares many elements with Thelema. And Crowley appeared to have thought so as well. By writing the Gnostic Catholic Mass as a celebratory rite of the OTO's 'central secret' he made Thelema a religion. He may have thought so long before he did this, as he so eloquently makes his point with this declaration he made regarding Liber AL:

> *Do what thou wilt shall be the whole of the Law! Refuse this, and fall under the curse of destiny. Divide will against itself, the result is impotence and strife, strife-in-vain. The Law condemns no man. Accept the Law, and everything is lawful. Refuse the Law, you put yourself beyond its pale. It is the Law that Jesus Christ, or rather the Gnostic tradition of which the Christian-legend is a degradation, attempted to teach; but nearly every word he said was misinterpreted and garbled by his enemies, particularly by those who called themselves his disciples. In any case the Aeon was not ready for a Law of Freedom. Of all his followers only St. Augustine appears to have got even a glimmer of what he meant.*
>
> *A further attempt to teach this law was made through Sir Edward Kelly at the end of the sixteenth century. The bondage of orthodoxy prevented his words from being heard, or understood. In many other ways has the spirit of truth striven with man, and partial shadows of this truth have been the greatest allies of science and philosophy. Only now has success been attained. A perfect vehicle was found, in the message enshrined in a jeweled casket; that is to say, in a book with the injunction "Change not as much as a style of a letter." This book is reproduced in facsimile, in order that there shall be no possibility of corrupting it. Here, then, we have an absolutely fixed and definite standpoint for the foundation of an universal religion.*
>
> *We have the Key to the resolution of all human problems, both philosophical and practical. If we have seemed to labor at proof, our love must be the excuse for our infirmity; for we know well that which is written in the Book: "Success is your proof."*

We ask no more than one witness; and we call upon Time to take an Oath, and testify to the Truth of our plea."—Chapter VIII - Genesis Libri Al - Equinox of The Gods – 1991, 93 Publishing

Once a group of people starts referring to a Holy Book as scripture, as Crowley indicates above, then you have a religion.

Further, in Magick Without Tears Crowley wrote, "To sum up, our system is a religion just so far as a religion means an enthusiastic putting-together of a series of doctrines, no one of which must in any way clash with Science or Magick."

Later, he clearly goes on to contradict himself in a letter to a student, where he states that calling Thelema a religion would "cause a great deal of misunderstanding, and work a rather stupid kind of mischief."

I believe that he was right on both counts: Thelema is some form of true Religion and religion certainly can lead to mischief. I posit that defining Thelema is, in itself, problematic because it must be individually defined. Like all people that are in a constant state of karmic evolution Crowley contradicted himself a lot. Either one has to dismiss all his handiwork as rubbish or one has to allow for a wide sort of opinions based on ALL of his work, and the work of the people he admired. What we COULD do without is the marginalization of individuals and/or organizations that see Thelema differently than whatever may be popular at the time.* When it is all said and done, we are all Thelemites after all. There should be enough Thelemic sectarianism that the need for any group to 'water down' their Thelema to make it palatable for everyone should never exist.

No one can argue that some remarkably stupid and cruel things have been done in the name of religion. But what of the hospitals, soup kitchens, foster homes, medical mission abroad, universities and the like that are also done in religion's name. A *real religion* must extend its benefit to outsiders if it is going to survive. Those adolescent, self-indulgent groups that only serve to benefit a few individuals while showing a complete disregard to social issues are simply posing and trying to impress themselves and their peers with what is little more than pseudo-mystical masturbation.

The idea of keeping Thelema hidden away from the 'profane' appeals to some people because of the air of mystery and secrecy that

* Pop-Thelema?

comes with such isolationism. This idea may sound rational as any other on the surface, but I don't see this as a compelling reason for not bringing Thelema to the largest number of people possible. In fact, keeping Thelema from people that can use it may be the greatest disservice to humanity we can make. Furthermore, the smaller the group, the less likely it is that it will draw in the sorts of individuals it needs the most. Thelema may not be ready for widespread distribution, but it never will unless we, its keepers, are willing to take it out of the darkness and bring it to the light where it belongs.

Speaking for myself, I tend to view his early comments to be the most valuable. It is obvious that Crowley allowed his unfortunate feelings about Christianity color his view of religion in general, and his early comments seem the most logical and informed, while in many of his later comments he appears, at least in my opinion, to have exercised creative license in his interpretations to justify his hatred for religion. Not that his hatred for Christian fundamentalism was unwarranted.

The religion of Thelema proposes the idea that physical existence begins with the interaction of two metaphysical principles. In the most prominent Thelemic Holy Book, The Book of The Law, these ideas are given form by association with the ancient Egyptian deities known as Nuit, the goddess of the night sky who represents unlimited possibility, and her lover Hadit, who represents the individual experience and is characterized as a Winged Serpent. The union of these two deities produces a phenomenon, which is identified with the Hawk Headed god: Ra-Hoor-Khuit, who represents the karmic law that dominates life. The Book of the Law is composed of three chapters dedicated to each of these three concepts which illustrate how they are to be worshiped.

In my opinion, one of the most significant characteristics of the Thelema is that these are, in many ways, the same archetypes which appear in various forms throughout all cultures and religious beliefs. It seems logical, then, that a Thelemic religion would indicate that all beliefs and religions are mirrors that reflect these metaphysical ideas to their adherents. Consequently, many Thelemites spend their lives seeking out these ideas by studying comparative religion.

The Law of Thelema hypothesizes the idea of a Personal Supreme Deity, which holds the reality constructs of each individual's spirituality, and reflects each individual's Gnosis. Thelemic doctrine encourages individuals to draw on a personal and recognizable experience with this God, which is individual to them, and which reflects their own True Purpose and Truth. The discovery of this Supreme Truth is referred to as "Knowing Ones True Will". It doesn't get anymore Gnostic than that!

This concept goes to further reinforce the idea that Thelemites should study the symbols of all religions and philosophies, since doing so will lead them to a greater understanding of one's self.

Should a Thelemite end up on a path that is not congenial with his or her True Nature there are consequences to face. One who subscribes to the Christian doctrine might equate this suffering with 'hell', or a separation from God.

Thelemic Practices

Whether alone or with peers, prayer, invocation and evocation, meditation, and comparative religion studies are all part of Thelemic religious practice. Each Thelemic Church has their own approach to the ritualization of their communal beliefs, but generally speaking there are Masses, the blessings of food, the adorations which correspond to the four stations of the sun, yoga, and the preparation for holy space.

Like many religions, Thelemic Churches, such as the Thelemic Gnostic Church of Alexandria celebrates many rights of passage, such as Baptism for Birth, Confirmation at puberty, Marriage, and finally, death. The birth, life and death of various Thelemic Saints are also celebrated, such as Francois Rabelais who was first to have coined the term 'Thelema' in conjunction with "Do as thou wouldst".

It is fair to say that presently there are various expressions of Thelema according to the temperament of the congregation and that these practices vary from group to group. Any religion whose holy book prohibits discussion and interpretation is subject to sectarianism in a big way.

And speaking of the prohibition of discussion:

We often receive letters from people complaining of the lack of clear-cut answers pertaining to Thelema. There are various reasons for this, one of which is a warning in Liber AL not to interpret the writings. Many people have taken this to mean that they shouldn't define beliefs or question assumptions. As one might imagine this makes it rather difficult for Thelemites to interact in social settings.

In its most basic form, a Thelemite is a person who adheres to the Law of Thelema, which like it or not,[*] is a philosophy first proposed by Catholic Priest and writer François Rabelais (1490 - 1553) in his literary works about a religious monk and a giant.

It basically states that people with good upbringing need little regulation since every action will be the right action; therefore he states that the only rule in his Abbey of Thelema will be "Do as thou wilt." Much of what he wrote was tongue-in-cheek criticism of some of the more ridiculous Catholic paradigms of his times.

---

[*]   And the "fundies" don't!

The idea that right action follows right thought is nothing new and is to be found at the heart of various Oriental philosophies.

Much later, Aleister Crowley* channeled a book called The Book of the Law in which it claimed: "The word of the Law is Thelema."

Thelema is a Greek word meaning 'will'. This is the 'divine will'. The Book of the Law states that "every man and every woman is a star" alluding to the divine purpose in every person. This purpose can be anything. When it is in accordance with the person's true nature, it is divine. Thelemites use these saying as greetings when they see one another, or in correspondence, beginning with "Do what thou wilt shall be the whole of the Law"

And ending with the second part of this law is: "Love is the law, love under will."

As might well be imagined, anything that can be interpreted as 'do what you want' usually is, and often times with dire results. Furthermore, it is easy to take the Book of the Law at face value. Without study and contemplation people are tempted to quote Thelemic Holy Books out of context in order to defend lack of responsibility or condone some of the greatest human vices, much to the detriment of everyone that happens to call themselves Thelemites.

The Order of Thelemic Knights espouses the idea that this Law invokes the greatest responsibility. We adhere to our own code of conduct and ethics which espouses the lofty concepts of soldiering. We study religion in order to come to a greater understanding of our own Thelema because we have observed that all religions are like links on a chain connecting us to our beginnings.

---

* Don't believe everything you read about him. He is the Prophet and his writings should be consulted often. Don't let the "Crowley experts" turn you off to Thelema.

Why Does Religion get such a Bad Rap?

If we accept that there is neither a heaven nor a hell, we renounce the idea of any power beyond the perception of science we then must accept responsibility for all we do in this life for there will be no form of atonement afterwards.

—Dominic Webb

It all begins with how one interprets religion. Again, I prefer to view religion as the celebration of the Spirit that is shared with people of mutual mind and agreed upon mission or paradigm. As I have said elsewhere, it can be an organized assault against the forces of the Demiurge. Generally speaking, many Westerners blow off religion saying that it represents one person's vision and for that reason it cannot be spiritually liberating. Often times this comes from the negative press that Christianity has received as a result of its corruption, or how we are forced into compliance with rules and law espoused by religious ideals that we do not subscribe to. In our own Thelemic communities the distaste for religion may also exist as a result of bad experiences with Thelemic clergy, or a misunderstanding by our clergy as to what their functions are. This is certainly is not the fault of religion, or all organized religion in general.

What does it mean to be religious? A religious person is an individual that sees value in fellowship and the communal celebration of ones spiritual ideals. Often times, one may feel that he or she can attain the price of enlightenment faster with a mentor, group of mentors or peers.

So what is 'God'? Who knows? I do know that arguing for the reality of "god" is just as fruitless as arguing against it. Crowley has said some very profound things about it, however, in a letter to a student:

If you tell me that an individual created the world, and placed men upon it with the seeds of evil in them, I cannot call that individual God, so long as I include the idea of Good in my connotation of God... if you wish to make your idea of God nobler, the way you do it is to make your mind nobler, and in particular to cultivate that noblest part of which you call God.

—*Crowley 1991*

This profound sentiment speaks volumes of the work laid out for Gnostic Thelemites.

There is no question that religion has done more to discredit the idea of 'God' than any other thing. Generally speaking, people are just plain mad at God* for the senseless suffering that has been caused in the name of religion. Obviously, religion is the conception of man. So how does one know if the priesthood represented by a church is walking the talk? A real priest or priestess is always mindful that they serve (and therefore represent, to some extent) the deity particular to the religious paradigm they follow. If someone behaves in a way which does not become that deity, then you can rest assured that they are clergy in word only. Look elsewhere.

Priests are teachers, consolers, counselors, and with any luck they have some understanding of the frailties of being human. If one is really fortunate, they may get clergy that has bothered to study the paradigm they claim to follow so that when a person in need approaches them they are able to communicate things that a person can put to use to improve their condition. A Jewish rabbi would not be much good trying to administer to a dying Catholic because the paradigm is different. Questioning the purpose of clergy is like questioning using intermediaries at all, such as psychologists and psychiatrists. It is the same thing, except for the priest deals with deeper, more personal issues.

Why bother with Clergy in the first place? When one is rebuilding a car it may be wise to ask the advice of a mechanic first. The area of spirituality is dangerously close to that of psychology. This is why I object to just anyone considering oneself clergy simply because they do something as mechanical as performing Mass. A priest is much more than that...or should be: because if we really believe that "there is no god but man" then clearly, the role of Thelemic clergy is to be a servant of the people.

Why couldn't some enlightened individual fulfill the role of clergy? I would hope, perhaps naively, that terms like 'enlightened individual' and 'priest' would be synonymous. At least that is our goal with our own clergy. An enlightened individual could (and they often do) fulfill that function: no question about that. But they are neither obligated nor checked against indiscretion. Let us examine the root of the word 'religion' which is 'religio' (Latin). Religio

* Usually the Christian one.

means 'to regulate' or 'regulated'. Clergy is 'regulated' by the paradigm of the Church which represents; his or her own deity; and the ideals of Church's congregants.

"But only the individual may take the journey!" or "The evolution of an individual's soul is not something that could occur under social pressure!" Sayeth the atheist. I find it curious that atheists should make references to words like 'soul' to support their arguments against religion. Perhaps we need an agreed upon definition for terms like 'soul' so that we might gain a greater understanding. Religion posits that a person's soul finds its place among its peers.

Clergy can be a mirror for the aspirant. If any initiation is to occur at all it because the aspirant allows it to occur in the first place. The priest or priestess just makes it easier by providing the appropriate information, celebration or by constantly exposing the congregant to the symbols he or she has adopted. Often times, initiation may take place when a priest or priestess asks the right question at the right time. But all of this requires training.

Fundamentalism gives religion a bad rap. Fundamentalism is a dangerous, sometimes fatal cocktail composed of a paradigm with a twist of tyranny and a splash of fanaticism. Initiation is a two way street. An enlightened creature will listen to opposing views and test his own beliefs in the light of conflicting paradigms. Consider this: nowhere in the bible does Jesus say that people should be slaves. He came to free people from the Pharisees and Rome. The people were told that they should do the same work that he has done. When he says that he is he only way to the Father® he is speaking of having attained to a station know as Tiphareth. With a little help from the Council of Nicaea, people today take that to mean that they should worship Jesus. This is an aberration of Jesus' teachings, but they are not Jesus' teachings.

Personality cults are not religions. They may try to pass themselves off as one, however. It is okay for a person to come up with a method to attainment. It is not okay to forget the message, ignore the work and worship the person. Consider other points of view from people who adhere to the same paradigm as the founder. Crowleyanity hurts the practice of Thelema as a philosophy, religion and way of life. Consider the Crowley's own thoughts on the matter:

I admit that my visions can never mean to other men as much as they do to me. I do not regret this. All I ask is that my results should convince seekers after truth that there is beyond doubt something worth while seeking, attainable by methods more or less like mine. I do not want to father a flock, to be the fetish of fools and fanatics, or the founder of a faith whose followers are content to echo my opinions. I want each man to cut his own way through the jungle. (Crowley, 1989)

Why do clergy get a bad rap? Perhaps it is because as a culture Westerners have no real tradition of their own. Maybe we don't respect our Holy Men and Women because we have learned to associate them with shysters, phonies, quacks, and posers. Maybe we ignore them and discredit them because they remind us of our own insincerity and laziness toward our spiritual salvation. Or perhaps we disregard them because we measure them against some unreal figment of the mythological Jesus? Possibly, it is because our recent memory of 'religion' or 'clergy' is marred by a group of very loud people who think that being a priest means being in control of people's lives?

Christians don't think they can be like Jesus because he was God and we're not. This reduces their religion to servile worship.

Thelemites should take a lesson from this.

A word of warning: Magick is hard. The Ministry is even harder because it deals with others. It takes effort most people aren't willing to put into it...but humans do like the titles that come along with the achievements: so much that they often covet them without having attained the achievement. In a way, I am surprised anyone wants to be a holy person at all. The only saving grace is that it really doesn't matter what anyone thinks or does...what is important is what we do.

Conscience and the Function of Guilt

*The sun is arisen; the spectre of the ages has been put to flight. "The word of Sin is Restriction," or as it has been otherwise said on this text: That is Sin, to hold thine holy spirit in! Go on, go on in thy might; and let no man make thee afraid.**

It is not easy to deduct the duties and rights of a priest in any way which is applicable to all cases. In most cases where we see an or-

* Aleister Crowley, Liber 837: The Law of Liberty.

ganized priesthood, the clergy is invested with *powers* rather than with *rights*. They are only given the authority to the exercise of these powers, such as the celebration of Mass, teaching, administering the other sacraments including the absolution of sins.

I will be using some language which may make some of you uneasy. If you are insulted by my use of certain Christian terms, rest assured that I am doing so because these terms have universal usage in the field of religion in general and they still describe certain phenomena more accurately than any other word. If one wants to be a student of religion one will have to get over whatever prejudices they might hold for specific sects. That is the only way to get an unbiased view of the heart of the paradigm. Furthermore, Gnosticism is so deeply rooted in mystical Christianity that we would do well by realizing that Thelema is just another link in a long chain of links, and that without Christianity we could not possibly have Thelema. I hope to use these words until you are sick of hearing them, and thus desensitize you to the boogieman in order to make it possible for you to contemporize those terms into your own modern practices without your having to reinvent the wheel, as it were.

Religio—from whence the word 'religion' originates, means "to be regulated" or "to regulate." It is to comply with the rules and regulations of the Church and its religious paradigm. Here we see that a Priest is a person who has agreed to be regulated by the church's dogma, and in return for the regularity, the church gives its clergy the right to exercise certain powers. A priest is religious.

As educators, priests provide instruction on the universal application of their Holy Books. Very few people I have met realize the awesome responsibility this is. Very few understand the practical application of their beliefs, and even fewer are capable of communicating these to one's congregation. If a stranger without any knowledge of Rabelais, Crowley, occult history or magico-religious archetypes were to approach you on the street to ask you what Thelema was, would you be able to describe it to them in a fifteen minutes conversation? If you manage to give that person an accurate description of our philosophy, could you answer questions about the history of your church? In these questions lies the template for a curriculum of religious studies with the emphasis on Thelemic Gnosticism.

A priest should be able to discern reality in the light of his or her paradigm that will, by necessity, be in harmony with his or her Holy Books. Teaching history and the spiritual explanation of reality are all duties for Priests, or elders as they were once called.

In the Christian churches (and this is to include many Gnostic ones as well), Priests deal with the absolution of sins. A word about sin: "It is said that we *are not punished for them, but by them.*" I wish I could remember where I read that.

Trying to deaden guilt or quiet the voice of one's conscience seems a very popular activity with Thelemites. We also succumb to our own flavor of peer pressure as we look to be the best Thelemites we can be. We naturally take our cues from our peers and from people we respect.

The entirety of an individual involves the conscience. It is a voice of reason, and the little Jiminy Cricket inside of all of us, and it does us very little good to squash the little green guy. For example: when you are going against your own true nature, you may hear this voice warning you against some action you might later regret, and oftentimes when we do those things we may indeed feel bad. Those feelings can come in the form of jealousy, feelings of inferiority, fear, codependency, and a loss of control in general, but how will we know if our first impulse is to silence them? By not analyzing these feelings to see if they hold any value we may be silencing the very voice that is trying to instruct us. We spend so much time calling it out and asking it for its guidance in ritual, Mass, meditation and, other magical techniques, but when it warns us that we are moving away from our core, we silence it, because somehow, somewhere we walked away thinking that a Thelemite who experiences guilt is no Thelemite. Perhaps guilt is what keeps us from doing the same mistake over and over again. Perhaps conscience is what tries to prevent the mistake in the first place.

Guilt, and sinning against one's self are all part of the course of discovering our True Will. It is important not to repeat mistakes. It is important to know where guilt comes from, as it can help us to understand ourselves better.

I have identified and categorized some popular sins for convenience, and regardless of which category they fall into, all feelings of guilt should be examined. Please note that I am using the word 'sin' here for effect and to help put many of our own phobias and badly formed ideas into perspective.

First, we have **religious sin**. This little creature is tenacious and often manifests as a result of some perfectly good dogma or social code that did wonderful things to advance the state of civilization... thousands of years ago. Here we see laws against eating pork, masturbation, homosexuality and anything else which did not result in making babies.* Tradition can be a problem when it can no longer be applied to current needs or events.

The second sin is strictly social and varies from one peer group to another. **Local sins**, such as guilt for not coming to Mass as often as people would like you to, are social sins. Or perhaps you are trying to do something perfectly natural for yourself within a social circle that frowns on whatever particular activity you are interested in. Whatever the case may be, these occurrences can also lead to feelings of guilt or shame. Everyone likes to be liked, and everyone likes to fit in.

The third, and in my opinion, the only sin worth indulging are **the sins we make against ourselves**. Turning one's back on the truth is spelled out for us in *Liber Librae*. Anytime we go against our own inner nature we feel badly...eventually...sometime. Pretending that someone doesn't have these feelings, or trying to oppress them can lead to a psychosis or worse. Surely, there are various examples you could come up with for this, so I won't bother you with details of my own observations.

So what does this have to do with priesthood? In Christianity, one of the functions of a priest is to act like an attorney for those poor souls that are afflicted by their sins. So how does this apply to us? We are neither psychologists nor mediators for the gods. But by simply knowing our religious paradigms well, we may be able to provide a release for those feelings when they paralyze the individual. Priests heal. We relieve suffering. The development of ethics will therefore be a necessary part of our studies.

Egregore, Atheism, Deism and Agnosia
Both the Atheist and Deist have their reasons for being as they are. Many of those reasons are perfectly reasonable and even logical. The Atheist believes it is impossible to prove the existence of God, and so therefore he must no exist. The Deist believes that being unable to prove something does not negate its existence: There is

* Read: Laborers.

212 The Ethics of Thelema

air, and it keeps us alive even though we are unable to see it. The scope of this manuscript is not to consider such philosophical conundrums, but to explore the issue of sincerity, fear, and ignorance.

We have observed and are surprised to learn that in many cases the atheist and deist hold God's love with such high regard that they feel threatened by the idea that He, She, or It might favor someone other than themselves. So intense is this fear that people have murdered other people for being the unfortunate recipient of Divine Wisdom or attention. You see, it is okay to pray because anyone can talk to God. But to have God speak back to the in the old days meant that one was a blasphemer or deluded heretic having been deceived by no one other than 'The Devil'.

The root of this problem appears to be jealousy. "Why doesn't God speak to me? Aren't I good enough? If God speaks to her or him, but wont speak to me, it must surely mean he or she is better and more worthy than me."

It is said* that Jesus was crucified for saying that he was the son of God; Mansur Al Hallaj, the Sufi poet was disemboweled for saying that God had spoken to him while he gazed at his own reflection in a mirror; Joan of Arc and countless others have died at the stake for having the great misfortune of hearing God's voice.† Today, society can no longer rid itself of these exceptional people by killing them. Instead they are ridiculed, medicated and locked up where they can no longer remind people of their own spiritual shortcomings.

The message is clear. People like to think of themselves as worthy, but only on the most superficial level and those that take their spirituality seriously threaten them.

Many atheists deal with these inadequacies by simply refusing to acknowledge the existence of something that he or she cannot conceive. Many deist deals with it by shunning or ridiculing anyone that appears to have succeeded spiritually.

The Gnostics called themselves "the perfected." The result was that others who wished the title wiped them out. Today we live in a godless society. Talk to God and you are praying. God talks back and you are psychologically challenged.

It is better not to hold an opinion at all, really. An agnostic can be ignorant of God, while the atheist refuses to accept the possibility of

---

* Wrongly.

† Or being on the wrong political side.

God's existence, thereby closing himself to the experience we refer to as Gnosis. Therefore, Agnosia is preferable to atheism.

Egregore: A kind of group mind created when people consciously or unconsciously come together for a common purpose. They are usually much more powerful when intentionally created and nurtured. Usually used in religious or magical context, egregores can be found anywhere that people come together for a common goal, such as a marriage, musical band, group of computer programmers, etc...Its efficiency is greater than the sum of its creators: it is the heart of the group, continuously engaging members which results in mutual evolution provided that members stay true to the mission for which they came together in the first place. It is capable of working independently to accomplish the group's goals. A properly prepared egregore becomes stronger through use and it can survive long past the existence of its creators. If members betray their egregore, it will leave the group. Really good ones can even lie around for centuries waiting for someone to stumble into it by way of some esoteric activity such as ritual. The members of such a group would inherit the esoteric wisdom of the group which originally created the egregore. An example would be the various Templar Orders which exist in modern times: they claim a lineage to the tradition via congress with the egregore of the original Grand Masters.

All initiatory institutions have a particular egregore whose survival demands certain things. In modern times Gnosticism has been confused with a lack of structure, rather than a spiritual experience. It is therefore often wrongly used as a reason to argue against canonization of any kind.

Religion and Community Building
Community is summed up in the dictionary as:
1. A group of people living in the same locality and under the same government.
2. The district or locality in which such a group lives.
3. A group of people having common interests.
4. A group viewed as forming a distinct segment of society.
5. Similarity or identity: a community of interests.
6. Sharing, participation, and fellowship.

One of the benefits of religion is that it provides community, which wouldn't be so important were real communities not so rare these days. Many of today's young people have no idea what a community really is, thanks to the overuse and abuse of the word in our day. Next to Brother, the word 'community' is the most abused word in our own incestuous society.

So what happened to community? People have become specialized by the very 'scientific' and industrial thinking that breaks down the universe into separate parts. Science has become a profitable tool for industry and capitalism demanded the use of resources for the sake of a few. This means that the communal unit had to be broken up to free up land and other resources owned by groups of individuals so that business interests could divide it amongst itself. We no longer have any ties to land or to our own survival,* but must rely on strangers to provide us with the necessary tools (jobs and education) to survive on our own—as individuals.

Nowhere is this plainer than in the United States, where its citizens fell hook, line and sinker for the idea of rugged 'individualism' which began as a call to responsibility during the depression, and later was converted into the cult of the individual. This lie that one person is an island to himself or herself, turned to be a perfect tool to divide people thereby weakening their position in society. Ironically, Americans only give lip service to this new philosophy of 'individualism' and are obviously predisposed to accepting something simply because it is popular. It is seen in advertising:

Be Original: Drink Dr. Pepper.

'Rugged Individualism' was a very popular idea…and still is, especially with Thelemites. This provides many of us with the necessary excuse to justify refraining from community building while dodging any appearance of laziness. To paraphrase a biblical proverb: God unites, the Devil divides. I do not think that Thelema's view of individualism is meant to divide.

Another example of this brand of this so-falsely called 'individu-

---

* Most "modern people" couldn't grow tomatoes in March, much less care for cattle. Landownership in the US is a sham evident by the taxes one must pay and pay and pay for the privilege of putting a fence around it. Everybody gets their pockets lined: No one appears to have the time or inclination to do anything about it.

alism' is the way our children have been taught that what they get out of life is entirely up to them. They have been told this because corporate interests generally abhor the idea that they should have to give something back to the people who help to grease the wheels. Government and corporate interests* do not want to be responsible to people. They only want to use them.

Community has given way to brutal competition, as every man and woman tries as hard as they can to get their 'piece of the pie', 'don't get involved' and 'look out for number one'. All of it is designed to get as much out of people in terms of labor and consumerism while having the added effect of preventing individuals from organizing. Solidarity is a barrier to the idea that corporate interests should be free to imposing their values on society. By promoting gratuitous individualism they are able to break bonds between people.

This flavor of American Capitalism is beginning to spread abroad as countries with no way to compete in the 'global economy' buckle under pressure to adopt the same draconian business practices that have become so common place here.

The answer is community. Religion provides the platform upon which individuals seeking a better life can come together to build a better life for themselves and help each other to accomplish a much more rewarding and rich lifestyle that they could on their own.

What Are Some of the Elements of a Successful Community?

1. **Spiritual Unity**—Every member of the community must feel a sense of duty and unity with other members. Each member sees himself as a necessary component, responsible for the health of viability of the greater whole. Constituents benefit by their participation within the community and the community benefits from each member's participation.

2. **Guardianship**—Provided that a person contributes to the greater good of the community there should be no discrimination. Members of the community should give one another the benefit of the doubt when there are suspicions of wrongdoing.

---

* Same thing.

3. **Honesty**—Everyone should be open to discussing issues, and if issues cannot be solved in a fraternal manner, then the entire community should avail itself of every resource to bring a resolution to problems. If there is one thing I have learned is that it isn't enough to ignore problems and require people to 'play nice'. A complete resolution is easy to secure when all parties are equally invested in the well being of the community.

4. **Compassion and Empathy**—Share what you have with others. Sharing diminishes narcissistic conduct. To eat while others go without, for example, communicates that one is not a part of the community.

5. **Old Goats**—They are the ones that hold the mysteries together and feed the egregore. It is because of their sacrifice that the community exists to begin with. Those that came before you are the pillars of the community and when they pass on from this life they will be part of the collective memory of the community. Therefore, they must always be remembered if the community is expected to survive beyond their physical death.

Some Things to Think About With Regards to Seeking Holy Orders

Religion helps to bring out what is best in man, but owing to the lack of knowledge of those who practice it and teach it, society has formed a negative opinion and it is presently far behind all the other arts.

A large percentage of the cause can be attributed to a lack of training, and the fact that in many Thelemic institutions one can be made a priest or priestess simply by raising ones hand. Much of the Thelemic clergy of today may dress and conduct themselves as clergy and even perform Mass, but for the most part they are little more than actors with a desire to be the center of attention. In reality, there are very few Thelemites that have the education, or bother to seek it in order to serve as true priests and priestesses.

The best clergy is made up of those rare individuals who have a "calling' for it, who seem to be naturally disposed to the service of their Church, and who are willing to study and work hard to be able to perform duties which are most aligned with their true nature. If one does indeed love the Church they would be best advised to look deep for the reasons that one wishes to join the ranks of the Priesthood, for if it is not an element of ones true nature their participation will serve to further degrade the idea of a Thelemic Clergy rather than fortifying it.

When learning comparative religion, one must put aside their personal biases in order to understand the importance of the paradigm. One does not need to be a Christian to understand the importance of Christ and the resurrection, nor is it required to be a Buddhist to appreciate the message of Siddhartha, but if one approaches the paradigm with contempt it will be impossible to appreciate why those things are important to its adherents, which makes for a lousy priest.

Sacred things are to be imparted only to sacred persons. It is a disrespectful, irreverent and sacrilegious to impart them unto the profane. When studying and learning from your teachers remember that you don't know everything, and that some times the germ planted in a student may take time to flourish. There is a huge difference between knowledge and opinion. The former leads to mastery, while the later will only result in ignorance.

On the Importance of Studying
Liber AL VEL LEGIS: The Book of the Law

It is little wonder that there have been so few comments on this work.

I: 36. *My scribe Ankh-af-na-khonsu, the priest of the princes, shall not in one letter change this book; but lest there be folly, he shall comment thereupon by the wisdom of Ra-Hoor-Khuit.*

This seems pretty clear, and yet Crowley changed and modified the text in various places. The original is heavily marked, complete sentences have been crossed out and new ones written over the old. Seems Crowley couldn't follow his own advice. This is one of his trademarks; it will appear, for in Chapter II paragraph 76 he is told:

4 6 3 8 A B K 2 4 A L G M O R 3 Y X 24 89 R P S T O V A L. What meaneth this, o prophet? Thou knowest not; nor shalt thou know ever. There cometh one to follow thee: he shall expound it... "

Anyone who has ever seen the original manuscript will clearly see that he did in fact try to solve the mystery. The page is marked up with a grid and a series of letters. Like most inquisitive creatures, he did try, but died without solving it as predicted in the text.

Chapter III paragraph 63 states: "The fool readeth this Book of the Law, and its comment; & he understandeth it not."

Who is the fool? Is it Crowley? Or is it every reader? It is important to determine who is being addressed in the text. Various references in the book are obviously commands made to Crowley himself, while others appear to have a more universal message.

Again in Chapter II, paragraph 40: "But the work of the comment? That is easy; and Hadit burning in thy heart shall make swift and secure thy pen."

Hadit makes it easy. So how is Hadit being used in the text? As a reference to ones Holy Guardian Angel? Is Aiwass speaking exclusively to Crowley, or to the reader?

And then we have the comment itself, which states:

The study of this Book is forbidden. It is wise to destroy this copy after the first reading. Whosoever disregards this does so at his own risk and peril. These are most dire. Those who discuss the contents of this Book are to be shunned by all, as centres of pestilence. All questions of the Law are to be decided only by appeal to my writings, each for himself.

'The Comment' came about in a way that most people could not even imagine. One of Crowley's students, Morman Mudd fell in love with Leah Hirsig* and wished to marry her. He argued that Liber AL describes "The Scarlet Woman" as an adulteress. This, he reasoned, means that she must be married. Norman, being the devoted student that he was, insisted that Crowley allow him to marry her so that she could cheat with Crowley and better fit the description in Liber AL. Crowley would have none of that, and eventually became so fed up with him that he wrote the infamous short comment just to shut him up. We've been stuck with it since then.

So the bigger question is not whether or not individuals should study and interpret this text, each according to their own level understanding. It is whether or not do that there can, or should be any agreed upon dogma based on the discoveries of such study. My hunch is that sectarianism is unavoidable, and that the day will come when those people who have everything to loose from an interpretation of Thelema that is honorable and proud will engage in battles of sorts with those of us that embrace those concepts. We all want a Thelemic world, and Thelema can manifest in one of two ways: think about it.

With all of the warnings in the Book, it is no wonder it has never been popular to engage in discussion. In fact, I have seen various interpretations of some of the more difficult passages, and in most cases these well meaning folks have been the subjects of much ridicule. Many so-called Thelemites love to throw stones, and some take refuge in the knowledge that the Master is dead and unable to interpret the Law they abuse. They hate it when someone reminds them that there are other interpretations which indicate that doing one's Will is a tremendous responsibility. They perpetuated he myth that only Crowley is entitled to speak of Thelema. This has given way to what I call the "Gerber Syndrome".

Abu Musa Jabir Ibn Hayyan, or Gerber, as the Europeans knew

---

* Who happened to be Crowley's Scarlet Woman at the time.

him, was an Arabian Alchemist who lived in what is now considered Iraq around 721 A.D. He made many advances in science, and was so well respected by his contemporaries that no one would publish any work which was not his. If Gerber didn't say it, it wasn't worth publishing: regardless of its importance. As a result, people abandoned the work, and at least on one occasion, some of the most important alchemical works were discovered and written by others under his name. One such writer became know as "The False Geber". His real name is unknown. He wrote under the Pseudonym "Geber," to gain respect for his own experiments and to assure the publication of his works at a time when book publishing was a difficult and expensive task that only the wealthy and well known could afford. He is believed to have been a Spaniard, and ironically, the originator of the most significant discovery of the Middle Ages: sulfuric acid.

We may one day see many 'newly found manuscripts' by Crowley yet. And like Hubbard, he may be one of those rare individuals who publishes more writing when dead than when alive.

When it comes to Liber AL, however, I don't think it should be interpreted for the masses. In fact, the comment reveals how we should approach the study of this book: "...each for himself." And this is the premise on which this entire recommended practice is based. I can testify to the benefit that I have personally received from studying this book and comparing it against other 'received' texts.

On the one hand, it seems to me our duty to unravel the mystery, at least for ourselves individually, since that is the only way that we can determine whether or not we are acting in accordance with the Law. On the other hand, Liber AL may be something of a time capsule, which will not surrender its contents until a predetermined time has arrived.

It is important to consider all of the facts about the book if we expect it to surrender its Truth, or a reflection of that Truth which belongs to each of us individually. I have often showed my displeasure with the meager myth building that takes place by the adherents of Thelema. We can in fact attribute at least a part of this deficit to the warning against interpretation. The other part, I suspect, has to do with a lack of interest. The one place where we can benefit from this vacuum of dogma is in the history of the Book itself. Some myths have started to become accepted within the Thelemic community, and much of this was instigated by Crowley himself. But let's attempt to use the method of science, at least at first, and stick to the historical facts that we know about this Book.

1. The book was 'dictated' on April 8, 9, and 10, 1904.
2. The text was a result of some magical work initiated by Crowley and his wife Rose Kelly.
3. Crowley was in Egypt at the time, and his consciousness was flooded with Egyptian and archetypes.
4. Crowley was a practicing Buddhist at the time he received the text.
5. Crowley despised the work when first received. He was repulsed by it, and would put it away forgetting it for many years.
6. The text has been heavily edited.
7. Some of the content in the printed text does not match what is written in the original writings. (Looks more like a squashed bug than a Tzaddy).

Like all holy books, *Liber AL* is littered with apparent contradiction, leaving the devotee to reconcile the instruction into a working paradigm. In the Old Testament we are told that God is loving, and then we see him playing fun and games with the Devil at the expense of his devout worshiper Lot. Similarly, in one part of *Liber AL* we are told that "Love is the Law," while in another we are to "stamp down the wretched & the weak." On one place "the Law is for all" while in another, we are the "chosen ones." It is amazing how many Thelemites are able to accept such contradictions without any further thought into the matter.[*] This lack of interest may be the root of all of the problems inherent in most Thelemic social experiments. The Law is either Love, or we trample down the weak. How we reconcile those two seemingly opposing ideas is important. Furthermore, I am sure that you have seen many for whom "Do what thou Wilt" means "do what you want", which does nothing but to devalue the importance of the Book to others that may have seen a spark of truth in it.

The Book of the Law contains a mystery. According to the text itself,

---

[*]   "Crowley said it, I believe it, that settles it."

one of its mysteries can be fully known. Others cannot. And yet the most benefit comes from the constant application of trying to solve the puzzle. Crowley himself knew this, and tried even though the text appeared to speak to him directly: "What meaneth this, o prophet? Thou knowest not; nor shalt thou know ever. There cometh one to follow thee: he shall expound it…"

A good place to begin trying to unravel the mystery is in the study of the Egyptian deities mentioned in the text. For example, 'Hadit'appears to be a mistransliteration of the name Hor Behedety (Horus of Behdet). He represents the omnipresence of Horus The Elder (Haroeris), who was adored in lower Egypt and is portrayed as a soldier deity and enemy of Set, shown in the familiar winged solar disk, usually seen topping important scenes in Egyptian art.

If this is correct, then what is the relationship between this Hor Behedety, Nuit and Ra-Hoor-Khuit? And most important, if Hadit is what defines the soul, or the spark of light inside all men and women, then perhaps by studying the relationship between Horus of Behdet and Set will help us to discover something unknown about ourselves? There are many ways that one could go. But the main thing that this illustrates is that no matter how 'received' one believes this book to be, it is clear that it was filtered through Crowley's symbol set, and this brings me to the next problem with Thelema: Crowleyism. I am sure that you know at least one Thelemite that thinks it is okay to be addicted to drugs, break oaths, or to spend other people's money just because Crowley did. This is a classic example of the dangers of confusing the Message with the messenger.

If you decide to do, as the Squires of Our Order are instructed you might find yourself with a greater understanding of this remarkable Book. It is very simple:

1. Get an electronic copy of Liber AL.
2. Copy it to your hard drive where you can edit it using your preferred text editor.
3. Divide those paragraphs to make room for your thoughts below each one.

It is that simple. This work will never end; if one is truly vested in the understanding of this text one could easily spend their entire life studying it. Remember that you are free to use meditation, contemplation, prayer and/or ritual to get your answers. I have often employed the use of some spirit to have certain passages explained. And here is the best advice that I can give you in this quest: study other religions. If you do this, as you study Liber AL, you will find some things in common which cannot be ignored.

Liber AL and the other Thelemic Holy Books show Crowley's unique arrangement of the same symbols used throughout the ages. One would do well to study medieval magic, mysticism, philosophy and religion so that they can possess the necessary tools to blend various elements of mystical and magical viewpoints in a way that is in accord with ones own nature as he did. This, to me, is what being Thelemic is all about.

In its short 100 years, the book has been interpreted, used, and abused by individuals in a manner inconsistent with its apparent message, and have applied its message to control others, rather than to liberate them. But there is a price to be paid for such a trespass:

There is great danger in me; for who doth not understand these runes shall make a great miss. He shall fall down into the pit called Because, and there he shall perish with the dogs of Reason. AL II:27

All interpretative work must begin with a predetermined set of presumptions: mine has always been that the *Liber AL* holds an lucid message, and that Law of Thelema contains within it the key to the survival of the human species; a noble warrior code; and the potential for numerous religious expressions for those few individuals that wish to celebrate their freedom, the joy of existence and solemnize the responsibility they have accepted for their own existence.

If I were asked to sum up the Book in a few lines, I would say that Chapter 1 appears to me to be a manifestation of the 'big picture'. A puzzle so large and magnificent that we are unable to grasps its magnificence. Chapter 2 looks as if it is showing us a piece of that puzzle so that we can see what one looks like, while being told that each and every one of us is a piece of that grand puzzle. Chapter 3 describes the inertia: The force and chaos that are generated as the living pieces of the puzzle struggle to find their own place.

What a magnificent Book.

The Padre Gal McLeod

I first encountered the good Padre on one of those BBS systems that was so instrumental in the tremendous interest in the occult which occurred during the 80's just as the internet made owner-operated networks obsolete. Nothing he had to say to me made me happy. In fact, I found much of his criticism toward Thelemites to be deliberately insulting. In one of our many online conversations I accused him of being the most anti-Thelemic person I had ever met, and pointed out that he didn't appear to like anything about Thelema, to which he replied that I was being typically Thelemic for shooting the messenger. "My criticism," he said, "is directed toward Thelemites, not Thelema. There is a huge difference, and this is part of the problem." A couple of days later he said it again, as if he wanted to make sure that I got the point which appeared to be so important to him: "My problem isn't with Thelema at all. I think Thelema is beautiful. My problem is with the so-called Thelemites."

Normally I would have simply blown a person like this off, but I continued the dialogue mainly because of his knowledge of things magical, and because I wondered how anyone could go back to Catholicism after having tasted the freedom afforded in Thelema, much less becoming a Catholic Priest. He was a walking, talking contradiction, but he had a lot of interesting things to say. To this day I have yet to meet a person so adept at the Enochian system and Goetia. He agreed to meet with me in person at the Mission San Diego de Alcalá to hand me the notes that follow below. One of the things that struck me the most about him was how hard he tried to make me feel comfortable. He was about 6 feet tall, weighed about 150 pounds and had the sort of bodyguard build that most people find intimidating, and he knew it. He was a perfect gentleman and a true Thelemic thinker. I often wonder where he is now; if he still walks amongst the living, or if ever really succeeded in embedding a piece of Thelema into his own, personal spiritual practices. The following are verbatim transcript of his notes:

Often times, the question we ask other individuals cannot be answered in any other form than by example, and this is particularly true when dealing with spiritual paradoxes. At first glance this may seem like an inadequate form of communication, but I am now tempted to repeat the familiar cliché:

"A picture is worth a thousand words."

We may look to the Thelemic Holy Book for advice only to find that *The Book of The Law (Liber AL vel Legis)* prohibits its interpretation.

You may believe that it is as easy as asking the average Thelemite what they think, believe and feel only to discover the ideological bankruptcy of a large majority of the Thelemic community. There is no common opinion pertaining to right action, no mythological cohesion. Without this, the Thelemic movement can never accomplish anything of lasting value. What little ideology may be contributed by younger Thelemites sounds much like social Darwinism and is one step away from emulating the skinhead philosophy. Many of the so-called "Intellectual" Thelemic factions are so far off the mark that the spiritual pre-pubescence is plainly visible.

Aleister Crowley believed Thelema to be a powerful religious-political philosophy based on the True Will of the individual. He himself made no efforts to hide his convictions or his ethical values, and yet Thelemic writers and teachers don't generally contribute anything new and generally leave their readers and students groping in the dark.

If one dares to illustrate the societal or communal impact of The Law of Thelema one is more often than not perceived as some sort of new aeon heretic. Say that Thelema might have been called something else were it not for Rabelais, and you are a "Rabelaisian Thelemite" that cannot stomach their version Law of Thelema or their limited interpretation. Disagree with their biased pseudo-scientific research, and you are an "anti-intellectual" that obviously hasn't read "The Dangers of Mysticism." Thelemites without honor have lashed out at writers who have spoken of Thelemic spiritual ideology. Lazy Thelemites have verbally battered authors who have implied the political implications of Thelema and the awesome social responsibility being a Thelemite entails. And yet when an interested party asks the Thelemic experts the simple question: What is Thelema? or What is a Thelemite? no one can adequately answer his or her question. For all of that intellectual superiority not a one can offer any clue to the simplest questions. In fact, one is usually conveniently directed to one of Crowley's essays. No one wants to think about this...much less voice an opinion which might not be well received by ones peers.

I am most interested in how Thelema has manifested in the religious and political Will of active Thelemites. Regrettably, Crowley is dead, and we cannot ask him how Thelema applies to today's world. I have found very few individuals that want to explore the subject in an intelligent manner and uncover its beauty. I am interested in the spiritual, magical, and philosophi-

cal impact of Thelema upon the world. I don't care about sex magick, collecting books, or conjuring Chthulu. I am too old to think of Thelema as a way to freak out my parents or use rituals to impress my friends.

I realize that these notes will never be published because when it comes to Thelema, there are no publishers interested in anything honest, truthful, or controversial. For the most part, the publishing of occult books has hit rock bottom. Thelemic books reflect the status quo that has been achieved in Thelemic circles. We have arrived at a place in occult history where nothing new can be published because the masses of consumers scream for more of the regurgitated crap already available. People want 'easy guides to' books because they neither have the time nor the inclination to invest in their spirituality. No one is expected to do anything but to blindly accept a mountain of superstition, and the only surrender is his or her mortal soul.

Reputable publishers only want to publish the work of dead people. They don't have to pay a dead person royalties. And the works of dead people sell really well, even if the instruction or advice is no longer applicable. So, it seems that the serious publisher only has two choices after all: publish crap for the masses, or to continually regurgitate the same stuff from long dead authors for the book collectors. We are, however, free to join the legions of Thelemites, who believe in nothing of value, or worse, that Knowledge and Conversation will occur while they argue over the stupidest, most insignificant childish crap on the various Internet elists. Your Angel is not attracted to the smell of moldy limited, numbered and signed first edition tomes.

What would you do if your god came to you in a dream, and said that the only way to achieve K&C was to surrender everything, save your home, and that you were only to labor long enough to provide your basic needs, and the rest of your time with Yoga? Seriously. It is worth thinking about, because that day may come, and if you turn your back on that message because you love your illusions of grandeur that door will be closed, and it will never open for you again.

Now, you might argue that the way to union is through riches, and that concept may be just as valid. But you will have to know your "want" from your "will." We can't all be rich and we can't all be poor. To thine own self be true. Do what thou wilt.

How much time do you or your magician buddies invest in your spiritual pursuits? (Reading, surfing the web, or getting into a flame war on the various Thelemic elists does not count.)

We might tell ourselves that we aren't required to worry about such things, since we live in the West where holy men are a dime a dozen and where, we are told, we can have our cake and eat it to. How many holy men or women do you know? Since every Tom, Dick and Harry Thelemite claims to be a magician, one would think that the streets must be littered with them. What have those long hours of dancing in your robes, learning old forgotten languages and collecting overpriced books done for you? Are you enlightened? Have any of these practices proven to endow you or anyone you know with spiritual gifts?

How you deal and process these difficult questions is a measure of your sincerity and your worth. The truth hurts. It is too painful to look at or acknowledge, so the ego becomes this gigantic justification machine which eases our conscience by shutting it up. The ego is like this kid that is constantly screaming in your ear so that you cannot hear anything else.

In the West, we follow the illusion of material gain. The goal is clear, and because people think they can have it all, they have learned to 'spiritualize' every aspect of their lives so that the word 'spiritual' has lost all meaning. The attraction is strong. Everyone who has ever wanted to experience 'God' knows that the Union is the most important thing there is, and yet the pull away from Work is so strong that most people will compromise what they believe in exchange for something that provides instant gratification. There is no time for investing. After all, society does not measure our worth based on how much one knows or how enlightened one is. Not even Thelemic societies.

Now you might be thinking that the Eastern renunciation is also an illusion, and you would not get an argument out of me. They are both illusions. But which illusion makes one a better person? And what illusion is more effective in bringing man to his God?

So I will ask you again: do you know any Thelemite that is a Holy Person or has spiritual gifts? Think about it. The proof is in the pudding after all.

Without self-honesty and sincerity there is no use even beginning this journey. Without those two things one can only imagine what the Promised Land might be like, and I suspect that the little justification machine is screaming pretty loudly into your ear right now:

"This guy is a nut. He is insane and doesn't truly understand Thelema." Or "the New Aeon Magician has to be able to bring his or her magick into every day life, which includes a career." That's fine by me. I am crazy. I must be, since I believe magick can change the world. I guess that is proof positive that you must be dealing with a psycho. But better to be delusional than insincere: "I'll pray after I finish this level of this computer game." I am tormented by those sorts of struggles just as everyone else is, and I have learned

to watch as the ego* tempts us into avoid doing exactly what we know deep down inside we should be doing. One has to possess the strength to face truth; to look at it in the face prepared to carry out that truth to its desired end.

The Prophet was a rich man. He never worked a day in his life. He has also said that magick is for the pursuit of the rich. Why?

Because only a rich person can afford to practice magick, meditate, pray and perform the necessary disciplines. Only a rich person has the luxury of time. Time is your most precious asset. It is not a renewable resource. You believe in reincarnation? Good for you! But what if you are wrong? What if this is the only pass at this we get? Perhaps reincarnation was invented to make people feel better about not doing what they know they should? "I'll get enlightened tomorrow...in my next life."

Some people I know have worked their entire life to try to achieve some financial independence so that they can do their magick. Sounds, good. You could try to be rich so that you could divorce yourself from your responsibilities, but your chances are pretty close to nil. And if you do achieve riches, chances are they will only distract you from your work. Of this I know a little. And if it takes you a lifetime, and you never really get there, then you have wasted an incarnation. Better luck next time... if there is a next time. A friend of mine said that a person that waits until everything is perfect before starting the magical path never starts the magical path. This is a world of shells, it is racked with imperfection.

Am I implying that everyone ought to be a holy person, or a magician? No. But if you say you are a warrior then I should see you fighting. If you say are a doctor, then I could see if you are healing. If you say you are a thief, then steal...but at least be honest with yourself, and do what is in your nature. Don't be a hypocrite, and don't straddle two fences, for it really is as Crowley says: if it is your Will to be a doctor, you will make a lousy painter. And whatever you find yourself to be, push that to the limit. Don't be lazy: it is your star, and deserves to shine brightly.

Trust me on this. You cannot serve two masters. I have tried.

---

* An enlightened mind is capable of watching itself think.

Nietzsche's Influence on Crowley

The fundamentalists, by "knowing" the answers before they start and then forcing nature into the straitjacket of their discredited preconceptions, lie outside the domain of science-or of any honest intellectual inquiry.

—Stephen Jay Gould

The phenomena of romanticizing Nietzsche to the extent that we see ourselves as superior beings surrounded by the sleeping masses may be a necessary prepubescent phase. For most people, they grow up observing the reality of life and grow beyond this to a deeper understanding of what it is to be human: Most people.

There are groups of Uber-Thelemites that like to use the works of Nietzsche in order to present Thelema in a way that justifies fascist inclinations. This is relatively easy for them to do because most people only understand Nietzsche's influence on Crowley insomuch as he is mentioned in the collects of *Liber XV.** The other Saints are often ignored since they don't serve to provide opportunists with much ammo.

The bulk of the work regarding Nietzsche's writing is, unfortunately dedicated to portraying him as a racist and madman at best, or a Nazi sympathizer at worse. This only serves to facilitate the work of portraying Thelema exactly the way the uber-Thelemite wants. In my opinion, this is a tragic injustice of the worst kind, for these people are largely responsible for the hundreds, maybe thousands of people that have turned away from Thelema never to look back again. Much of it is done intentionally, because they have really bought into the entire deception, or because they only have the shallowest interpretation of Crowley and Nietzsche's work but have no ethical problems with dragging Thelema, Crowley and Nietzsche's name through the mud in order to win some imaginary contest. One can only imagine the karmic consequences.

Anyone that wants to avoid being duped into accepting this supposed form of 'Thelema', will have to have at least a layman's understanding of Nietzsche's ideas. His ideas are scattered in various places throughout The Book of the Law. We can choose to stop peeling back the layers as soon as we come up with the sort of The-

* The Mass for the Gnostic Catholic Church, or Ecclessia Gnostica Catholica.

lema we can live with, or we can keep digging to discover its most deeply hidden secrets. Crowley himself did not appear to have known the depth of the philosophy he heralded in 1904. This is, in fact, prophesized by the Book itself. This, combined with his unfortunate hatred for all things dealing with Christian fundamentalism, must have affected the message and every comment he made upon it. We can begin to posit just how deeply this message was filtered through Crowley's biases.

As for Nietzsche, he was a brilliant but under appreciated writer who was shunned by his contemporaries for being too literary while others saw him as too abstract. In other words, his work defied academic labeling during his time, and continues to do so today. He was and important and a radical thinker during his time, and much of what he wrote appealed to Crowley, partly due to his ultra-puritan Christian upbringing. Nietzsche influenced his concept of the universe, as we shall see.

In contrast to Western philosophy, which identifies the physical body as a lesser part of the human experience, Nietzsche went against the accepted duality conception of separated physical and mental worlds, by insisting that the mental/spiritual planes could not be truly separated from the physical.* In other words, he believed the rational mind to be a component of the whole and not a separate or superior virtuous component. As a result, he tended to value the automatic and uncontrolled impulses emanating from physical passion as well as darkest regions of the unconscious mind where they originate.

In 1871 he wrote *The Birth of Tragedy*. Here he boldly states that the true creative genius of the artist resides in those unconscious impulses, and not in the lucid or calculated rational faculties. He criticized the classic philosophies of Socrates and Plato, both of whom postulated the existence of a more virtuous world than the one in which we presently live. These ideals, Nietzsche preached, were responsible for the degeneration of the human condition and the wholesale betrayal of the Earth.† There is no longer an above or below.‡ He went on to further postulate that the reason for de-

---

*   Liber AL I:8
†   Liber AL I:26 and I:58
‡   "As above so below." "Kether is in Malkuth, and Malkuth in Kether." Liber AL
    I:4, I:22

valuating the physical world is fear* of life's uncertainties, suffering and the ultimate end that awaits all of us. It is this inherent fear that causes people to seek shelter in imaginary worlds promising shelter and peace: usually after death, where they can continue to live as they do now.† He viewed this wishful thinking as a weakness, and sang the praises of those strong individuals that could take adversity in stride, even going as far as stating that a strong person would welcome such suffering.‡

He coined the phrase *live dangerously,* saying that death is what defines life itself; sickness, health; poverty, richness; pain, joy and so on. He wrote that life must be embraced in its totality.

He received a lot of criticism in his *Beyond Good and Evil* for his infamous musings on "Master" and "Slave" moralities.§ According to Nietzsche, human beings develop into two dominating categories. Master Moralities are highly developed self-confident individuals possessed of physical and intellectual strength, and will naturally rule over things and other people. For these individuals, pride is a virtue rather than a vice.¶ They are generally opposed to humility, modesty, sympathy, pity,** patience and kindness. People who act according to those values belong to the Slave Morality category that tends to thrive in oppressed populations. But if we look at his own life, we see a man that cared deeply for other people. He took care of wounded soldiers, which subsequently led to his becoming ill with diphtheria and dysentery which subsequently led to a painful assortment of health difficulties for the rest of his life…and ultimately, his death. Nietzsche was a walking-talking contradiction.

Nietzsche was not against religion. He simply thought of *all* religious/metaphysical systems as necessary evils that instilled in individuals the discipline necessary to drive Western civilization out of the darkness, but attributed the Slave Moralities specifically to Christianity. "God is dead," he said—not to make a statement about the existence of God—but to make an observation about His or Her role in a universe observed in purely scientific terms. After all,

---

*   Liber Librae. Paragraph 7 – Liber AL III:17
†   See Crowley's "The Dangers of Mysticism."
‡   Liber AL I:32
§   Liber AL II:58
¶   Liber AL II:77
** Liber AL II:48

what is the difference between an unobservable God and a God that doesn't exist? No longer must Science bend its yoke to Religion when there is a conflict between them.*

In *The Joyful Science,* section 125, Nietzsche goes on to explain God's death, not in his own voice, but as a character he referred to as a madman. The 'madman' goes on to scream at the sleeping masses, that WE killed god. Science killed God the way video killed the radio star. We are His assassins, and the murder weapon is Science, and we have become his replacement: "Shall we not have to become gods ourselves to seem worthy of it?"† Science is Nietzsche's proverbial forbidden fruit: the fruit from the Tree of the Knowledge of Good and Evil that God warned Adam and Eve against in Genesis. Here is the irony. We haven't answered Nietzsche's question. We have clung on to Science as the new religion and new god, but we have not determined god's role in this new world...and IT is still out there...waiting. The archetype still exists and hasn't been reassigned or reinterpreted. This is why everything is so wrong.

The Humanists, Nietzsche claims, hypothesize that nothing will change once man realizes that God has died, and that the same forms of integrity and improvement will continue to be perpetuated by humanity. In other words, man will take on the role of the God he killed.‡ Nietzsche obviously disagrees, since as we have seen above, he lumps all of those qualities under the Slave Morality adhered to by the weak people. Here, Nietzsche appears to be cutting off his nose to spite his face. Wouldn't those qualities he finds so objectionable continue to be used so long as they further our goals? Doesn't that now make them qualities of the Master Morality?

The Existentialist, on the other hand, was seriously disturbed by Nietzsche's proclamation of God's death. Clearly, they thought, man cannot be trusted to do the right thing in the absence of any imposing moral values or conventional ethical structure. Now, without God's unmovable authority man is free to determine right and wrong for himself.§ This apparently, must have appealed to Crowley tremendously.

In fact, some philosophers since Nietzsche thought that the death

---

*   "The Aim of Religion, The Method of Science."
†   "There is no god but man." Also, Liber AL I:11, I:21, II:23, II:78
‡   "There is no god but man."
§   "Do what thou wilt shall be the whole of the Law."

of God via Science would herald a new religion with a more realistic value system than the religious ones based on superstition. Crowley appears to have had similar notions.

In his own autobiography, Ecce Homo, How One Becomes What One Is, Nietzsche questions his own greatness. "why am I so wise?" "why am I so clever?" "why am I a destiny?"—with these words Nietzsche finished one of his last works. In this book he describes himself as "a follower of the philosopher Dionysus, the god of life's exuberance."

The problems with Science as religion are pretty obvious. By definition, science must treat every observable fact equally valuable or valueless. It must be value-neutral. This makes Science dangerous because it must, by necessity, remain unfettered by any moral judgment or refrained by any ethics that would interfere with its being impartial. One doesn't have to look very far back to see the numerous atrocities committed under the name of Science, or the apparent lack of concern for the outcome that this impartiality affords it.* "Love is the law, love under will" seems to balance things out quite nicely, and makes it possible to use Science as a system to further spiritual goals as well as a foundation on which to form an ethical system based on scientific facts.

The element of 'Love' is missing from Nietzsche's writings. Not so in Crowley's work, if we bother to look closely beyond his own contradictions. Crowley adopted Nietzsche's declarations: There is no God. Man has freewill. Man should be passionate. Social conformity only serves to hold man back. Conventional morality† and the interests of others should not restrain the individual. Masculinity, strength, and passion are qualities of the highest person.

Now there is more life behind me, than there is ahead. The young idealist beginning to discover the possibilities of his own existence dwells in that larger area. One of the most profound things I have learned about being human is that there's no real difference between Nietzsche's Master and Slave moralities. People move in and out of those modes as their Will dictates. They are simplified forms of the Yin and Yang, black and white, the large and small,

---

* Consider how much consideration went into the decision to unleash the first atomic bomb. Science now faces other ethical dilemmas in the form of cloning and the use of DNA.

† Not all morality, as the uber-Thelemite would have us believe.

the above and below, and the all-begetter all devourer Ouroboros which simultaneously swallows itself into the infinitely small point, and pulls itself out of his own mouth expanding itself into the un-limited. There are only slave and free mentalities. The desire to become a Master is a true sign of a 'Slave Mentality'.

We are free to use the ideas of philosophers such as Nietzsche to examine the beliefs of people that adhere to them. In fact that is why they are models. But you see, the sword blade cuts both ways. If the goal is to further Scientific Illuminism, then one mustn't be a boob about it. Seems to me the first step is to determine whether or not the philosopher whose ideals we appreciate, actually truly lived according to his or her own beliefs. Then, we should look to determine whether adhering to those ideas really generate the re-sults that they said they would. Then, we have to understand that a person isn't going to be right 100% of the time,* nor should those failures diminish the validity and effectiveness of other ideas. And finally, we have to consider that we are not them, and that the best that we can hope for is to discover some part of their philosophy that we can use to discover our own truth. We must consider, test and evaluate all these things before we can even begin to 'judge others to see if they have gnosis'. Otherwise, you are only being an intellectual bully, and no one really likes a bully...except for other bullies.

It is easy for the Uber-Thelemites to use something like Thelema or the writings of Nietzsche to justify being a jerk or to divorce themselves from any social involvement or responsibility what so ever. That is the easy part. It should be no surprise that Thelema is so popular with the socially inept. It is much harder to study and practice Thelema without any lust of result. Without any motive outside of scientific curiosity to see if it does indeed offer the solu-tions to today's problems as Crowley stated so many times through-out his life.

There is no doubt in my mind that *Liber AL* was indeed a 're-ceived' text. But it is ridiculous for anyone, much less a scientific il-luminist, to assume that it would have manifested in the same man-ner had Crowley not been exposed to the giants listed as Saints in his Mass. To get the truth from the Book of the Law (especially the comments) one has to consider all things: Which points are be-

* Liber AL I:56

ing directed to Crowley, specifically? Which parts are intended for Thelemites? Which passages are referring to humanity as a whole? How much of the message of the Book itself, or the comments are biased by the events in Crowley's own personal life? One simply has to learn to read in between and then beyond Crowley if they are interested in getting to the precious stones buried in the text.

Conclusion

As has already been said, Karma Yoga is building and standing by ones own moral/ethical code based on ones true nature. Some Thelemites have questioned the need for ethics in Thelema in light of the axiom: "Thou hast no right but to do thy will." Clearly, Crowley saw the need for ethics or we might have never seen documents such as *Duty, Liber OZ,* or *Liber Librae,** a wonderful list of Saints in his Gnostic Catholic Mass, nor would he have broached the subject so often in letters to his students.

Knowing ones True Will is simultaneously liberating and limiting. In fact, very few are bold enough to make the earnest effort to pull back the layers of illusion to arrive at their True Self. Even fewer still possess the sincerity or inclination to act upon that discovery once it is made. "Thou hast no right but to do thy will." That is the only right we truly have.

In between faith and destiny we will find freewill, that unfortunate curse of God upon man for having had the audacity to make himself judge over good and evil. Freewill, we are told, will eventually lead us to our own undoing because of our 'imperfect human nature' will prevent us from choosing the right course.

I posit a much brighter outcome. Nietzsche said it best: God Is Dead…and we have killed him with science. We cannot undo what has been done. We decide what is right and what is wrong using only the facts. No longer will science have to adjust its findings to conform to superstition. What we have today is an opportunity to shed all false notions. "The aims of religion and the method of science" will help us to rediscover our inner compass. In doing so the human race will become perfected and we will plot the appropriate course. Thelema can lead humanity to the realization of our own divinity, and that awareness is the key to all that ails us. An ethical man must always do the right thing. This 'right thing' will originate with right thought and then manifest in right action…and that 'thing' is no less than the manifestation of our True Will.

---

*   MacGregor Matthers authored *Liber Librae.* Crowley embraced this text and is often credited for having penned it.

Bibliography

Angelo, Thomas A. and Cross, K. Patricia (1993) *Classroom Assessment Techniques: A Handbook for College Teachers,* Jossey-Bass Publications

Bates, Daniel G. and Fratkin, Elliot M ((2002) *Cultural Anthropology* Allyn & Bacon

Bierce, Ambrose (2002) *The Unabridged Devil's Dictionary,* The University of Georgia Press

Chesterton, Gilbert (1959) *Orthodoxy,* Doubleday & Company

Crowley, Aleister, *The Libri of Aleister Crowley,* http://www.hermetic. com/crowley/ including *The Law of Liberty, Liber Librae,* etc.

Crowley, Aleister (1986) *777 and other Qabalistic Writings of Aleister Crowley,* Weiser Books

Crowley, Aleister (2004) *The Book of the Law | Liber AL vel Legis,* Weiser Books

Crowley, Aleister (1989) *The Holy Books of Thelema,* Weiser Books

Crowley, Aleister (1942) *Liber OZ,* s.n.

Crowley, Aleister (1998) *Magick: Liber Aba : Book 4,* Weiser Books

Crowley, Aleister (1976) *Magick in Theory and Practice,* Dover Publications

Crowley, Aleister (1991) *Magick Without Tears,* New Falcon Publications

Crowley, Aleister *The Libri of Aleister Crowley* http://www.hermetic.com/ crowley/ including *The Law of Liberty, Liber Librae,* etc.

Crowley, Aleister; Neuburg, Victor B.; Desti, Mary (1999) *The Vision and the Voice With Commentary and Other Papers: The Collected Diaries of Aleister Crowley, 1909-1914 E.V. (Equinox),* Weiser Books

Crowley, Aleister, (author), Symonds, John (Editor), Grant, Kenneth (Editor) (1989) *The Confessions of Aleister Crowley: An Autobiography,* Penguin

Fortune, Dion (2000) *The Mystical Qabalah,* Weiser Books

Frater U.D. (1990) *Practical Sigil Magic,* Llewellyn Publications

Graves, Robert (1960), *The Larousse Encyclopedia of Mythology,* Batchworth Press Limited

Jung, Carl *The Psychology of the Child Archetype*

Jung, Carl (1970) *The Structure and Dynamics of the Psyche (Collected Works of C.G. Jung, Volume 8),* Princeton University Press

Jung, Carl (1985) *Synchronicity,* Routledge

Kaplan, Aryeh (editor) (1997) *The Sepher Yetzirah,* Weiser Books

Lévi, Éliphas (1990) *Dogmes et Rituels de haute magie,* Bussière "Liber Libræ Sub Figura XXX"

Nietzsche, Friedrich (2005) *The Anti-Christ,* Cosimo Classics

Nietzsche, Friedrich (2005) *Beyond Good and Evil,* Digireads.com

Nietzsche, Friedrich (1974) *The Gay Science,* Vintage

Rawls, John (1999) *A Theory of Justice,* Belknap Press

Vivekananda, Swami (1999) *Karma Yoga: the Yoga of Action,* Vedanta Press

Recommended Reading

Alvarado, Louis (1991) *Psychology, Astrology & Western Magic,* Llewellyn Publications

Buber, Martin (1990) *The Way of Man: According to the Teachings of Hasidism,* Citadel Press)

Crowley, Aleister (1986) *777 and other Qabalistic Writings of Aleister Crowley,* Weiser Books

Crowley, Aleister (1998) *Magick: Liber Aba : Book 4,* Weiser Books

Fortune, Dion (2000) *The Mystical Qabalah,* Weiser Books

Godwin, David (2002) *Godwin's Cabalistic Encyclopedia,* Llewellyn Publications

Johnsen, Linda (1994) *Daughters of The Goddess: The Women Saints of India,* Yes International

Kant, Immanuel (1960) *An Immanuel Kant Reader,* Trans. and Ed., with Commentary by Raymond B. Blakney; Harper Books

Kaplan, Aryeh (editor) (1997) *The Sepher Yetzirah,* Weiser Books

Koltuv, Barbara Black, Ph.D (1987) *The Book of Lilith,* Nicolas-Hays Inc.

Lukeman, Alex (1993) *What Your Dreams Can Teach You,* Llewellyn Publications

Moore, Robert and Gillette, Douglas (1991) *King, Warrior, Magician, Lover: Rediscovering the Archetypes of the Mature Masculine,* HarperOne

McLean, Adam (1989) *The Triple Goddess: An Exploration of the Archetypal Feminine,* Phanes Press

Qualls-Corbett, Nancy (1998) *The Sacred Prostitute,* Inner City Books

Regardie, Israel (1995) *A Garden of Pomegranates,* Llewellyn Publications

Soho, Takuan (1986) *The Unfettered Mind,* Kodansha International

Szekely, Edmond Bordeaux (1981) *The Teachings of The Essenes from Enoch to The Dead Sea Scrolls,* C.W. Daniel Co.

Scholem, Gershom (1968) *Zohar: The Book of Splendor,* Schoken Books

Ueshiba, Morihei (1992) *The Art of Peace,* Shambhala Publications

Wilson, Robert Anton (1986) *Ishtar Rising,* Falcon Press

Zhuge, Liang and Ji, Liu (2005) *Mastering The Art of War,* Shambhala Publications

Who Is Gerald Del Campo?

Gerald Enrique del Campo (b. 1960) is a poet, musician, songwriter, photographer, magician, philosopher, author, and lecturer on occult and religious topics. He was born in Córdoba, Argentina on January 14, 1960. He immigrated to the United States with his parents when he was eight years old.

Gerald del Campo attended Catholic School in North Hollywood, California when he first arrived to America. During his early school years he showed a special aptitude towards science, mathematics, languages, and religious-philosophical studies. At a very young age, he asked to be prepared for the Catholic Priesthood, but over the years his enthusiasm for Catholicism faded. He began corresponding with the various Rosicrucian Orders, the Martinists, the Center for Self Realization, and an assortment of other groups. During this period he had become acutely aware of an occult movement which was taking place in the 1970's mostly from the warnings of his teachers, and became interested in the subjects of comparative religion, philosophy and metaphysics, all of which led to his fascination with the occult itself.

In 1975, when del Campo was 15 years old, a complete stranger handed him The Book of the Law, which altered his course dramatically. This led him to the direction of Aleister Crowley's writings and Thelema.

From 1982 till 1986, he studied Enochian magic with David Kennedy, Israel Regardie's personal secretary. In 1987 he joined Ordo Templi Orientis, where he eventually became Master of RPSTOVAL Oasis. Later he served that Order in the capacity of Quartermaster and volunteered to serve an eleven year term with the OTO's Electoral College. From 1988 until 1990 he was a member of the College of Thelema and studied under Phyllis Seckler. In 1989, he was a founding member of the Temple of Thelema. In that same year he joined Fraternitas Lux Occulta and studied under Paul Clark. In 1998 he became a member of The Hermetic Order of QBLH. He founded the The Order of Thelemic Knights, a Thelemic charitable organization based on the virtues soldiering and chivalry as exemplified by Templarism on August 23, 1999.

In August 2006, due to conflicts within the Order, Gerald del Campo resigned from the OTO after 20 years membership.

Timeline of Major Events

Joins Ordo Templi Orientis 1987

Becomes a student at the College of Thelema 1988 - 1990

Founding member of Temple of Thelema 1988 - 1989

Master OTO RPSTOVAL Oasis 1989 - 1995

Member Fraternitas LUX Occulta 1988 - 1989

Ordo Templi Orientis Quarter Master 1989 - 1992

Ordained Priest in EGC by Lon DuQuette in Los Angeles on August, 4 1991

New Aeon Magick: Thelema Without Tears is published March 21, 1993

Served as senator in Ordo Templi Orientis Electoral College 1993-2004

New Aeon Magick is adopted by the Pagan Student Alliance at the University of Texas, Austin in 1997.

Member QBLH 1998-2002

QBLH Education Committee 2000 - 2001

Founding Member of Aleister Crowley Foundation 1998

Founder and Grand Master of Order of Thelemic Knights August 23, 1999

New Aeon English Qabalah Revealed is published July 4, 2001

Consecrated Bishop by Ecclesia Gnostic Catholica Hermetica, January 1, 2003

Adopted Tau Apollonius as name January 1, 2003

Founder and Patriarch of the Thelemic Gnostic Church of Alexandria January 1, 2003

Education Committee North American College of Gnostic Bishops June 6, 2003 -2006

Became head of Aleister Crowley Foundation 2004

Ethics committee North American College of Gnostic Bishops March 2, 2006

Resigned from the OTO after 20 years membership August, 2006

Writings

Mr. del Campo is a prolific writer who is concerned with the positive and responsible promulgation of the Law of Thelema. Many of his writings have been translated into various languages and some have become either recommended or required reading at various universities around the world.

The following list includes some of his more popular writings in the areas of Thelema, religion, philosophy, and mythology which have appeared in various magical journals are listed in order. They do not include his poetry or dissertations on photography, brewing, or technical writings:

On Animal Sacrifice (1985)
Latin Banishing Ritual of The Pentagram (Winter of 1986)
On the Use of Blood in Ritual (1986)
De Matrimonium et Reconciliato Inter Ingenium et Motus et Fructus Coniunctio Summ (1987)
On The Use of Blood in Ritual (1988)
The Problem With Secular Democratic Politics (July 4th 1992)
New Aeon Magick: Thelema Without Tears (published March 21, 1994 (First edition 1994, Llewellyn Worldwide - Second edition Luxor Press 2000)
Introduction To Qabalah (published on the web in 1996, and becomes recommended reading for a class on Jungian Psychology at the University of Cape Town, South Africa.
Officium De Sacerdotium 1998
Alchemy: The Struggle for Immortality (published on web site in 1998, and it becomes required reading for "Egyptian Chemistry" at the National University of Singapore from 1998-2003
Rabelais: The First Thelemite (1999)
St. Joan of Arc (1999)
Saladin (1999)
Sir William Wallace (1999)
Malcolm X (2000)
Crazy Horse (2000)
Rosaleen Norton (2000)
Mansur al-Hallaj (2000)
Emiliano Zapata 2000)

Hypatia of Alexandria (2000)
The Progression of The Ego Into The Self via The Law of Thelema 2001)
To Gnow or Not To Gnow (March 2001)
Chivalry Is Not Dead (2001)
Why Thelema Implies Responsibility (2001)
After 9/11 (2002)
On The Importance of Studying The Book of The Law (2002)
To All Children (2002)
New Aeon English Qabalah Revealed (Luxor Press 2001)
Basic Techniques for Performing Sex Magick (2002)
Why Does Religion Get Such a Bad Rap? (2003)
A Short Article of The Subject of Thelemic Gnosticism (2003)
A Brief Introduction to The Religion of Thelema (2003)
Bakhti and The Order (2002 for OTK)
The Sword (December 2002)
A Short Treatise on Buddhism (2002)
A Short Article on The Unfolding of Thelema (2003)
There is No God But Man - Really? (2003)
Soldiers Are Soldiers (2003)
Doing and allowing those to do what one does best (2006)

About Concrescent Press

Concrescent Press is dedicated to publishing advanced magickal practice and Pagan scholarship. It takes advantage of the recent revolution in publishing technology and economics to bring forth works that, previously, might only have been circulated privately. Now, we are growing the future together.

Colophon

This book is made of ITC New Baskerville and Baskerville Old Face using Adobe InDesign, Illustrator and Photoshop. The cover was designed and the body was set by Sam Webster. The illustrations were drawn by the author.

Visit our website at
www.Concrescent.net

CPSIA information can be obtained at www.ICGtesting.com
Printed in the USA
BVOW081414200912

300979BV00001B/27/P